MARINE INSURANCE—THE PRINCIPLES

A reconstruction of Edward Lloyd's coffee house.

The servery (left) and the fire place. The servery from which coffee was dispensed is equipped with coffee grinders, coffee pots, jugs and other utensils of the period. The hot water boiler hangs over the fire and coffee pots stand on the trivet in front to warm.

MARINE INSURANCE
Vol. i — THE PRINCIPLES

by

ROBERT H. BROWN, A.C.I.I., M.Inst.A.M.

Lecturer at the City of London Polytechnic
Chief Examiner in Marine Insurance for the
London Chamber of Commerce
Examiner for the Institute of Chartered Shipbrokers
Examiner for the Institute of South African Shipbrokers
Author of
"Dictionary of Marine Insurance Terms"
"Marine Insurance Abbreviations"
"Marine Insurance—Cargo Practice—Vol. 2"
"Marine Insurance—Hull Practice—Vol. 3"

WITHERBY & CO LTD
5 PLANTAIN PLACE
CROSBY ROW
LONDON, S.E.1. 1.Y.N.

MONUMENT
SERIES

©

Witherby & Co Ltd 1968

1st edition 1968
2nd edition 1973
3rd edition 1975

ISBN 0 900 886 07 2

PRINTED IN GREAT BRITAIN BY
NORTHUMBERLAND PRESS LIMITED
GATESHEAD

FOREWORD

"For Angling may be said to be like the Mathematics, that can never be fully learnt, not so fully but that there will still be more new experiments left for the trial of other men that succeed us."

IZAAK WALTON,
from the *Compleat Angler*

IF Izaak Walton had had any experience of underwriting, he would surely have joined marine insurance with Angling and the Mathematics. It is frequently as exasperating as a bad day's fishing, and, to the newcomer, as mystifying as the new Mathematics. Very few of us can claim that it is fully learnt.

Today we are all aware of the importance of proper training for every job. The Government, with its Industrial Training Act, has insisted that the new entrants to industry are properly taught.

Underwriters and brokers are all convinced that we shall only retain our position as the centre of world insurance if our technical knowledge equals our experience.

Mr. Brown, with his experience as lecturer, tutor and examiner, has written a book which will appeal to everybody concerned with marine insurance.

For the experienced, how valuable it is to be reminded of what they once knew, but have since, perhaps, forgotten. For the future A.C.I.I., how vital to know how an examiner looks at the subject, and what he thinks are the most important aspects to study. But the greatest appeal of this book will be to those in the industry who have, for various reasons, been unable to complete, or even to start, academic study of insurance, who have been scared off by the dryness of the technicalities of previous books on marine insurance. This book, by combining the description of the practice with the principles on which the practice is based, will not only give the reader a sound knowledge of the way the business is conducted, but will give such a grounding that the reader will be encouraged and well equipped to face the many problems of this absorbing subject.

PAUL DIXEY
Lloyd's Underwriter.

AUTHOR'S PREFACE

DESPITE the large number of people actively engaged in the practice of marine insurance very few of its practitioners have attempted to write a textbook on the subject. This may be because those that have been produced are of such excellent quality that no other work has been deemed necessary. In company with many of my contemporaries I studied these works in my student days, and I am grateful for the help I received from them. I feel that without this background I could never have undertaken this present task and I, therefore, wish to acknowledge an indebtedness to Harold Turner's "Principles of Marine Insurance", Victor Dover's "Handbook", Payne's "Carriage of Goods by Sea", the study courses of the Chartered Insurance Institute, and the handbooks published by the Institute of London Underwriters.

Very wisely these earlier writers have concentrated on the well established principles of the subject, backed by case law, thereby establishing a basic foundation for the young embryo practitioner. Nevertheless, such Principles are little more than the established practice of the past, and it seems to me that it is time that many later developments are brought within the range of text books and that the standard practices of today should be recorded. I realize, of course, that this may lead to severe criticism if it is thought that I propose to introduce some form of rules of conduct, and I would like to make it clear that I intend only to place on record that which is commonly practised for the benefit of those who have been unable to acquire this knowledge by years of experience. It is true that experience is the best teacher but to gain experience takes time, and in this progressive age time is something we cannot afford to expend.

In my aim to introduce modern practice I propose to write this work in two stages. The first of these gives the principles of the business, but necessarily embraces some fundamental practices which properly belong in this section. The second stage relates to the practice of Cargo Insurance, Hull Insurance, Freight Insurance and Marine Reinsurance.

I trust that this method of approach will enable the student more readily to understand the subject.

R. H. BROWN
London 1968

AUTHOR'S NOTE

IN writing this book on Principles of Marine Insurance I have
deliberately avoided unnecessary reference to law cases prior to
the Marine Insurance Act, 1906. The reason for this is that the
Marine Insurance Act, 1906 codifies the law up to 21st December,
1906, so that reference to the relevant section of the Act replaces
reference to earlier law cases. In the very few instances where I
have quoted an early law case this has been done to illustrate, or
to add emphasis to, a point rather than to establish an authority.

I take this opportunity to acknowledge with gratitude the valuable
assistance and constructive criticism in the preparation of this
work given by my very good friend and colleague J. K. Goodacre,
A.C.I.I., also the interest shown and advice given by Desmond
Baker, A.C.I.I., and many other colleagues in the London market.

Further I would like to express my appreciation to Lloyd's
Information Department for their co-operation and help.

R.H.B.
1968

REVISED EDITION 1975

The world of marine insurance has coped with many changes
in recent years. Even the principles on which practice is based
have been challenged, clarified or revised. The result is that this
book has now been updated to incorporate these changes. Although
I still believe that students, in the early stages, become confused
with law cases, I have incorporated reference to some legal decisions
to enable one to examine the legal findings on which a principle
is based. Reference to "Marine Insurance Claims" by J. K.
Goodacre will give details of such court cases. I am grateful to
Ken Goodacre for allowing me to draw freely on the information
contained in his excellent book.

R.H.B.,
London, 1975.

CONTENTS

CHAPTER 1

THE PRINCIPLES OF MARINE INSURANCE

Introduction and the Credit System

IN the early days of the human race man was limited in his travel and, consequently, in his knowledge of other lands by his inability to cross the seas which obstructed his path. Although men of those lands bordered by food producing waters designed and built craft for their immediate needs they feared to leave the sight of land, and so did not venture very far. Of course, those people who lived upon the mainland of the continents were not so hampered and many of them travelled vast distances in search of new lands and knowledge, taking with them trading goods to pay for the journeys and thus opening the well trod trading routes from Europe to India and China and vice versa. Such methods of trading demanded large, well protected caravans and were expensive expeditions, so that it was not long before the Mediterranean traders began to design vessels capable of crossing the Mediterranean and the era of the Phoenician traders began. Eventually these enterprising traders extended their activities beyond the Mediterranean and even visited the shore of Britain in search of tin and iron. The Britons of those times, so many years ago, had not the knowledge to build ships of any size, although as an island race such vessels would have greatly increased their range of knowledge and their trading prospects.

It was not until well after the Roman conquest that the practice of shipbuilding began to take shape but, once the possibilities were realized, the British people forged ahead to build larger vessels and ventured further and further from the island's shores. The enthusiasm for seafaring was in the blood of the nation by Elizabethan times and, encouraged by the Queen, the Elizabethan sailors made the feats of British seamen known and respected throughout the world. Nevertheless, lack of communications and the lone voyages of those sailors made them vulnerable to the hazards which beset them, so that to undertake such a voyage was an adventure not to be undertaken lightly, thus was born the expression "marine adventure".

The vagaries of the winds, remember all vessels were sailing vessels at that time, and the distance between trading countries would mean that an adventure would sometimes take several years

1

to complete. It was common practice for a trader to own his own ship, or fleet of ships, and to load that ship with trading goods destined for a particular port. In some cases the trader would himself be master of the vessel but in the case of large trading "houses" it was customary to employ a master for the vessel and to send along a "supercargo", a trusted man who was responsible for the trading activities of the vessel. The plan was for the vessel to proceed to its destination port where the supercargo would dispose of the merchandise and purchase other goods for a further port. Since the supercargo and master would take the vessel to the nearest place where a profit would be made it would probably be many years before the ship returned to its home port for the owner to realize on his investment.

One cannot simply stand still in commerce and wait several years for each transaction to show a profit but unless the trader, or merchant as we shall now call him, had vast resources he could not undertake several concurrent voyages. The only answer to the problem was to obtain financial backing so that, on the security of his ship and goods with the anticipated outcome of the adventure, the merchant would obtain credit by an advance in cash. The Lombards, who settled in London in the twelfth century, were largely responsible for this system and many of the London merchant banks today owe their origins to the enterprise of these Italian settlers. Lombard Street, the centre of the banking world in London, is named after them. Although the credit system of the time solved the immediate problems of the merchant it had one vital snag. The loan was secured on the ship, cargo and anticipated profit but this was a nebulous form of security since if the vessel failed to return the security would be extinguished. The advancer of the money was in effect "underwriting" the adventure because he stood little chance of a reimbursement of his money if the vessel failed to return. Many moneylenders were not prepared to advance money on such a loose form of security even if offered a large share in the profit of the adventure, because such were the hazards of sea voyages in those days that a great risk was involved in the transaction. It became commonplace for the merchant to obtain an undertaking from a further financier who, while not actually advancing cash, was prepared to guarantee the financial outcome of the adventure in return for a "consideration". The consideration might be in the form of a payment called the "premium" or it might be a percentage of the profit of the adventure. In any event, this was the birth of marine insurance.

The need to formulate a set of rules for the conduct of marine insurance in Elizabethan times led to the enacting of an Act on the subject in 1601 and an illustration of the encouragement to "adventure" is contained in the preamble to that Act in pointing out that it is better for many to bear the loss by way of insurance, in the event of misfortune, than for the luckless owner of the vessel and/or merchant to suffer alone. In this respect the Act states "it cometh to pass that upon the loss or perishing of any ship there followeth not the undoing of any man, but the loss alighteth rather easily upon many men rather than heavily upon few, and rather upon them that adventure not, than those that do adventure, whereby all merchants, especially the younger sort, are allowed to venture more willingly and freely".

The Credit System of Today

When the credit system first began the need was to finance both the outfitting of the vessel and the outcome of the adventure, the vessel and cargo frequently belonging to the same person or merchant house but, with the passage of time, the merchant has ceased to have his own vessels and, due to the increased size of cargo ships, is seldom able to utilize the whole cargo space of one vessel at one time. Hence, the system of trading from port to port by a vessel for one merchant has virtually ceased to exist. In most instances the merchant of today sells his goods by sample or description, and the sea voyage is merely the delivery of goods already sold. There are still instances where goods are sent "on consignment", that is, for sale at destination but the credit system is not concerned with these. The merchant selling his goods overseas receives a letter of credit, which may be in the form of a bill of exchange, agreeing to pay on delivery of the goods. To reduce the sending of cash the international banking system allows for transactions of this nature to be dealt with through the banks. The merchant, upon receipt of the letter of credit, can present this to his bank which will obtain payment in due course from the buyer's bank, on which bank the letter of credit was drawn. If the merchant requires an advance this can also be arranged provided he deposits with his bank the necessary shipping documents for the goods. The documents of title will be required as these give evidence of ownership and shipment of the goods, being the export invoice, which shows the price, quantity and quality of the goods, and the bill of lading, which shows the terms of the contract of affreightment and the accepted condition of the goods when shipped. In addition, the bank will require the letter of credit giving authority for payment and, if the consignee so stipulates in the letter of credit, the bank will also require a marine policy effected on conditions. The bank will demand that a policy be presented if an advance payment is made. A certificate issued off an open cover may be acceptable to the bank as sufficient evidence of insurance.

Export Credits Guarantee Department (E.C.G.D.)

Whilst the credit system provides for the advance of money and the marine policy protects against financial loss resulting from physical loss of or damage to the goods, both the merchant and the bank are in a vulnerable position if the buyer fails to pay for the goods for any reason. Some buyers set up irrevocable credit in their own banks to cover the cost of the goods and many merchants are loathe to sell except against such guarantees. The Government is desirous to encourage exports but realize that many exporters could not accept orders on credit unless payment was guaranteed. The Export Credits Guarantee Department is a Governmental department set up under the auspices of the Board of Trade to provide insurance facilities to cover non-payment by importers of goods exported from the United Kingdom on credit. For "specific" cases separate application must be made to the Department, acceptance being based on the circumstances of and in the Country of import. The object of the Department is to provide cover in event of insolvency of the consignee or non payment due to civil disturbances and other causes, being where payment is delayed or prevented by exceptional circumstances rather than where no payment at all is likely, for the latter could be of no advantage to the Country. It is customary for regular shipments to be covered under a "whole turnover system" where the whole turnover is accepted in principle and declarations are made and automatically covered as each shipment goes forward, in much the same way as the "open cover" system in cargo insurance. Once covered by the E.C.G.D. the seller can obtain an advance from a bank in the ordinary way, if required.

Quantitative and Qualitative Control

As has been stated earlier, in modern commerce it is customary to sell goods overseas by means of description of quality or sample. The buyer under English law is protected if the goods delivered are not of the quantity or quality represented, but a foreign buyer may find it difficult to enforce any rights he has in this respect. In the case of large sale contracts, especially those arranged with the import departments of foreign Governments it is customary to insert a clause providing that the buyer shall retain a fixed percentage of the purchase price against inspection of the delivered goods. If the goods are not up to the quantity and quality represented the retention becomes forfeit.

Although there is no established insurance market for insolvency other than the E.C.G.D., some large cargo covers contain a "quantitative and qualitative control" clause. This clause provides for reimbursement to the seller of the retention if forfeited but is only accepted by insurers in the belief that any lack of quantity or quality would be due to loss or damage during the voyage.

The buyer may find it difficult to negotiate a sale on the above basis but if he wishes to protect himself he may obtain a "performance bond" from an insurance company which has the effect of paying a similar amount to that which he would have retained had the goods been delivered below standard under a sale contract with a quantitative and qualitative control clause.

Sale Contracts

Before leaving the subject of sale contracts it would be advisable to consider the meanings of the standard F.O.B. and C.I.F. contracts. F.O.B. means "Free on board" and C.I.F. means "Cost, insurance and freight". The principal difference is the time when title to the goods passes from seller to buyer, for one needs to establish who has responsibility for and rights in the goods at each stage of the voyage. When goods are sold F.O.B. the seller is only responsible for, and only has the rights in, the goods until they are loaded on the carrying vessel. The seller is responsible for paying all expenses and arranging transit until the goods are on board. It is also the seller's right and responsibility to arrange insurance up to this point. Once the goods are on board the buyer takes over all rights and responsibilities, including payment of freight and arrangement of insurance. Under the C.I.F. sale contract the seller undertakes to arrange and pay for all costs of delivery and insurance to destination because the buyer has paid for these in the sale price. A similar contract, where the buyer prefers to arrange his own insurance, is the "C & F" contract. Under both these contracts the consignee has no responsibility until he takes delivery of the goods. Where the goods are sold under a C.I.F. contract the insurance policy is assigned to the consignee and he can claim under the policy as though he had arranged the insurance himself.

Need to Insure

There is no compulsion under English law for a merchant to

insure his goods. The credit system often requires that he must arrange insurance, but apart from this it would appear to be common prudence for the merchant to insure his goods whilst in transit. It follows that, whether or not the merchant obtains an advance under the credit system, it is customary for him to arrange insurance. Further, without insurance, it would be necessary for the merchant to set aside a large sum of money to cover possible losses, which money could be profitably employed in the merchant's business.

The shipowner, equally, would feel it pointless to hold large sums in reserve against possible future losses, when, for a relatively small outlay, he could protect himself by insurance.

CHAPTER II

MARINE INSURANCE MARKETS

SINCE the origins of marine insurance can be traced to the mercantile practices in London during the sixteenth century, it is not surprising that the development of marine insurance as a business took place in London so that, by the middle of the seventeenth century many financiers were specializing in the underwriting of marine adventures. Nevertheless, each underwriter acted strictly on his own, using his personal fortune and resources to back the outcome of the adventures he chose to underwrite. These underwriters eventually formed the community which founded Lloyd's and many of their traditional practices exist today. The student would do well to acquaint himself with the history of Lloyd's, although it is not necessary to remember the actual dates stated in the history given below, for a knowledge of this past will enable him more readily to understand the reasons for the practices of today. The London market contains many Insurance Companies but it was much later that the Company market as we know it came into existence and adopted many of the usages and customs of Lloyd's.

Lloyd's

The seventeenth century underwriter was a person of sound financial reputation. His personal fortune had to be adequate to meet his commitments and his integrity had to be beyond reproach. This was the era when many businesses found a sound basis on which to practise and "honour" was an absolute necessity in all good business transactions. Law cases tended to be drawn out and few businessmen would consider entering into transactions where the commitments of either party were liable to have to be decided in a court of law. Consequently, there was little documentation involved in underwriting transactions. Details of the cover required were written on a slip of paper and the underwriter simply entered the amount he was prepared to underwrite and initialled it. Nevertheless, where credit was needed the person making the advance would need

.ething more than an undertaking binding in honour only as
.urity for his loan. In such cases a policy was written by hand, as
, evidenced in the wording of the present day "S.G." form of policy
oy the words "And it is agreed by us, the Insurers, that this Writing
or Policy of Assurance shall be of as much Force and Effect as the
surest Writing or Policy of Assurance heretofore made in Lombard
Street, or the Royal Exchange, or elsewhere in London".

At first, transactions would be negotiated in the private residence
of the underwriter but, as business grew, this method became incon-
venient and, following the practice of the day, the underwriter would
spend his time in one or other of the many coffee houses which were
becoming popular as meeting places in London in the seventeenth
century.

Edward Lloyd owned such a coffee house which was situated in
Tower Street close to the Pool of London. At the time the Pool, that
part of the Thames just below London Bridge, was the part of the
river where all ships visiting London moored to discharge and load
cargoes. Today few ships berth at the wharves in the Pool. Probably due to its proximity to the river and the world of shipping,
the coffee house became a favourite meeting place for underwriters and their associates, and was soon well known as the
centre for marine insurance. According to the Information Department at Lloyd's the earliest record of the existence of Lloyd's coffee
house was dated 1688 but it must have been operated before that
date. In 1691 Edward Lloyd moved his premises to the site now
occupied by No. 16 Lombard Street where it remained until 1785,
although Edward Lloyd died in 1713 probably without realizing the
worldwide prestige his name would achieve by its association with
marine insurance.

Edward Lloyd was quick to realize the advantage of a reputation
which would attract custom and so went out of his way to encourage
association of underwriters on his premises. He provided his patrons
with writing materials and set up a rostrum in one corner of the
coffee house. From this rostrum a boy, called the Kidney, would
make announcements of importance to the customers. To increase the
facilities he had to offer, Lloyd published a news sheet in 1696 in
which he included details of shipping movements and other matters
of interest. After a while the news sheet was discontinued following
difficulties arising from inaccurate reporting of proceedings in the
House of Lords. In 1734 a new newsheet called "Lloyd's List" was
published and issued to subscribers. It was issued weekly until 1740
when it was issued every Tuesday and Friday, and cost subscribers
three shillings per quarter payable at the Bar of Lloyd's Coffee
House in Lombard Street. The list contained details of stock prices
and current rates of exchange in addition to details of the movements

of ships. This paper later became the "Lloyd's List and Shipping Gazette"; but has now reverted to its original title of "Lloyd's List".

In 1769 a gambling element in the Lombard Street coffee house caused the underwriting fraternity to move to a new coffee house in Pope's Head Alley. This establishment was called the "New Lloyd's Coffee House" and was set up by a waiter, from the old coffee house, named Thomas Fielding. By this time the underwriting fraternity was growing rapidly and binding itself into a sort of club which needed its own premises so that in 1771 a committee was elected from the members, who then numbered some 79 merchants, brokers and underwriters. It was the duty of this committee to set up premises and a sum of money was subscribed by members to this end. Eventually, following the personal efforts of John Julius Angerstein, the association of underwriters moved into rooms in the Royal Exchange in the year 1774 where they remained for more than a century, except for a period when the Royal Exchange was being rebuilt following a fire in 1838.

The Lloyd's of today is a society, incorporated by Act of Parliament in 1871, with amendments contained in the Lloyd's Acts of 1888, 1911, 1925, 1951. The first Lloyd's building was erected in 1928 but, once again faced with overcrowding, a new building was erected in Lime Street shortly after the Second World War, occupying a site devastated by bombing during that war. This new building contains an underwriting room 340 feet long and 120 feet wide with a surrounding gallery floor. Marine, motor and aviation business is conducted on the ground floor while other non-marine business is mostly transacted on the gallery floor. It is important to note that the Corporation does not underwrite insurance contracts but merely provides facilities for its members to conduct their own business. From the mere handful who formed the first group of members to elect a committee in 1771 the number of underwriting members has increased to approximately 6,000, including both men and women members, and these elect a Committee comprising sixteen members to conduct the affairs of the Corporation. A Committee member serves for four years. Each year four members retire, being replaced by a further four elected members. A retiring member must not be re-elected until a year after his retirement. The Committee members elect their own Chairman and two Deputy Chairmen annually.

Following the traditions of Lloyd's each underwriting member is responsible up to his full personal fortune to meet his/her commitments. At one time Lloyd's membership was restricted to British males, elected to Lloyd's at the discretion of the Committee. However, today, Lloyd's will give consideration to women and foreign nationals who apply for membership. Each applicant, before election, is required to deposit a substantial amount with Lloyd's as security against his/her failure to meet future commitments. In addition, a means test is applied to satisfy the Committee that the personal assets of the member are adequate. These requirements are based on the anticipated annual premium income, and activities on behalf of the member are restricted to a premium income compatible with the wealth requirements. To quote an example, it was announced in 1975 that members wishing to underwrite an annual premium income in excess of £150,000 would, in addition to lodging an increased deposit, have to comply with a range of increasing means tests up to a maximum of £175,000 for British and Commonwealth names and £235,000 for foreign nationals. With the aim of increasing the capacity of the Lloyd's market, to meet a greater flow of business, it is proposed to introduce a new class of membership in 1976. The new category will allow British "names" in the U.K. to show substantially lower wealth level (£37,500). Naturally, such a member would be bound by the underwriting restrictions applying to this level (e.g. he would be restricted in his premium income) and his deposit requirement would be no less than any other member. In practice, each underwriting member is termed a "name".

Within the Lloyd's community there are a number of underwriting agencies. These are not, in fact, underwriters but are accounting organisations established, with the blessing of the Committee of Lloyd's, to take care of the underwriting activities of "names"; the majority of whom have no knowledge of insurance. An agency groups a number of the "names" it represents into a syndicate and appoints an active underwriter to represent the syndicate. The liability of each name is "several and unlimited". This means that each name is liable to the full extent of his/her personal means to meet his/her proportion of claims attaching to the syndicate and that membership of a syndicate in no way reduces the extent of the member's liability. Each name is responsible for an agreed proportion of risks accepted on behalf of the syndicate and no name has any responsibility to make good losses that another name on the syndicate is unable to meet. The majority of underwriting members take no active part in the business of underwriting, leaving this to the member appointed to represent the syndicate. This active underwriter is usually a member of the syndicate but he can be an employee of the syndicate, in which case he is salaried and has no personal obligation to meet the commitments of the syndicate.

The active underwriters, with their assistants, occupy seats at "boxes" in the Underwriting Room. These "boxes" are designed from the traditional seats in the old coffee houses, although, in the modern Lloyd's, the high wooden backs are replaced by glass partitions. The "Club" atmosphere is still preserved and the public are not generally admitted to the "Room". Only members, associates, and annual subscribers of Lloyd's are permitted to enter the "Room" so that merchants and shipowners must approach a Lloyd's Broker if they wish to place their business at Lloyd's, as only such a broker can approach the Underwriter on their behalf. Whilst women may be admitted as underwriting members at Lloyd's they are not permitted personally to transact business in the Room. Nevertheless today women brokers can be seen in the Room.

The annual premium income at Lloyd's is over £700,000,000 and the liability undertaken to attract such an income must be fantastic. This liability is assumed by the Underwriting members and although the Committee, representing the Corporation, has no responsibility for the debts of the members, it is, nevertheless, careful to preserve Lloyd's good name. Before election to membership as an underwriting member each applicant must satisfy the Committee of his financial standing and, upon election, submit to an annual audit to show that his underwriting assets are sufficient to meet his commitments. Under the Insurance Companies Act, 1958 the audit must be conducted by an auditor approved by the Committee. The Department of Trade and Industry prescribe a form of certificate which the auditor must issue. The Audit was not introduced by the Act but had been in existence since 1908 without legal compulsion.

An interesting illustration of Lloyd's maintenance of tradition exists in the use of a rostrum in the "Room" from which the "caller" makes important announcements, and calls the names of persons whose attention is required by others either inside or outside the "Room". It is customary to call brokers in this manner. When news of considerable importance is to be announced the "caller" rings the Lutine Bell to command attention. Two strokes are given for bad news or one stroke for good news. The frigate "Lutine" was lost off Terschelling in a violent storm in 1799, going down with all hands and an estimated £1,400,000 in gold bullion, all insured at Lloyd's. Subsequent salvage produced about £100,000 in bullion and various relics. The bell was hung over the rostrum at Lloyd's, and is still traditionally hung permanently over the rostrum today.

Lloyd's buildings, both new and old, house the offices of many of the Corporation's departments, as well as the Committee Room, Captains' Room and Nelson Room. The attendants at Lloyd's are easily recognized by their long red cloaks and top hats. They are traditionally called "waiters" following the origin of their duties in the old coffee house.

Shipping intelligence is received from Lloyd's Agents, coast radio stations and shipowners. Details of casualties are published on the Casualty Board in the Room. Such details, together with other information, is passed to Lloyd's of London Press Ltd. This independent company, with considerable printing and publishing facilities at Colchester, Essex, reproduces the information in a number of publications which are in regular use throughout the insurance market. A list of these is given below: —

LLOYD'S LIST

Published Daily (Monday to Saturday inclusive)

This daily newspaper provides a world wide service of news of interest to the maritime, insurance and transportation industries. Regular articles are published on freights and finance, ship sales, United Kingdom and Continental ports, etc., etc., and there is a weekly technical review. World shipping movements, maritime and aviation casualties, strikes, labour disputes, details of exceptional weather conditions, navigational hazards, etc. appear daily. Also published are details of ships expected at U.K. ports and ships in port.

LLOYD'S SHIPPING INDEX

Published Daily (Monday to Friday inclusive)

This publication lists, in alphabetical order around 20,000 merchant vessels on overseas voyages and shows the type, owner, flag, classification society, year of build, gross and net tonnages, the current voyage and latest reported position of each vessel. Up to 4,000 alterations to voyage information are made each day. Where appropriate, reference is made to recent casualty reports which have been published in Lloyd's List.

LLOYD'S VOYAGE RECORD

Published Weekly

This publication also lists vessels in alphabetical order, but gives a comprehensive coverage of arrivals and sailings at all ports of call on current voyages rather than the latest reports. By filing copies of this publication it is possible to keep complete records of vessels' voyages.

LLOYD'S LOADING LIST

Published Weekly

An exporters' guide showing vessels due to load in U.K. ports for all parts of the world with receiving and sailing dates and names of loading brokers. Sailings given approximately 28 days ahead. Cable rates, latitude and longitude and local time shown against all ports. Also shows services operated by road transport operators and shipping and forwarding agents.

Free supplements: Lists of Consular Requirements of all countries and Loading Brokers issued periodically; Cargo by Air giving details of U.K. internal services and services outward from the U.K. to all parts of the world—issued monthly.

LLOYD'S LAW REPORTS
Published Monthly
These Reports specialize in maritime and insurance cases heard in the English Courts and include important decisions given by the Scottish, Commonwealth and United States Courts. Although shipping cases feature prominently, insurance, aviation and commercial actions are also included.

The reports are of particular interest to all concerned with commercial law in that four-fifths of the judgments reported will not be found in any other law reports. A feature of these reports is the introduction to the case, which contains, where necessary, a paraphrase of the pleadings, extracts from relevant documents and a summary of Counsel's arguments. The index to each Part contains a precis of each decision reported and these, together with ample cross-references, facilitate the search for cases. All back volumes from 1919, when the reports first commenced, are available from stock.

LLOYD'S MARITIME AND COMMERCIAL LAW QUARTERLY
International legal developments reviewed in a manner which appeals to the businessman and lawyer. Incorporating: —
* Articles on topical legal points from contributors throughout the world.
* A unique case-note service, setting out, under classified headings, details of important decisions by the superior Courts of other States.
* Texts of relevant international conventions and details of foreign legislation.

LLOYD'S WEEKLY CASUALTY REPORTS
It has been found convenient for record purposes to republish weekly, in handy book-size form, the casualty reports which have been printed in Lloyd's List each day. Reference to these Reports is simplified by the publication of an index each quarter.

LLOYD'S SURVEY HANDBOOK
This important work of reference, which was first published in 1952, has been greatly enlarged and, besides affording information as to loss and damage to a larger number of commodities, sets out authoritative views on principal causes of damage. The book is designed to be of practical use in shipping and insurance circles, as well as to those concerned in the handling of cargoes generally.

DIGESTS OF LLOYD'S LAW REPORTS

These volumes contain condensed reports of all the cases reported in Lloyd's Law Reports during a period of five years. As the reports are arranged under subject-matter headings, the Digests provide both a comprehensive index to Lloyd's Law Reports and case-books on the various aspects of shipping, insurance and commercial law.

Thirteen Digests have been published to date covering the period 1919 to 1970.

LLOYD'S MARITIME ATLAS

In the compass of a small Atlas it is impossible to plot every port of the world, but all the more important ports are shown in Lloyd's Maritime Atlas. To illustrate congested areas to full advantage, inset maps have been introduced where practicable. Reference to the full and geographically arranged list in Section II enables the relative positions of ports and places not marked on the maps to be readily ascertained; this section also indicates on which map or maps the various places may be found.

Many ports shown in the Atlas—and more particularly in Section II—are not to be found in any of the usual atlases or works of reference.

16 two-colour maps are incorporated.

LLOYD'S CALENDAR
Published Annually

Lloyd's Calendar is published annually and contains general information on shipping and marine insurance. Its contents include copies of Lloyd's Standard Form of Salvage Agreement, Standard Forms of Policies, articles on general and particular average, salvage operations. There are articles on the automated merchant vessel report (AMVER) system, a new approach to the presentation of radar information, big economic advantages from container ships, safety legislation and many other items of general interest.

Associations and Services connected with Lloyd's

The Salvage Association was formed in 1856 and has its head office in Lloyd's building. It is not entirely a Lloyd's concern, the controlling committee being composed of representatives of many marine insurers. The Association provides expert technical assistance regarding salvage and arranges surveys of damaged ships, cargoes and other maritime property. Surveying offices and agents maintained in many ports are subject to the control of head office. The Association does not maintain salvage vessels or equipment but is able to assist in the negotiation of salvage contracts and the resulting awards. It is a non-profit making concern and was incorporated by Royal Charter in 1867.

Lloyd's Average and Recoveries Department acts for both Lloyd's Underwriters and Insurance Companies in the collection of general average refunds and deals with the distribution of such refunds and also of recoveries obtained in connection with cargo claims which have been paid by insurers in collision cases. In addition the Department investigates the possibility of recoveries from carriers and other third parties and disburses any recoveries obtained to insurers. The Department is also concerned with general average guarantees.

Lloyd's Agency Department is concerned with the activities of Lloyd's Agents (see later in this chapter) and incorporates the Settlement of Claims Abroad Department, which processes claims under CPA policies and certificates.

Lloyd's also maintains a Claims Bureau and Policy Signing office, details of which appear in the chapters relating to claims and policy signing.

Other Lloyd's services include an Advisory and Legislation Department, a Membership and Service Group, an Agency Department and an Information Department. There are also Underwriters' Associations which act for Lloyd's Underwriters in all technical matters and generally represent the Underwriters in matters pertaining to their business.

The London Company Market

Although many of the well established Fire Offices of today were founded in the sixteenth and seventeenth centuries, the Companies tended to leave the insurance of marine adventures in the hands of the Underwriters at Lloyds. In 1680 a Dr. Nicholas Barbon and others started a Fire Office which later became the "Phoenix". A Friendly Society for mutual insurance against fire was established in 1684 and "The Amicable Contributors" or "Hand in Hand", also a Fire Office, was established in 1696. It is probable that the enormous losses suffered in the Great Fire of London in 1666 made the public very fire insurance conscious which provided a sound basis for the establishment of Fire Offices but there seems to have been little encouragement for the commencement of a Company market for marine insurance. Records show, however, that there was an Office of Insurance, in the Royal Exchange in 1555, which wrote marine risks. There were a number of small private Companies which attempted to enter the marine insurance field but, probably due to lack of funds, these did not last long. The collapse of the Government sponsored South Sea Trading Company. "The South Sea Bubble", also probably disillusioned the investing public at the time. The first major steps towards establishing a Company market took place in 1720 when, following a campaign launched in 1717 by men with marine interests and a discontent for Lloyd's system, two Companies "The London Assurance" and "The Royal Exchange" were incorporated by Royal Charter and for the next 100 years or so these two Corporations held a monopoly of the London Company market in marine insurance. There were other Companies operating outside London in Belfast and Dublin, while private underwriters operated in Liverpool, Manchester, Greenock, Bristol and Glasgow. In the early nineteenth century the "Alliance", a fire office, formed the "Alliance Marine" and following the Joint Stock Act of 1844 several more Companies were formed leading eventually to the extensive Company market which we have today. Not all these Companies are with us today because many suffered from the effects of the first World War and the subsequent depression of 1926 during which period several Companies ceased to operate.

The marine insurance Company of today is a Joint Stock Company with a liability limited to its assets as declared to the Department of Trade and Industry. It must be remembered that the Lloyd's Underwriter has no such limit of liability. The Company may be part of a group of Companies or it may stand by itself. In either event, it is the practice for the Company to build up vast reserves in investments to cover its commitments. Annually, announcements of the financial state of the Company are required by law to be published and the large brokerage firms make a study of these figures to protect their clients' interests, although they are under no obligation to do so. Whilst some of the Mutual Societies, the shareholders of which are the policy holders, have marine departments, Company mutual insurance is not common in the marine market. The majority of Companies each have a board of directors which appoints an underwriter to accept business on behalf of the Company. The title "Underwriter" is given out of courtesy for the Company Underwriter does not, in fact, have any personal liability for the risks he writes. He is a salaried employee of the Company, and it is the Company which is liable for the commitments undertaken by the Underwriter.

Apart from these differences, the Company and Lloyd's Markets work very well together using similar systems and with little discrimination from brokers. Several Companies have underwriting rooms in Lloyd's building and others are situated in the same area of London, thus providing a compact market for the broker on his daily rounds. British Insurance Companies are subject to the provisions of the Insurance Companies Act (1967) which lays down minimum financial assets that must be maintained by the Company as a margin of safety against insolvency. Companies that are unable to comply with the requirements of the Act are ordered by law to cease underwriting.

Markets Outside London

Although London has been the centre of the marine insurance industry for centuries it is not the only place in the world where marine insurance is underwritten. There is a thriving market in Liverpool where the Liverpool Underwriters Association has been in existence since 1802, although there is little doubt underwriting went on before that date.

Starting as individual underwriters who merged into syndicates, the Liverpool underwriters finally formed Companies so that it is exclusively a Company market today, working in close association with the London Company market. Representatives of the commercial world in Liverpool, including shipowners, marine insurance brokers and average adjusters, assembled in 1802 to form the Liverpool Underwriters' Association. The Association provides a comprehensive information and intelligence service to members and provides underwriters with a forum for discussion and consideration of marine insurance matters, as well as facilities for liaison with kindred organizations. The Association acts as Lloyd's shipping correspondents in Liverpool, reporting to Lloyd's Intelligence Department the movement of all ships passing in and out of the Port of Liverpool. With the aid of shipowners and merchants the Liverpool Underwriters helped to form the Liverpool Salvage Association in 1857, which Association, unlike the Salvage Association, owns the equipment and salvage vessels it operates.

The Glasgow Association of Underwriters and Brokers operates on similar lines to Lloyd's and it is interesting to note that this Association was largely responsible for the Glasgow Salvage Association which amalgamated with the Liverpool Salvage Association in 1923.

Working in London, one tends to consider foreign insurance Companies as little more than a reinsurance market and this conviction is strengthened by the enormous amount of foreign direct business which flows regularly into the London market. Nevertheless, there is a substantial Company market in most of the financially developed countries in the world which, in addition to extensive reinsurance activities, accepts a large volume of direct business, much of which is, however, reinsured in London. One of the reasons why much of this business is not immediately apparent to us in

London is because many countries restrict the export of direct insurance business and insist it be offered to their own market first. In certain States in the U.S.A., for instance, legislation only permits the direct insurance business which is surplus to that which can be absorbed in the U.S.A. to be placed outside the Country.

The Marine Insurance Broker

It is a distinct advantage to the underwriters at Lloyd's that the public are not admitted to the "Room" to negotiate the insurance cover they require. Instead, a member of the public, whether he be a merchant, shipowner or other proposed assured, must employ the intermediary of a Lloyd's broker and the underwriter finds he is negotiating with a person well versed in the laws, customs and practices of marine insurance. Not all brokers are Lloyd's brokers but any other broker may engage the services of a Lloyd's broker to place business at Lloyd's for him. Before admission to Lloyd's the broker, wishing to become a Lloyd's broker, has to satisfy the Committee of Lloyd's that he is a suitable and satisfactory person to become an authorized Lloyd's broker. Once admitted, he describes himself as such by using the term "and at Lloyd's" on his notepaper and on the name plate identifying his premises. He is issued with a "ticket" authorizing him to enter the "Room", upon payment of the necessary subscription, and he may arrange for employees to represent him in the actual negotiations. Each such employee must be issued with his own "ticket" naming him as a substitute for the broker who employs him. Although the employee is not personally responsible for the obligations of the broker he is, nevertheless afforded the courtesy title of "broker" by his associates in the market so that the "broker" we meet in practice is usually the substitute for the broker who employs him. It is, therefore, the employer who is the "broker" discussed in the following paragraph.

As has been stated, not all brokers are Lloyd's brokers but in the eyes of the law every broker has the same responsibilities to his Principal. The broker is the agent of the proposed assured, *not of the insurer* with whom he places the insurance. Even though the insurer pays the remuneration to the broker, called brokerage, as a deduction from the premium the broker still remains solely responsible to his Principal, the assured. Once a broker agrees to accept a proposal to negotiate an insurance he becomes the agent of the assured and is subject to the laws of agency. If he is negligent in his duties, whereby his Principal is prejudiced, the Principal may sue him for damages. The broker is deemed to be an expert, well versed in the laws and customs of insurance and the insurance market in which he practises. He does not guarantee the solvency of the insurer and cannot be held liable for a loss which the insurer does not meet, except where he has been negligent in placing the insurance and such negligence resulted in the insurer not meeting a loss which would have been paid but for the negligence. The broker is under no obligation to accept the proposal to negotiate nor to complete the placing. He must use his best endeavours, skill and knowledge of the market to obtain the best cover at the most reasonable rate of premium. If he accepts the proposal to negotiate on behalf of the proposer but is unable to effect the insurance or complete the placing he will customarily approach another broker to assist him. If he is still unsuccessful after using all his resources the broker must immediately advise his Principal of his failure and this before the risk attaches, although in the latter case where the broker receives his instructions from his Principal just before, or even after, the risk attaches, the broker could not be held liable in event of a late advice of failure to place the insurance.

The broker, whether "at Lloyd's" or not, does not discriminate in favour of either the Lloyd's or the Company market. His duty to his Principal comes first and he places the insurance in, what he considers to be, the best market for that particular risk. In fact, the risk may be shared between both markets. Although the broker is not responsible for the solvency of the insurer most large brokerage concerns keep a close watch on the financial status, as published, of the Companies in the market.

Lloyd's Insurance Brokers' Association

Lloyd's Insurance Brokers' Association exists to protect the interests of its members. Every Lloyd's broker is eligible for membership and the majority are members. By arrangements with Lloyd's Underwriters' Association and the Institute of London Underwriters, representing the Company interests, the Association distributes official notices to its members. There are two sections, being marine and non-marine respectively, with each section having its own Chairman.

Corporation of Insurance Brokers

As the "Association of Insurance Brokers and Agents" this organization was founded in 1906 and incorporated in 1910. It later became the "Corporation of Insurance Brokers", being thus incorporated in 1919. Having its headquarters in St. Helen's Place, London the Corporation exists to safeguard the interests of its members and to encourage practices designed to elevate their status. At one time membership was almost exclusively non marine but, gradually the marine brokers are finding it an asset to become "incorporated".

Lloyd's Agents

When Lloyd's was incorporated by Act of Parliament in 1871 it was given power to appoint Agents of the Corporation in all parts of the world. Nevertheless, this power is given by English law and has no effect where the country, outside the jurisdiction of English law, decides not to permit Lloyd's agents to operate within its boundaries. This limitation has been imposed in some areas, probably due to the intelligence service operated by the agents, but it is true to say that a Lloyd's agent has been appointed in most of the world's larger ports and in many small ports. It is essential to appreciate that the Lloyd's agent is an agent of the Corporation, and, since the Corporation does not underwrite, nor does the Lloyd's agent. His duty is to provide a service for the shipping community as a whole. When a ship is in distress or goods are landed in a damaged condition the Lloyd's agent can be called upon by the master to assist in arranging surveys and in other matters. In this way the agent is helping all insurers covering the ship and goods whether or not they be Lloyd's underwriters. He issues certificates of survey and, if the policy so provides, may settle claims, receiving a fee for his services. In addition the Lloyd's agent promptly and regularly transmits information regarding shipping movements and conditions in his area, directly to Lloyd's Intelligence Department, thereby assisting Lloyd's to publish accurate and up-to-date information about world shipping.

Marine Insurance Company Agents

In order to expand their scope of activities most large Companies appoint agents to represent the parent Company provincially and in many of the major cities overseas. These agents may be appointed solely to represent the parent Company but the majority of such agents are business firms operating in the area who undertake the agency as part of their business. In this way, one firm may hold several agencies for different Companies. The Company agent, unlike the Lloyd's agent, underwrites business on behalf of the parent Company. His agency appointment stipulates limitations on the type of business and the maximum amounts to which he may commit the Company. Any business outside these limits must be submitted to the parent Company for approval before acceptance. The agent is generally empowered to settle claims, although, once again, settlement in certain cases is subject to Head Office approval. As remuneration for his services the agent is entitled to retain a commission from the premiums he collects on behalf of the Company and, usually, receives a profit commission based on the profit accruing from the business written by him.

Institute of London Underwriters

The Institute of London Underwriters is an organization which represents the interests of its members in the London marine insurance Company market. Its membership comprises more than 100 Companies including the principal marine insurance Companies. The "Institute", as the organization is called in the market, was incorporated in 1884 and until recently only British and British controlled Companies and Corporations were eligible for membership. A committee, elected from the members, runs the affairs of the Institute. The purpose of the Institute is to further the interests of insurance by co-ordinating facilities regarding wordings, clauses and conditions and to find grounds for common agreement on problems affecting the insurance market. Principally the Institute concentrates on marine business.

Committees are formed which include Lloyd's Underwriters as well as members of the Institute, to decide on matters affecting the whole market and to make recommendations to the market based on their findings. The Institute provides facilities for these Committees to meet. The Technical and Clauses Committee and The Joint Hull Committee are two such Committees. The "Returns Bureau" (The Joint Hull Returns Bureau) operates under the auspices of the Joint Hull Committee for the benefit of the whole market and authorizes "Lay up" returns for both Lloyd's and Company underwriters. In addition to its services to insurance, the Institute administers a Policy Signing Office and a "Claims Payable Abroad" service on behalf of its member Companies.

The marine insurance clauses drafted by the Technical and Clauses Committee are published by the Institute. These "Institute Clauses" are widely used throughout the world.

CHAPTER III

EFFECTING MARINE INSURANCE

Definition of Marine Insurance

FROM the earliest records of law cases in marine insurance the decisions of these cases have been used as precedents to uphold contentions in subsequent legal issues. It was such legal decisions that served to establish the interpretation of many practices and these became the customs and usages of the marine insurance industry. To clarify any misunderstandings it was decided to codify these legal decisions in the Marine Insurance Act of 1906 which came into operation on the first day of January 1907. This Act codified the Law relating to Marine Insurance as at 21st December 1906 and is now the basis of the marine insurance principles of today.

In theory, the purpose of any form of insurance is to replace that which has been lost. It is not intended that the assured should make a profit from his loss but that he should merely be in no worse position than he was before the loss occurred. Obviously, it is not practicable to expect the insurer to replace an object which is lost, nor is it reasonable to expect him to remove the damage thus restoring the damaged object to the whole sound object. As a compromise, any recompense must be of a monetary nature and this system of reimbursement is called "indemnifying". Bearing this in mind, it is easier to appreciate the definition of marine insurance as it appears in Section 1 of the Marine Insurance Act, 1906, which states that by a contract of marine insurance "the insurer undertakes to indemnify the assured, in manner and to the extent thereby agreed, against marine losses, that is to say, the losses incident to marine adventure". In Section 3 the Act defines a "maritime adventure" and "maritime perils" and it states that where ship, goods or other movables are exposed to maritime perils there is a marine adventure. Such property is then called "insurable property". The Act includes in a marine adventure "the earning or acquisition of any freight, passage money, commission, profit or other pecuniary benefit or the security for any advances, loan or disbursements" where any of these is "endangered by the exposure of the insurable property to maritime perils". In the same section the Act provides that any liability to a third party incurred by the owner or person responsible for the insurable property is embraced in the definition.

Many of these expressions may be unfamiliar to the student reading of marine insurance for the first time but will be explained in later chapters. For the moment, the student is advised merely to note where he can find the official definition of marine insurance. Regarding the definition of maritime perils, this will be fully discussed in the chapter on marine perils later.

Effecting Marine Insurance

A merchant, shipowner or other person seeking marine insurance cover may approach a Company underwriter directly and many merchants do, in fact, transact their business in this manner. To effect the insurance with an insurer at Lloyd's it is necessary to use the intermediary of a Lloyd's broker so that it has become the practice for the proposer to approach a broker and engage his services whether or not the insurance is to be effected with Lloyd's. Upon receipt of instructions from his Principal, the proposer, the broker outside the London market will arrange cover by telephone, by means of an agency or by mail with his various contacts; but if he is a London broker, that is, in most cases, a Lloyd's broker, he will follow a well established procedure.

The broker, in his office, will accumulate the facts of the insurance to be effected and will set these down on a piece of stiff card. This document is termed the "slip" and it occupies a very important position in the negotiation of a marine insurance contract.

In 1970 Lloyd's introduced a "standard" slip to the London market and from September 1971 the use of the standard became compulsory for all insurances placed by Lloyd's brokers. The standard slip can comprise two or more panels, at the broker's option but each panel must be exactly 4.75 inches wide. The broker has a choice of two standard lengths; being exactly 8.27 inches or exactly 10 inches. The standard format for "placing" detail is not compulsory in a marine original slip but if the insurance is effected on a slip with the placing detail other than in the standard format, then an off slip must be prepared for signing and accounting purposes; such off slip conforming with the "standard" in every respect.

The "slip" is used to obtain the agreement of one or many insurers to underwrite the insurance. The number of insurers anticipated depends on the monetary value of the subject matter of the insurance and the amount of cover required. The minimum size for a standard slip is 2 panels but the broker will use a slip comprising more than 2 panels if he anticipates that a smaller slip will not be adequate for his purposes.

Having prepared his slip, the broker will select the section of the market in which he anticipates the type of risk involved will be readily acceptable. Many insurers specialize in particular types of insurance and thereby achieve considerable knowledge of the peculiarities of such risks. Such an insurer may be a Lloyd's Underwriter or a Company Underwriter. In any event, such an underwriter achieves not only knowledge but a reputation in the market for his judgement in accepting and rating his specialized type of risk. Such is the reputation of the insurer in the market that once his initial is on the slip the broker has little difficulty in finding other underwriters to follow his lead. This specialist underwriter is known in the market as a "Lead" or "Leader" and it is part of a broker's duty to know the recognized market "Leads". The broker takes his slip to the "Lead" and negotiates the insurance contract with him. This practice of negotiation is called "broking" and it is at this point that the rate of premium is decided. The "Lead" agrees the rate with the broker and impresses his Syndicate line stamp on the slip if he is at Lloyd's (A Company Underwriter does the same with his Company stamp). The Syndicate stamp is a box that contains the Syndicate number, a three letter pseudonym and a row of 12 small boxes in which the underwriter's reference is entered. Where an active underwriter represents more than one Syndicate two or more Syndicate numbers and pseudonyms will appear on the same Syndicate line stamp with the percentage applicable to each Syndicate number indicated. Within the line stamp the underwriter will insert his "line". His "line" is the amount or percentage of the risk that the underwriter is prepared to accept on behalf of his Syndicate. The relationship of the Leader's line to the whole risk is indicated at the foot of panel 2, so that any following underwriter can readily see the basis of the Leader's written line and act accordingly; each following line being written on the same basis. The impression of a line stamp on the slip has the same effect as if the underwriter had initialled the slip. At this point the contract is *concluded* between the "Lead" and the assured (M.I.A. 1906 Sect. 21). Having obtained his "Lead" the broker proceeds to other insurers who will follow the leading underwriter by accepting the rate agreed and inserting their acceptance, initials and details of reference. The broker will continue around the market until he has placed 100% of the value to be placed. At this point the placing can be said to be completed and the broker can notify his Principal accordingly. Although the placing is not completed until the whole amount of the value required has been "taken up" the contract with each individual insurer and the assured is *concluded* as the insurer initials the slip so that a slip with, say, six insurers on it is a slip with six separate contracts agreed and concluded. Even if the broker fails to complete the placing the contract with each signifying insurer stands as concluded.

It is seldom that a broker is unable to complete a placing but if he is having difficulty he may request the assistance of another broker who may be able to place the balance of cover for him. Far from being unable to complete, it is more likely that the broker will find a wider market than he requires. It is a recognized practice for the broker to utilize this wider market by placing considerably more than the amount of cover required. A broker receiving instructions to place £5,000 may, in fact, place £10,000. This is called "overplacing" and is so widely practiced that the Leader would be surprised if the slip was not overplaced and would wonder whether, perhaps, he had not given proper consideration to the risk since, apparently, other insurers were not very willing to follow him. The broker will always overplace the insurance for this reason and, also, because it widens his market for future insurances of a similar nature. If the risk is a very desirable one, overplacing helps the broker to give part of the insurance to those insurers who have helped him in the past with a line on a more undesirable risk. This helps maintain the good relations which must exist for a broker to be successful. There are many occasions when an insurer, not really anxious to accept a particular insurance, will write, what is called, an "oblige line" for a broker to help him in a particularly difficult placing. Further, the insurer likes the practice of "overplacing" because it helps to spread the risk of insurance over a wider market and this is one of the basic principles of good underwriting.

There is another circumstance where overplacing may take place quite unintentionally even if the broker did not decide to place more than the amount required. Let us suppose that, as in the example above, the broker has £5,000 to place. This £5,000 is on goods which it is anticipated will be shipped in a few days. He places this amount but, for the purposes of this example, does not overplace. When the actual shipment takes place only £4,000 of goods are actually shipped so the total insurers' liability has been reduced to £4,000, hence it follows that the broker has overplaced by £1,000.

In either event the broker is not empowered to remove any of the insurers from the slip. If, for any reason, the assured does not accept any of the insurers, which is his prerogative, the broker would have to reapproach that insurer to have the line deleted, but he could not simply delete it himself. Nevertheless, the amount on the slip is greater than the amount at risk, and, to bring it to the correct amount, the broker must reduce each line so that the total is for the correct amount. This reducing of the line is usually done when the policy is prepared for signing. The practice of having a policy signed is called "closing" the insurance and the practice of reducing each line is, therefore, called "short closing".

It is important to note that, whilst the broker is empowered to *reduce* all the lines proportionately he is not empowered to *increase* any of the lines. If, for any reason, the line of any insurer is to be increased the broker must ask the insurer to accept the increase and the insurer himself must make the alteration and initial it.

The art of broking calls for considerable skill and diplomacy for the broker, whilst maintaining a good relationship between himself and the insurers, must always remember that he acts as agent for his Principal, the assured, and must have his interests at heart.

It was stated earlier that the "slip" holds an important position in the effecting of a marine insurance contract. It also holds a peculiar position in the eyes of the law. The placing slip is often termed the "original" slip. Some people believe the origin of this expression to have derived from the fact that it incorporates the original instructions of the broker's principal; but it is more likely that the term came into common use to differentiate between the placing slip and the "off" slip copy of the placing slip which the broker usually prepares for signing and accounting purposes (termed the "signing slip"). In itself, the original slip has no legal validity as a contract (M.I.A. 1906 Sect. 22). By initialling the original slip the insurer merely indicates his intention to accept the insurance and to issue a policy in accordance with the conditions and terms on the "slip". The slip is, however, the basis of the contract and even though the contract is binding in honour only, it is deemed to be "concluded" when the insurer initials the slip (M.I.A. 1906 Sect. 21). The conditions of the contract cannot, however, be presented for consideration in a court of law until they are embodied in a properly executed policy of insurance because the slip is only "prima facie" evidence of the contract. In theory, an insurer could refuse to issue a policy and no action could be taken against him should he repudiate liability under the contract, but this would be folly on his part for no broker would offer him business in the future, and he might as well resign from underwriting. So conscious is the insurer of his position of honour, in practice, that policies are frequently signed after a loss is known to have occurred.

Once the policy has been issued the slip may be used as evidence (M.I.A. 1906 Sect. 89), and the court may even order the policy to be rectified to conform with the intentions shown by the slip.

Important though the slip is, it is merely the broker's instrument for placing the insurance and once this has been achieved the slip becomes of secondary importance as the legally enforceable policy takes over as soon as it has been signed.

However, for practical purposes the slip is used, often without the need to produce the policy, for the processing of endorsements relating to additional and return premium and for claims and refunds of claims. In cargo insurance practice it is customary to use slip policies in some circumstances in place of formal policy documents.

Once the slip has been initialled the broker will return to his office and pass it to his office colleague to deal with the remainder of the procedure. When the office staff have completed their duties the slip will be filed for future reference. Although the broker has completed his part in the matter the slip may be very useful to him in the future. If he has a similar insurance to place he will require that slip, and others like it, to use as a "guide" to show him where he is likely to find a ready market. The broker will show the "guide" slip to the insurer to remind him that he wrote a similar risk before and to indicate the amount of his acceptance on that occasion. Provided the "guide" slip is for an insurance which has proved profitable the insurer will be more ready to accept a similar amount on the new risk offered to him and to write it at the same rate of premium. This saves a great deal of time in negotiations. It is because "original" slips are constantly being removed from the files for this purpose, that most brokers like to keep a file of duplicate slips. Few insurers take kindly to initialling both an original and a duplicate so it has become the practice for most brokers to keep photo copies of all slips on file.

In some brokerage offices it is the practice for the broker to carry out all negotiations with his Principal as well as place the insurance. In other offices the office staff negotiate with the Principal and prepare the slip for the broker. In either case, where a big contract is involved, the Marine Director of the office will often negotiate with his Principal and, himself, obtain the "lead" on the slip, although he may delegate some, or the whole, of this work to his senior broker.

Whichever system is used the broker must immediately inform his Principal of his success in placing the insurance. This is done by word of mouth, telephone, cable, telex or in writing. If it is by word of mouth, telephone, cable or telex, it is customary to confirm this in writing. A covernote is prepared and sent with the letter. The covernote has no legal value as an instrument to be used against the insurer, nor can it be used against the broker, in law, since it is merely an advice. Nevertheless, once the policy has been issued the covernote can be produced as supporting evidence in a case against the broker for negligence.

In some cases the Principal may have asked the broker to simply obtain a quotation. The broker usually has quotations from various insurers noted on small, separate pieces of white paper and puts up the most reasonable of these to his Principal for his consideration. Although the broker could easily advise his Principal of the lowest of these quotations because he is not obliged to complete the placing in law, it would be unwise of him to put up a rate to his Principal unless he was sure he could complete the placing at that rate. It is an honourable practice amongst insurers that no insurer will quote one rate to one broker and a different rate to another on the same risk. The insurer is not bound to honour a quotation, since there is no legal contract in force, but no insurer would think of going back on his word once given. Marine insurers and brokers enjoy a mutual trust of which they are justly proud.

Policy Signing

Once the covernote has been issued and the broker's Principal advised of completion of the placing, the slip is filed. It is customary to number the covernote and the slip for identification and ease in filing. If the insurance is on cargo the broker must wait for a "closing advice" from his Principal, telling him the actual amount shipped, before he can take any further action. If the insurance is on a ship there is no need to wait and the brokerage office staff can proceed, immediately, with closing of the insurance. Few brokers like to part with the original slip whilst the policy is being signed so, to avoid this, a "signing slip" is prepared. This is a typed copy of the original slip, although in some cases it is handwritten, which is initialled by the leading insurer and is merely an authorization for the policy to be signed. There is a market agreement which provides for policies to be signed on presentation of a signing slip initialled by the leading underwriter only.

The drafting and preparing of a marine insurance policy requires considerable technical knowledge and, because of its importance as a legal document, the policy must be carefully checked by the signing authority before it is finally signed. Each insurer's initial on the slip constitutes a separate contract and, in theory, one could have a separate policy for each contract. This would prove unwieldy and expensive so that, over the years, systems have been introduced to make provision for several insurers to have their subscriptions set down on one policy form. Such a policy is called a "combined" policy and is the most common form of policy used. Lloyd's realized the importance of a combined policy many years ago and instituted a system for all Lloyd's underwriters on any one slip to have their subscriptions set down in a combined policy form and this policy to be checked, signed and sealed, on behalf of those underwriters, by the Lloyd's Policy Signing Office. The policy bears the seal of Lloyd's Policy Signing Office but this does not mean that the Corporation accepts any liability under the policy. The seal merely makes it clear that the Corporation has issued the policy on behalf of its members as indicated inside the form. It must be remembered that, although it is on one form, the combined policy represents a separate contract with each insurer (M.I.A. 1906 Sect. 24—Sub 2) and, although the seal is used in practice it is not a legal requirement (M.I.A. 1906 Sect. 24—Sub 1).

In 1942 the Institute of London Underwriters, representing a large section of the Company market, introduced a similar Policy Signing Department to give its members the same economic advantages in policy signing enjoyed by Lloyd's underwriters.

There are two signing and accounting procedures available at L.P.S.O. (the I.L.U. uses the same procedures). The main procedure is termed "Separation". This requires that the Broker prepares his slip for signing and accounting purposes and submits this, with a premium advice note, to L.P.S.O. as Stage One. This allows the accounting side of the operation to be completed, without the delay necessitated by preparing and checking a policy. Once the slip has been processed in Stage One it is numbered and dated, then returned to the broker who initiates Stage Two later. In Stage Two of the Separation Procedure the broker submits the slip already processed, with the policy form to L.P.S.O. where the policy is checked, signed and sealed and returned with the slip to the broker. Where no delay in premium payment will result the broker may use the S. & A. Procedure, instead of the Separation Procedure. In the S. & A. Procedure there is only one stage; the broker submitting both slip and policy in one operation and L.P.S.O. carrying out both signing and accounting in one procedure flow.

On occasions the slip may include lines written by Companies which are not members of the Institute of London Underwriters. In such cases the broker will not issue a signing slip for any of these non-Institute Companies but, instead, he will complete a "closing slip". The closing slip is a printed form issued, in blank, by the Company which leaves spaces for the insertion of the closing details required by the Company. This closing slip is sent to the Company which prepares and issues a signed policy. Where there are several non-Institute Companies involved it is possible for the broker to prepare a combined policy for all these Companies and, by obtaining authorizations from the other Companies, the broker will have the policy signed by the leading non-Institute Company, on behalf of the other Companies.

N.B. More detailed information regarding policy signing and accounting can be found in Volumes 2 and 3.

CHAPTER IV

PREMIUMS, ADDITIONAL AND RETURNABLE PREMIUMS

Premiums

THERE are two parties to a marine insurance contract. These are the insurer, who agrees to bind himself to the true performance of the contract, and the assured, who agrees to pay the consideration for the performance. This consideration is, in fact, the sum of money paid or payable to the insurer and is called "the premium". The premium is vitally important to the insurer for it is from his premium income that he accumulates the funds set aside to meet possible claims. The difference between premium income and claims, less overheads, represents the insurer's profit. It follows that the insurer must use all his skill, judgement and knowledge to ensure an adequate premium income but, at the same time, not to underwrite business which may result in large claims, thus reducing the profit ratio. In non-marine insurance actuarial tables are used to give a reliable guide for the assessment of adequate premiums and, from this guide, a fixed minimum for premium rating is derived which is called a tariff. Companies which use the tariff are called "Tariff Companies". The use of tariffs has not been introduced into marine insurance. Traditionally, the marine insurer uses his personal skill, judgement and knowledge to assess the premium to be charged. Such judgement is gained by experience and, for this reason, the premium is assessed by the leading insurer on a slip. The other insurers simply follow the leader and accept the premium rate assessed by him.

The rate of premium for any particular type of insurance will remain, more or less, constant but the premium derived therefrom will be higher or lower depending on the sum insured. If the insurer stated the actual premium on the slip he would have to make a calculation with the sum insured in each case. To avoid this necessity the rate of premium is shown as a percentage. This percentage is then applied to the sum insured when the insurance is closed. For example, let us assume the rate for a particular type of insurance is 0.25%. This then, is called the "rate" and this rate is used on all similar types of insurance written by that underwriter. If the sum insured on one slip is £1,000 the rate of 0.25% will produce a premium of £2.50. If the sum insured on a second slip is £2,000 the rate of 0.25% will produce a premium of £5.00. In practice the expression "rate" is always used to refer to the premium rate.

When the contract is concluded, that is when the insurer accepts the insurance, the rate is agreed but no actual payment takes place at this time. If a proposer approached an insurer directly the Company underwriter would require the premium to be paid for a single insurance at the time of accepting the insurance. This is a common practice in non-marine insurance but most marine insurance is effected through the intermediary of a broker and for the broker to pay each insurer the premium when he placed the insurance would not be practicable. If one considers the practices of overplacing and subsequent reducing one can see how cumbersome and impracticable such a procedure would be. The insurer dealing directly with an unknown proposer is justified in protecting himself by demanding the premium with the proposal but, usually, the broker is so well known to the insurer that he is happy to leave the matter of premium payment on marine insurance to be settled at a more convenient time.

The insurer, therefore, must look to the broker for the premium and the Marine Insurance Act, 1906, places this responsibility squarely on the broker in Section 53, subsection 1. This onus lies on the broker whether or not he has actually received the premium from the assured. To protect the broker in event of non-payment subsection 2 of the same section in the Act gives the broker a lien on the policy. This lien entitles the broker to retain the policy until he receives the premium and charges from the assured. The broker may also exercise the lien to obtain payment of any other outstanding balance of insurance accounts although this latter cannot be exercised if the broker has reason to believe the balance to be due from an agent of the assured and not directly from the assured.

While Section 53 subsection 1 of the Act places responsibility for payment of the premium directly on the broker it, at the same time, relieves the broker from responsibility for claims payment and places this responsibility directly between the insurer and the assured. Therefore, if the assured authorizes his broker to collect a claim on his behalf the broker is empowered to do this but without the authorization the broker has no entitlement to collect a claim. In fact, the assured may instruct an entirely different broker to collect a claim, as frequently happens when a policy has been effected overseas and is assigned to a consignee in England in which case the consignee will usually instruct his own broker to collect the claim. Since the broker, exercising his lien on the policy for premium payment, has no authorization from the assured and no rights in the policy he cannot use the policy to collect a claim thus offsetting the overdue premium against the claim. In practice, where a broker deals regularly with a Principal he seldom feels the need to exercise his lien and for practical purposes he settles balances due to or from the assured at regular intervals, say monthly or quarterly.

In practice, it is difficult for the broker to exercise his lien. Whilst, to some extent, he may be able to do this with a hull policy, most cargo insurance is effected by means of open cover and certificates replace the policy for most practical purposes. The assured holds the certificate and where this provides for claim settlement on production of the certificate, as is often the case, the broker's lien on the policy would have no effect. However, if the lien *can* be exercised effectively it prevents the assured using the insurance as a form of collateral security to obtain a loan or advance payment and will encourage prompt payment of the premium to the broker.

Delay in premium payment has been of serious concern to underwriters for many years and, in recent years, attempts have been made to encourage early settlement. The "terms of credit" system introduced at Lloyd's requires that the premium be paid within 5 months of the month designated on the slip by the leading underwriter. Usually, the month so designated is the month in which the risk commences, but, in some cases, this may be adjusted to allow a longer period of credit.

In view of the policy being issued to the broker before the premium is actually paid to the insurer, Companies do not show any receipt for the premium on the policy. Lloyd's on the other hand, do state in the policy form wording which constitutes an acknowledgement of receipt of the premium. Section 54 of the Marine Insurance Act, 1906, states that this acknowledgement of receipt of the premium is conclusive of the receipt between the insurer and assured but not between the insurer and the broker. This is another good reason for the broker not to release the policy to the assured until the premium is paid.

Because the broker is entitled to a lien on the policy the assured cannot demand the policy to be delivered directly to him by the insurer where a broker has effected the insurance, nor is the insurer, in such cases, empowered to deliver the policy directly to the assured. The insurer must always pass the policy to the broker, leaving him to deliver it to the assured at his discretion.

Brokerage

Although the broker is the agent of the assured he is remunerated by the insurer. This remuneration is called "brokerage" and the broker is entitled to deduct his brokerage from the premium before he pays it to the insurer. In addition to the brokerage the broker may deduct an allowance for discount to the assured as encouragement for due payment. A further allowance was given to the broker in 1935 to cover increased overheads. Both the brokerage and further allowance are given on condition that no part of them is given away to the assured. A broker may share his brokerage with another broker or agent but it is an understanding that he does not give any of it to the assured. Apart from the broker's allowance the brokerage and discount are common to all marine insurance contracts. Special arrangements are made for brokerage and discounts on reinsurances. The following examples show how the brokerage, discount and allowance is calculated on direct hull and cargo insurance respectively.

	Hull		*Cargo*
Gross Premium	U.S. $100·00		U.S. $100·00
Brokerage 5% o.g.	5·00	5% o.g.	5·00
	95·00		95·00
Assured's Discount 10% on net	9·50	10% o.n.	9·50
	85·50		85·50
Broker's special allowance ½% o.g.	·50		
		2½% o.n.	2·14
Net Premium	85·00		83·36
Gross Premium	100·00		100·00
Net ,,	85·00		83·36
Total deductions	15·00		16·64
	(or 15%)		(approximately ⅙th)

In calculating the net premium for cargo insurance it has become the custom for the broker to simply deduct 1/6th from the gross premium, paying the balance of 5/6ths to the insurer. The broker's calculation is as follows:

		Gross Premium $100·00
⅙th	=	16·66
Gross Prem.	$100·00	
− 5%	5·00	
	95·00	
Client's Allce.		
10%	9·50 9·50	
	7·16	

	Summary:	Gross Premium	$100·00
		Client's Allce.	9·50
			90·50
		Brokerage	7·16
			83·34

It will be noticed that by this system the insurer on cargo business receives $83·34 in place of the $83·36 which is due to him but despite this small loss to the insurer this practice of calculation is accepted throughout the market.

Deferred Premiums

In hull insurance the premium on a ship can be very big and the shipowner may prefer not to pay it all at once. In such cases, the insurer may agree to accept the premium in instalments. This is called "deferred account" or "deferred premium" and one aspect of this system of payment is that the discount to the assured is reduced from 10% on net to 8% on net. More detail of the operation of the deferred account system can be found in the books on Hull insurance and Reinsurance.

Additional Premiums

When goods are insured on a particular voyage the premium rate may be (say) 1·00% and, provided the risk remains constant, the insurer will continue to charge 1·00% for the same type of goods on that particular voyage. If some new hazard is introduced into the risk the insurer may "load" the basic premium. Let us say this "loading" is 0·25%, in which case the premium rate for the voyage with the increased risk becomes 1·25% and the premium is then said to be "loaded". If the additional hazard is only temporary, once it ceases to exist the premium rate for subsequent voyages will revert to 1·00% and will no longer be loaded. This does not mean that once the rate is fixed at 1·25% it can be automatically reduced to 1·00% if the reason for the loading ceases to exist before the voyage commences, although the assured could raise a good argument for a reduction in the rate. It simply means that when a similar risk is offered to the insurer, after the additional hazard has ceased to exist, the insurer will reduce the rate to 1·00% and no longer apply the loading.

A "loading" is *not* an additional premium. An additional premium is an extra premium to be charged, over and above the basic or the loaded rate, when a certain state of affairs exists. In practice, an additional premium is not charged at the time the contract is concluded because it is usually in respect of a risk which may be anticipated as likely to happen but which need not necessarily happen. Therefore, when the contract is concluded the basic rate is agreed and a provision is made for an additional premium to be charged if a certain circumstance occurs. If the circumstance does not occur no additional premium is charged. In most cases an actual rate or a set scale is specified when the contract is concluded but where this does not happen the Marine Insurance Act, 1906 (Section 31) protects the assured from an exhorbitant charge by stating that the additional premium must be reasonable and in deciding what is reasonable Section 88 states that this must be a question of fact. This latter means that all facts, including past experience of similar situations, must be taken into account to determine what is reasonable.

Obviously, without the additional premium the extra risk would not be covered by the policy, so it follows that an additional premium is charged for the cover of something not normally covered by the policy. Since neither party knows for certain that this additional risk is going to arise it is said to be "held covered" should it occur. In marine insurance, the term "held covered" is, generally, only used to apply to such probable additional risks.

There are two notable exceptions to the above use of the term "held covered". One being on the occasion when a broker offers an insurance to an underwriter on, say, a Friday. The insurer may wish to consider the risk more fully or require enquiries to be made before finally committing himself. The broker, on the other hand, may fear the risk might attach over the weekend and a loss occur. The insurer will probably agree to "hold covered" his line over the weekend. If a loss occurs the insurer will be honour bound to meet that loss. If no loss occurs the insurer can decide on Monday whether or not he will accept the line. The second exception is more common and occurs when a long term contract is due for renewal. The broker may not be in a position to present the renewal slip on or before the renewal date and, to prevent the insurance expiring, he will take the expiring slip to each insurer in turn who, if he is prepared to renew, will write "Renewal h/c" and initial it.

Let us now take three examples to illustrate the application of a "held covered" provision and the relevant additional premium:
Example 1. Goods are insured from A to B at 1·00% and the insurance terminates when the goods are delivered to the warehouse at B. The assured anticipates long periods of hold up in the destination warehouse before he can dispose of the goods and is concerned about the fire risk since the marine policy will have ceased to operate. He does not want to effect a separate fire policy because he is not certain about the hold up taking place. The answer is for the marine policy to continue if and when the goods are held up in the destination warehouse, but only for fire risks. Let us assume the marine insurer agrees to this and applies an additional premium of 0·075% for each thirty day period or part. The policy will show "Additional periods held covered at destination warehouse against fire risks only at an additional premium of 0·075% for each period of

thirty days, or part thereof". The assured will pay the basic rate of 1·00%, but not the additional premium, and the policy will be delivered to him. In due course, the goods will arrive and the consignee will know if, and for how long, the goods are held up in the destination warehouse. When the goods finally leave the warehouse the assured will notify the insurer and the additional premium will be calculated and paid. The effectiveness of this system depends largely on the honesty and good faith of the assured for, unless there is a loss under the policy, the insurer is unlikely to know whether there has been any warehouse risk at all. Nevertheless, the system seems to work very satisfactorily, being another illustration of the good faith which persists between the marine insurance market and commercial interests.

Example 2. Goods are insured from A to B and are to be carried by a named vessel or one of a specified class. In practice a classification clause[1] is used in the long term insurance contract to ensure that carrying vessels are up to the required standard as anticipated by the insurer when he accepted and rated the risk. While the assured will do his best to ensure the goods are carried by the specified vessel or by a vessel of the required class he cannot always control this and, to protect him from being uninsured, the insurer will agree, on conclusion of contract, to "hold covered" other vessels. In the absence of any special specified rate of additional premium the expression "held covered" means "held covered at a premium to be arranged" and M.I.A. 1906 Sect. 31 comes into operation. This type of additional premium is called "Overage" because it is in respect of vessels of over 15 years age or not fully classed. In many cases a set scale is agreed for "over-age" vessels but where there is no scale the broker negotiates the rate for the additional premium with the leader on the slip which rate must, of course, be reasonable.

Example 3. It is common practice for a ship-owner to keep premiums down by agreeing to limit the area of navigation of his vessel. These navigational limits are specified in the policy as an express warranty and if the warranty is breached the insurer is discharged from liability as from the date of the breach (M.I.A. 1906 Sect. 33). The assured would not like his insurance simply to cease from the date of the breach of warranty if the vessel happened to go outside its navigational limits and, therefore, arranges with his insurer to "hold covered" the breach at an additional premium which, customarily, is already agreed. If the vessel goes outside the navigational limits the insurance continues and the assured pays the relevant additional premium, but if the vessel stays within the navigational limits no additional premium is payable.

[1] For details of the Classification Clause see Vol. 2.

Returnable Premiums

When a proposer gives the instructions to his broker to effect an insurance, or when he approaches a Company directly himself, he is considering the possibility of loss in the future and is concerned with covering himself in event of that loss occurring. The insurer must consider the risk in the same light and charge a premium accordingly. It may happen that the risk does not take place or that, even if it does, it may do so in such circumstances that the insurer would have charged a lower premium. The assured may then feel he has been unjustly overcharged and that he is entitled to a return of part or whole of the premium. In deciding whether, in fact, a return of premium is due there are certain fixed principles to be taken into account and these are laid down in the Marine Insurance Act, 1906 Sections 82 to 84.

The first of these Sections is merely incidental since it simply provides that once a premium, or proportionate part, becomes returnable it may be recovered from the insurer if already paid or retained if not already paid. It should be remembered that Section 53 of the Act makes the insurer directly responsible to the assured for returnable premiums, but Section 82 gives the right to an agent (a broker that is) to retain a returnable premium where he has not paid the premium. This would appear to be contradictory but the problem is probably purely academic since there has never been an instance recorded where a broker retained a returnable premium without crediting it to the assured and the assured took action against the insurer for it.

Section 83 deals with return by agreement and Section 84 deals with return for failure of consideration. We will leave Section 83 for the moment and consider Section 84 first.

Earlier it was stated that the "consideration" is the amount paid or payable to the insurer. This is true because the premium is the consideration for the performance of the contract but also the performance of the contract is the consideration for the premium. When Section 84 of the Act refers to "consideration" it means it as the performance of the contract, hence it deals with circumstances where the performance of the contract fails. Obviously, if the performance of the contract fails the insurer does not pay any losses and, if this is merely due to circumstances outside control of the assured, it is only reasonable that the premium should become returnable. Nevertheless, the performance of the contract may fail for a number of reasons and not all of these would entitle the assured to a return of his premium.

If there has been any fraud or illegality the consideration would undoubtedly fail but the assured could hardly expect a return of his premium. The law would be condoning a fraudulent act if it allowed the guilty party to recover the premium which he had put forward as part of his fraudulent activity. But, if there is no fraud or illegality on the part of the assured or his agent then the assured is entitled to a return of the premium he has paid, or is liable to pay, in event of failure of consideration. An example will best illustrate the meaning of this form of failure of consideration. Goods valued and insured for £1,000 are to be shipped on a voyage from A to B. Before the shipment takes place the sale contract falls through and the goods are not sent for shipment and are, therefore, never imperilled. Accordingly, there is a failure of consideration and the whole premium is returnable. If the shipment did take place but only £500 value was shipped half the premium would become returnable.

The Act makes provision for the premium to be returned where the policy is void. A void policy is one which is inadmissible in evidence in a court of law. It is difficult to envisage how this could arise without fraud or illegality and the Act states that the premium is not returnable in the latter event. A P.P.I. policy (see Chapter 5) is void but if the insurer is prepared to stand by his obligations in "honour" the assured could hardly expect to have his premium returned. Once again this is little more than an academic exercise for, if a policy is void and inadmissible as evidence, how does one sue for a return of premium?

In the example above reference is made to the subject matter of the insurance (the goods) never having been imperilled. This means never having been exposed to peril. Most policies on cargo contain the phrase "lost or not lost". In some cases the insurance may have attached, that is the voyage started, before the contract is concluded and a loss may have occurred. By using the expression "lost or not lost" the insurer agrees to cover the assured for that loss also, provided the assured is not aware of the loss or, if he is, provided the insurer is also aware of it (M.I.A. 1906 First Schedule, Rule of construction No. 1). If the assured effects the insurance on the basis of "lost or not lost" and the assured then finds the goods had already arrived before the contract was concluded he is not entitled to a return of his premium. The Act does say that if the insurer was aware that the goods had arrived safely the premium *is* returnable, but this is unlikely to occur because there would seem to be no purpose in the insurer accepting the insurance.

The remainder of Section 84 is concerned with insurable interest, gaming and wagering policies, unvalued policies and double insurance. Although those will be dealt with in detail in subsequent chapters it is necessary to touch briefly on these matters now so far as they relate to returnable premiums, in order to conclude a summary of the principles of returnable premiums as provided in Section 84 of the Act. To claim under a marine policy the assured must have an insurable interest at the time of loss. If he has no interest he cannot claim so the premium becomes returnable. But, this rule does not apply in respect of gaming or wagering policies. The law frowns on policies effected by way of gaming or wagering and will not acknowledge their existence. In fact, since 1909 the effecting of such policies has been illegal but this was not so when the Marine Insurance Act was drafted so the Act discouraged those who effected such policies by making the premium non-returnable.

In practice the majority of marine policies are valued, that is to say, the value is agreed, is expressed as such in the policy and is conclusive of the insurable value whether or not it is correct. In such policies there can be no question of the premium having been paid on a higher value than is at risk. But, if the policy is not "valued" and the sum insured is greater than the actual amount at risk there is over-insurance and the premium in respect of the amount over-insured is returnable. The same principle is applied when there is innocent double insurance. This may occur when a seller insures the goods and the buyer, unaware of the seller's action, also insures them. If the earlier, presumably the seller's, policy has borne the entire risk or has paid the full sum insured there can be no return of premium on that policy. Otherwise, in event of double insurance the premium is proportionately returnable. In practice it is customary to avoid complications by cancelling the second policy outright and returning the premium on that policy.

We now come to Section 83 of the Act which deals with returns by agreement. Earlier, it was shown how the insurer agrees to "hold covered" a possible but not necessarily probable risk on agreement for the assured to pay an additional premium if the risk takes place. In the same way that an assured may anticipate the possibility of an increase in risk he may also anticipate the possibility of a reduction in risk, so that since the insurer is entitled to an additional premium in event an increase in risk it is reasonable that the assured should expect a return of premium for a reduction of risk. The insurer appreciates this and in such cases agrees in the contract to give a return of premium should the anticipated circumstance take place.

The most common form of return by agreement occurs in hull insurance. The hull underwriter charges a rate commensurate with the full navigational risks which it is to be anticipated the vessel will encounter. It is customary to insure a ship for a period of 12 months and it is likely that the ship will be "laid up" out of commission for part of the period of the insurance. When a ship is laid up the risk to the insurers is drastically reduced and the rate charged on the policy is much higher than would have been charged for a lay-up risk. Therefore, it is customary for all hull time policies to contain a clause providing for return of part of the premium in event of the vessel being laid up. The minimum period of lay up to qualify for a return is 30 consecutive days and the return is calculated by deducting a percentage retention from the annual navigating rate and allowing 1/12th of the difference obtained as a return for each full period of 30 days. The amount deducted is termed a "port risk retention" or, alternatively, a "lay up retention". In practice, the retention is based on the policy premium and varies according to whether the vessel is under repair or not during the lay up period (i.e. 20% not under repair or 40% under repair). The calculation is subject to a maximum and minimum retention. All returns are paid to the broker net of 15% discount, even in the case of deferred account where the original premium is net of 13·1% only. The broker pays the assured the exact amount received from the underwriter. It is important to note that no returns are payable until the policy expires and are then payable only subject to the vessel being safe on such expiry. The term "and arrival" is used in the policy, by the side of the returns provision, to indicate this. Further details of lay up retentions and return calculations can be found in the book on the practice of hull insurance (see Volume 3).

Hull policies also customarily contain provisions for a return of premium in event of the policy being cancelled before the expiry date.

In certain types of cargo insurance the insurer may agree to a return of premium in event of no claims for a particular section of the insurance. This is to encourage the assured to accept a high premium rate overall but to do his best to see that no loss occurs which could be prevented by exceptional care. An example of this can be seen in the insurance of rejection risks. In some Countries the import regulations are strict and are rigidly applied. The U.S.A. are particularly outstanding in this and they have a Governmental department which employs inspectors to examine all foods and drugs imported. Regulations, as to minimum standards of purity and quality, are laid down and any imports which do not reach these standards are rejected. This practice of examining food on import is not confined to the U.S.A. but the rigidity of the application of the U.S.A. regulations leads exporters of certain foodstuffs, mainly fruit products from the Mediterranean, to seek insurance against rejection. There is no ready market for the risk, but some insurers will accept it provided they are offered the ordinary marine insurance as well. The rate will be an overall rate for both marine and rejection risks with a provision that, in event of no claims for rejection throughout *all the season's policies*, a return of premium at a fixed rate will be paid. In some cases the return of premium may not be based on the whole season's policies, but this is a matter for negotiation when concluding the contract.

Insolvency of the Insurer

Before leaving the subject of premiums and returnable premiums it would be as well to have a reminder of the position of each of the parties involved in event of the insurer becoming insolvent. In practice the strict audit to which a Lloyd's underwriter submits annually makes it very unlikely that a Lloyd's underwriter would become insolvent.

The Companies each have an annual accounting system, whereas a Lloyd's underwriter has a three year accounting system, but these systems are merely to establish the profit and loss ratios and do not necessarily reflect the solvency of the insurer. Where a Company is insolvent it is unable to meet its liabilities and its affairs are placed in the hands of a liquidator. The liquidator has no power to write insurance nor to issue policies. It is said in legal circles that it would be "ultra vires", that is beyond his powers, for a liquidator to issue a policy. Therefore, if any slip has been written but the policy not issued the insurance is simply void. If the policy has been issued the broker is responsible for the premium in accordance with Section 53 of the M.I.A. 1906, even though he knows the insurer can no longer meet any claims, or at least can only meet them in part. The same section provides that the insurer is directly liable to the assured for claims and returnable premiums. The broker is agent of the assured and, as such, is not responsible for the solvency of the insurer. If the insurer becomes insolvent the assured cannot sue the broker for negligence because he placed the insurance with that insurer. The broker always states the names of the insurers in his covernote and it is up to the assured to refuse to accept any particular insurer. Most large brokerage concerns keep an eye on the published annual accounts of the Companies with whom they place business and do their best to ensure that the business is not placed with a Company of doubtful solvency. They may even meet claims out of their own resources but it must be remembered that there is no responsibility on the broker to do this.

CHAPTER V

INSURABLE INTEREST

THE purpose of a marine insurance contract is to reimburse the insured for a loss suffered as a result of the operation of an insured peril. To suffer a loss the assured must have an interest in the insured property exposed to peril. If the assured has no interest he can suffer no loss and there is nothing to reimburse. It follows that the assured under a marine insurance contract must have an insurable interest and if he has no interest nor a reasonable expectation of acquiring such interest the policy is void (M.I.A. 1906 Sect. 4). In fact, not only is the policy void but a person effecting such a policy has contravened the Marine Insurance (Gambling Policies) Act, 1909 and is liable to suffer the penalties imposed by that Act.

In other branches of insurance the proposer must have an insurable interest when the insurance is effected. This principle does not apply in marine insurance. The assured in a marine insurance contract need not have an insurable interest at the time the insurance is effected but he must have a reasonable expectation of acquiring such interest and he must have an interest at the time of loss. This latter is important because if the assured's interest has not attached or has ceased before the loss occurs he cannot claim under the policy. He must have an interest at the time of loss to claim (M.I.A. 1906 Sect. 6). Cargo policies are customarily assigned with the passing of the interest in the goods from one party to another and it would be impracticable for each of the parties to the assignment to claim on the same policy separately because each had an interest at different times in voyage. Also it would prove difficult to discover exactly when a loss occurred in the case of goods which arrive damaged. To overcome this difficulty the standard policy form always contains the words "lost or not lost". If an insurance is effected with the term "lost or not lost" contained in the policy but the assured is aware of a loss occurring prior to the attachment of his own interest the insurer is not liable for that loss unless he also knew of it when the contract was concluded (M.I.A. 1906 Sect. 6), but where neither party was aware of a loss when the contract was concluded and the policy is assigned the rights in the policy pass to the assignee and he can claim for a loss which occurred before his interest attached.

42

Apart from the use of the "lost or not lost" provision an assured who has no interest at the time of loss cannot acquire such interest after he is aware of the loss (M.I.A. 1906 Sect. 6).

Section 5 of the Marine Insurance Act, 1906 is very important for it defines insurable interest which is one of the fundamental requirements of insurance. The section is reproduced below and should be carefully studied.

"Marine Insurance Act, 1906 (Section 5).

(1) Subject to the provisions of this Act, every person has an insurable interest who is interested in a marine adventure.

(2) In particular a person is interested in a marine adventure where he stands in any legal or equitable relation to the adventure or to any insurable property at risk therein, in consequence of which he may benefit by the safety or due arrival of insurable property, or may be prejudiced by its loss, or by damage thereto, or by the detention thereof, or may incur liability in respect thereof".

It can be seen from Section 5 that the assured must stand in such relation to the adventure that in event of misfortune he may suffer some form of loss. If he cannot suffer a loss then he has no insurable interest.

The person who has such an interest in the subject matter of the insurance has an insurable interest. Therefore, in practice, the subject matter of the insurance is always called the "interest". The subject matter in a cargo policy is the cargo and this is called a "cargo interest". The same applies to an insurance on a ship where it is customary to show the interest as "Hull and Machinery" and this is called a "hull interest". In practice marine insurances are segregated into two broad categories. These categories are "Cargo Interest" and "Hull Interest" respectively. Cargo interests embrace all types of interest related to the cargo whereas Hull interests, obviously, embrace all types of interest related to the ship. Some interests are difficult to place in any one of these categories and the tendency is to call the interests of the cargo owner "cargo interests" and those of the shipowner "hull interests". One may even hear them referred to as "cargo-owner's interest" and "shipowner's interest" without actually relating them to either Cargo or Hull category.

The following examples should help the student to categorize the particular types of interest.

Cargo Interests

Ownership—The owner of the goods "stands in a legal and equitable relation" to the goods "in consequence of which he may benefit by the safety or due arrival" of the goods "or may be prejudiced by their loss, or by damage thereto or by the detention thereof". The owner, therefore, clearly has an interest in the goods and this interest continues so long as he has title to the goods. This still applies even if the goods are security for a loan. The extent of his interest is what he actually paid for the goods but this may be increased by additional interests as follows below.

Shipping Costs—When the cargo owner sells his goods he must pay the costs of having them carried to the consignee's destination. This cost is called "freight" and in most cases freight is paid by the cargo owner in advance, being non returnable in the event of the goods not being delivered. When freight is paid in advance, and is non returnable, the cargo owner has an insurable interest in such freight (M.I.A. 1906 Sect. 12).

Insurance Charges—When effecting insurance on the goods the assured pays a premium. If the goods are lost he cannot recover the premium but if they are not lost the price he receives from the consignee will include the seller's premium. Since such premium is lost in event of the goods being lost the cargo owner has an insurable interest in the premium (M.I.A. 1906 Sect. 13).

Anticipated Profit—A seller of goods expects to make a profit on the sale and the price due to him from the consignee will include this profit. If the goods fail to arrive the seller loses his profit so he has an insurable interest in the anticipated profit.

Partial Ownership—Where a cargo owner has title to only part of the consignment he has an insurable interest in respect of that part and any charges or profit attaching to it (M.I.A. 1906 Sect. 8). It is not difficult to establish the extent of partial ownership when the consignment consists of clearly marked containers, as in the case of canned foods being carried as a bulk consignment for a number of owners and Section 72 of the M.I.A. 1906 makes provision for the apportionment of loss in such cases.

Defeasible Interest—The seller of goods has an insurable interest in the goods until title passes to the buyer, which may occur after the commencement of the voyage. When title passes the seller's interest terminates. This sort of interest, which may cease during the currency of the voyage for reasons other than maritime perils is called a "defeasible interest" (M.I.A. 1906 Sect. 7). No return of premium is payable if the interest is terminated during the currency of the policy.

Contingent Interest—When title passes to the buyer the seller's interest terminates and the buyer's interest attaches. Sometimes the sale contract contains a clause giving the buyer the right to reject the goods because of delayed delivery or for other reasons. If the buyer exercises his right under the clause the buyer's interest terminates and reverts to the seller. This sort of interest, which attaches during the currency of the voyage on the happening of a contingency, is called a "contingent interest" (M.I.A. 1906 Sect. 7).

Bottomry and Respondentia—These are both insurable interests which are of little more than academic interest today. Both are concerned with loans obtained by the master during the voyage to enable him to complete the voyage. Modern communications make it possible for the master to contact his owners for instructions and money but communications were not always as good as they are today. The master would be forced to offer the ship, freight and even the cargo as security for a loan under a Bottomry Bond or, in the case of Respondentia, the cargo alone would act as security for the loan. If the security was lost the loan was not repayable so the lender had an insurable interest in the outcome of the adventure to the extent of his loan (M.I.A. 1906 Sect. 10).

Forwarding Expenses—It is not unusual for a contract of affreightment (the contract by which the carrier agrees to carry the goods) to contain a clause allowing the carrier to discharge the cargo short of the destination port or over-carry it to a further port if, for some reason, it cannot be discharged at the destination port. When a carrier exercises his rights under the clause the cargo owner must make his own arrangements and bear the expense of getting the property to its destination. The carrier may even be entitled to charge additional freight for overcarriage. The ordinary policy does not cover these expenses but the cargo owner has an insurable interest in them and can insure the expenses if there is a market available. The most likely situation where these expenses arise occurs when the destination port is strike-bound. When the likelihood of such a loss becomes apparent it is probably too late to interest an insurer in the risk. To protect themselves many regular shippers (the "shipper" is the cargo owner or consignor) arrange an insurance for 12 months at a time to cover all shipments against loss by "strikes expenses".

A similar type of expense occurs when goods are discharged short of destination because the approaches to the destination port have become icebound. Each year in the autumn the St. Lawrence freezes and ships have to deviate to other ports if the freeze comes earlier than anticipated. When ships are liable to sail for such ports in late summer cargo owners become concerned at the additional expense they might incur if the cargo is discharged short of destination and seek insurance. This is called "ice deviation risk" and the insurance pays £X per ton on cargo discharged short of destination due to ice risks. The insurer always requires a warranty in the insurance that the vessel sails not later than a certain date.

Commission—An agent acting for the cargo owner on a commission basis may insure the commission he expects to earn when the goods arrive. This is provided for in Section 5 of the Act by the words "may benefit by the safety or due arrival of insurable property".

Liability—To incur a legal liability there must be a degree of negligence. Since the cargo is in the care of the carrier under a contract of carriage any liability incurred in relation to the cargo would lie with the carrier. It is possible for the owner of a dangerous cargo to incur a liability to the carrier but this is a contractual liability and is not usually the subject of marine insurance. In practice it is not customary for insurance on cargo owner's liability to be effected in the marine market.

Cargo Specie—There are so many different types of cargo, each with its own special underwriting problems, that a sizeable book could be written to cover them all. One, however, does bear mentioning here, namely "cargo specie". The reason for selecting this particular interest is that many underwriters keep separate statistics for specie. "Specie" is an embracing term covering all sorts of valuable cargo. It covers gold bullion, other precious metals, precious stones, bonds, share certificates, money in coin and currency in notes. The term can be used to cover items similar to those named but is not used to cover "objets d'art" or "fine arts", such as valuable porcelain, sculptures and paintings.

Hull Interests

Ownership—The shipowner, naturally, has an insurable interest in the ship which he owns. This interest is shown in the policy as "Hull and Machinery". Sometimes this can be seen as "Hull, Machinery, and Refrigerating Machinery". The reasons for these methods of description of the interest will be explained later when we consider "valued policies".

Partial Ownership—The part owner in a ship has an insurable interest in the value of the part he owns. Today this hardly ever applies but at one time the ship was considered divided in 64 parts and several owners, in partnership, would each own one or more 1/64ths of the ship. Most ships today are owned by large shipping concerns. These shipping concerns have a board of directors and shareholders. A shareholder in a Shipping Company has no insurable interest in the ships owned by the Company.

Insurance Charges—The shipowner usually insures his vessel for a period of twelve months. He pays the premium when the policy is issued and recovers it in the freight he earns during the ensuing 12 months. If the vessel becomes a loss during that period the freight earning ceases so the shipowner is unable to earn the premium in respect of the balance of the 12 months premium. Because he may lose the premium in this way he has an insurable interest in the premium and may insure it. Since the premium is deemed to be recovered in the freight earned the insurable interest reduces as time goes on so it is customary to reduce the sum insured in the policy by 1/12th each month. If the sum insured in the premium policy is £1,200 at inception after 6 months it will have reduced to £600 and in the last month of the insurance it will stand at £100. This type of interest is generally called "Premiums Reducing Interest". Of course, if the policy is for a voyage the premium does not reduce but one is unlikely to come across a voyage policy on premiums in practice. In theory, the shipowner is expected to replace the lost vessel and to insure the replacement. He will want to recover, from the loss, sufficient premium to pay for the new insurance which is another reason why he has an insurable interest in his premium.

Charterer's Interest—Where a person requires the use of a complete vessel either for a voyage or a period of time he usually charters the vessel. This means he hires the vessel under either a voyage charterparty or under a time charterparty. He might even hire the vessel under a charterparty by demise, in which case he leases the vessel. Under an ordinary charterparty the charterer simply has the right to have his goods carried by the vessel, but he has no possession or control of the vessel so has no insurable interest in it, the shipowner remaining responsible for the ship. Under a charterparty by demise, however, the charterer provides the stores, fuel, master and crew, and the possession and control of the ship are with the charterer. Here, the charterer has an insurable interest in so far as he is responsible for the loss of or damage to the vessel. This latter form of charterparty is unusual today.

Charterer's Freight—Where a charterer pays money in advance for hire of a vessel there may be a provision in the contract that no part of the hire money is returnable in event of loss. Alternatively, the charterer may not pay in advance but may agree to pay £X per day for a given period even if the vessel is lost or damaged during that period. In both circumstances the charterer has an insurable interest in the money paid or payable.

Freight—Where packaged goods are carried the shipper pays the money for the carriage in advance. This money is called advanced freight. The definition of the word freight can be found in the first schedule to the Marine Insurance Act, 1906. Advanced freight is not returnable generally so the insurable interest is vested in the cargo owner. In certain cases the freight on bulk cargoes is payable on the amount discharged at destination. The amount discharged is called "Out-turn" and since the freight is payable on the out-turn it is not payable until the ship has discharged so if any loss of cargo occurs there is a loss of freight. Hence, the shipowner has an insurable interests in this freight. Because freight is seldom at the shipowner's risk many shipowners use their freight interest to effect a separate insurance for 12 months on "total loss only" terms with freight as the interest. In event of a total loss this policy provides an additional amount to the hull policy proceeds.

Disbursements—During the course of a voyage a master may find it necessary to expend sums of money for the furtherance of the voyage. Such "out of pocket" expenditure is called "disbursements" and, in theory, these amounts are recovered in the freight payable at destination. The shipowner has an insurable interest in disbursements but, in common with freight in modern practice, this interest is rather nebulous because so much freight is paid in advance. As in the case of freight the shipowner tends to use disbursements as the interest in a policy to provide an additional amount to the proceeds from the Hull policy. (See "P.P.I. Policies".)

Mortgagee's Interest—Many a shipowner finds it necessary to mortgage his vessel to obtain money for running his business. Such a shipowner retains his insurable interest in the ship even though it is security for a loan. The mortgagee, the person who lends the money, also has an insurable interest in the ship to the extent of his loan and the charges due on the loan (M.I.A. 1906 Sect. 14).

Contractual Liability—A shipowner who carries goods, other than under a charterparty, is called a "common carrier". The common carrier enters into a contract with the cargo owner whereby he is absolutely responsible to the cargo owner for loss of or damage to the goods whilst in his care. There are certain exceptions which excuse the carrier from liability, but, apart from these, the carrier can incur a contractual liability for loss of or damage to the goods. This liability to the cargo is an insurable interest (M.I.A. 1906 Sect. 5) but is not insured in the ordinary market. It is one of the interests that is insured with a P & I club.

Third Party Liability—There are two parties to a contract. Any person outside a contract is a third party. Liability to one party of a contract by the other is called a "contractual liability". Liability to a person outside a contract is called a "third party liability". There are many ways in which a shipowner may incur a third party liability and in all of these he has an insurable interest. The only form of third party liability insurable in the ordinary market is that which is consequent upon collision. In practice, all hull policies contain a clause providing cover against collision liability. This clause constitutes a separate contract and the sum insured in the policy is, in effect, repeated for this contract. In the Institute Time Clauses, Hulls, the limit of indemnity is 3/4ths of the liability with a further limit of 3/4ths of the insured value. It follows, that if the insured ship was responsible for a collision and also became a total loss the policy would pay a maximum of 3/4ths of the insured value in respect of the collision liability and, in addition, the full insured value in respect of the total loss. Other third party liabilities include loss of life, personal injury, damage to wharves, piers, buoys and other objects, liability for statutory removal of wreck and infringements of rights of harbour authorities and others. These other third party liabilities are not covered in the ordinary market but may be covered by P & I clubs. It is of interest to note that the laws of some Countries provide that the collision liability of an offending ship is extinguished if that ship is a total loss in the collision.

P & I Interests—There are many insurable interests which the shipowner cannot insure in the ordinary market. It has become the practice for shipowners to join mutual clubs to protect themselves from loss in respect of these interests. Such mutual clubs are called P & I clubs. The abbreviation means "Protecting and Indemnity" though very often the expression "Protection and Indemnity" is used. The club covers the 1/4th collision liability not borne by the market, loss of life, personal injury, damage to harbour wharves and other objects, removal of wreck, infringement of rights, quarantine expenses, shipwreck indemnity to master and crew, liability to cargo and other interests not covered by the ordinary marine insurance market. Where small craft are concerned and in the cases of ship construction and port risks the ordinary marine market underwrites P & I interests but, otherwise, it leaves them to the clubs.

Incidental Interests

Master's and Seamen's wages—In theory the master and seamen could lose their wages in event of loss of the adventure so the Marine Insurance Act allows them to insure these. (M.I.A. 1906 Sect. 11). In practice, however, the law protects masters and seamen from loss of wages in event of shipwreck so the shipowner has the insurable interest as part of his shipwreck indemnity interest, which he covers in a P & I club.

Reinsurance—The insurer undertakes a liability when he accepts a "line" in an insurance policy. He, therefore, has an insurable interest insofar as he is liable in event of loss in the adventure. He may reinsure the whole or part of his line with another insurer. If the original insurance is on full conditions he may reinsure on full conditions or on limited conditions, that is, he may reinsure an "All Risks" insurance either as "All Risks" or, say, "Total Loss Only". He cannot, however, reinsure on wider conditions than the original insurance. He cannot reinsure a "Total Loss Only" policy on "All Risks" conditions.

P.P.I. Policies

The abbreviation P.P.I. means "Policy Proof of Interest". Under an ordinary marine policy the assured has to prove his interest exists at the time of loss to substantiate a claim. By its terms a P.P.I. policy forgoes the need for the assured to prove his interest at the time of loss. The mere production of the policy is deemed sufficient proof of interest. It must not be assumed that the assured need not have an interest. He must *have* an insurable interest. It is only *proof* of the interest which is waived not the need to have an interest.

There are many interests which the assured would be loathe to insure if collection of a claim depended on proof of interest at the time of loss, for such interests are so nebulous that to prove insurable interest could be a lengthy and costly process.

Increased value in cargo is an example of an interest which is difficult to prove. Let us suppose a cargo of wool is sent from Australia to London for sale in the Wool Market. The dealer who owns the wool sells it en route for £2,000. The buyer obviously expects it to bring more in the market on arrival and insures this estimated increase on an increased value policy. If the cargo is lost before arrival the buyer cannot prove that he would have realized the anticipated profit and so cannot prove his interest in the increased value. Clearly the only form of policy he could effect is a P.P.I. policy.

Disbursements and Anticipated Freight are interests which are also of a nebulous nature. The shipowner cannot prove the amount of disbursements he will incur in advance and neither can he prove that the amount he insures for anticipated freight is the actual amount he would have earned if the vessel had not been lost. Actually, the shipowner *could* prove the amount of disbursements he had paid, if the receipts are not lost with the ship, and where anticipated freight is in respect of charterparties or a current voyage he could prove his interest. It has become the practice, however, for the shipowner to utilize his interests in disbursements and anticipated freight to effect a P.P.I. policy on T.L.O. (Total Loss Only) terms, thus recovering an amount as increased value of the ship in event of a total loss, without the need to prove his interest. To avoid abuse in this field all hull insurers insist on a warranty in the hull policy limiting the amounts which can be insured on this basis.

While the P.P.I. policy only foregoes *proof* of interest the law does not see any difference between a policy which foregoes proof of interest and one where no interest exists at all. The Marine Insurance Act, 1906 in Section 4 draws no distinction between the two and declares them both equally void. It deems such policies to be effected by way of gaming and wagering. When a policy is declared void it cannot be accepted as evidence in legal proceedings. It follows, that a P.P.I. policy is binding in honour only and neither party can enforce legal rights. The assured cannot sue the insurer who refuses to pay a claim and the insurer cannot sue the assured for any recovery due in respect of a claim paid. Further, a broker effecting a P.P.I. policy on behalf of his principal, cannot be sued for negligence in effecting such a policy.

The Marine Insurance Act, 1906 is a civil code and imposes no penalties for contravention of its provisions. Where a person effects a P.P.I. policy the Marine Insurance Act, 1906 merely declares it void. On the other hand, the Marine Insurance (Gambling Policies) Act, 1909 was introduced to stop gaming and wagering and does impose penalties if it is contravened. Any person who effects a marine policy where he has no insurable interest, nor a reasonable expectation of acquiring such interest, contravenes the 1909 Act. A shipowner's employee, not being a part owner, who effects a policy which forgoes his duty to prove insurable interest is also guilty of contravening the 1909 Act. A broker who knowingly effects such a policy on behalf of his principal is equally guilty of an offence and is subject to the same penalties as his principal. On summary conviction, the penalties, for an offence under the Marine Insurance (Gambling Policies) Act, 1909, are imprisonment, with or without hard labour, for a term not exceeding 6 months or a fine not exceeding £100. In either case the guilty party must also forfeit to the Crown any monies received under the contract.

Because a policy with a P.P.I. clause is declared void by the terms of the Marine Insurance Act, 1906 it was, at one time, thought that by removing the clause the policy could be made a legally valid contract. For this reason, it was customary to attach the P.P.I. policy by means of a pin instead of gumming it to the policy as is done with other clauses. The idea was that by simply unpinning the clause the policy could be made valid. This theory was tested in the case of "Edwards (John and Co.,)—v—Motor Union Insurance Co. (1922)" in which case the judge held that a policy which was sterile at inception would not be made valid by any subsequent action. It is an indication of the persistence of customary practice and the reluctance to change that many brokers and insurers today, over 50 years after the court decision, still attach the P.P.I. clause to the policy with a pin.

It must be emphasized that the assured under a P.P.I. policy *must have an insurable interest* otherwise he contravenes the Gam-

bling Policies Act. The P.P.I. clause merely does away with the need
to *prove* that interest. Where it is alleged that the assured has no
interest and a case is brought under the Marine Insurance (Gambling
Policies) Act, 1909, the assured has the right to defend himself by
proving his interest. By so doing he merely avoids any penalty but
this proof does not make the policy legally valid. Whether or not
the assured proves his interest the P.P.I. policy remains void at law.

Although the underwriter waives proof of interest in the case
of a P.P.I. policy he does not waive evidence of loss. Of course,
this would appear to defeat the object of waiving proof of interest
for it would seem difficult to provide evidence of loss without
proof of interest. In practice, there is no problem for a P.P.I. policy
will undoubtedly relate to some other policy and payment of a
claim on that other policy is usually sufficient proof of loss for
the underwriters subscribing the P.P.I. policy. For example, a
P.P.I. policy covering "increased value of cargo" will, probably,
bear the words, "to pay as cargo". This means that when the main
policy covering the cargo pays a total loss the underwriters on the
P.P.I. policy pay the sum insured thereby.

Double Insurance

If an assured deliberately insures the same risk twice for the
purpose of making a profit on the insurance he is, obviously, committing a fraudulent act. Neither the insurer nor the law can condone
such an action so certain rules are laid down in the Marine Insurance
Act, 1906, regarding double insurance. Not every case of double
insurance is fraudulent for it can happen that a person effects an
insurance not knowing that it has already been effected on his behalf
by some other person. An example of this would be where a supplier
effects an insurance to cover the goods and the forwarding agent,
unaware of the supplier's arrangement, also effects an insurance to
cover the same goods. The forwarding agent would not be aware
of the supplier's policy until it emerged in the process of assignment,
at which point the consignee would find himself with two policies
covering the same insurance, but with different insurers. The Marine
Insurance Act, 1906, in Section 32, defines double insurance as
existing where "two or more policies are effected by or on behalf
of the assured on the same adventure and interest or any part thereof, and the sums insured exceed the indemnity allowed" by the Act.
In sub-section 2 of the same section the Act states the rules to be
applied where double insurance occurs. The assured is given the
option, unless the policy provides otherwise, to claim payment from
the insurers in such order as he may think fit, provided that he is not

entitled to receive any sum in excess of the indemnity allowed by the Act. So far as is possible the assured will claim from one policy only and arrange for the other to be cancelled. In practice, it is not always that simple, and in some cases, claims may be made separately on both policies quite inadvertently. One claim being made by the assured and the other by a person acting on his behalf with the other policy, neither knowing of the other's action. Should the assured be over-indemnified by way of double insurance he is deemed to hold the excess amount in trust for the insurers who will decide between themselves in what manner the refund is to be allocated.

In Section 32 (2), where the Marine Insurance Act gives the assured the option to claim from either insurer as he thinks fit, there is the qualification "unless the policy otherwise provides". It would appear unlikely that an insurer, not knowing of any double insurance, would make such a provision in the policy so that the point needs some clarification. The marine insurer may be aware of some over-lapping insurance, that is, another policy attaching during part of the marine transit and covering the same, or part of the same, risks. An example of this would be a Fire Risks policy covering the goods in a warehouse at the loading port. The assured would have a permanent policy covering all goods of his which are in the relevant warehouse during a period of 12 months. The marine policy would probably attach when the goods leave the inland premises for transit and would thus embrace the period in the port warehouse, whilst the goods await shipment. The marine insurer who is aware of the existence of the fire policy might insert a clause in the contract providing that any claim for fire loss, whilst the goods are in the warehouse, must first be made on the fire policy, thus only the excess of the amount recoverable on the fire policy being claimable on the marine policy. It is not unusual for the fire insurers to make a similar provision so there is a danger of the assured finding himself in difficulties in event of a fire loss.

Co-insurance

Where two or more insurers each cover part of an insurance there is said to be co-insurance. In an ordinary marine insurance policy there are usually several insurers. Each insurer enters into a separate contract with the assured and no one insurer is responsible for the liabilities of any of the other insurers in the policy. Although this type of co-insurance is commonplace it is not the sort of insurance to which we refer when considering the term co-insurance. We are more concerned with the circumstance where a broker has placed as much as possible in his home market and offers the balance of the insurance to an overseas market. When a broker places an insurance in his home market all the following underwriters accept the terms and conditions agreed by the leader. The broker wants the same terms and conditions accepted by the overseas insurers and puts the insurance to them on those terms and conditions, whereby the overseas insurers agree to follow the broker's home market. This practice is so similar to that adopted for reinsurance placings that it is advisable for the broker to make it clear that it is a co-insurance, for there are vital differences between the relative positions of reinsurer to reinsured and co-insurer to the assured. A reinsurer is responsible only to the reinsured for losses, never directly to the original assured. If the reinsured does not pay a loss the reinsurer is not liable and the unsatisfied original assured cannot pursue his claim against the reinsurer. On the other hand, a co-insurer is in exactly the same position as the, so called, original insurer in that he can be directly sued by the assured since his contract is between himself and the assured not between himself and his co-insurer. The foreign co-insurer has merely accepted the same terms and conditions as the home market insurer and, otherwise, is not concerned with the activities of the home market insurer. The assured who carries part of the risk himself, that is he insures only part of the total amount at risk, is a co-insurer. Further, where a deductible is applied to claims on the policy the assured is a co-insurer for the amount of the deductible. However, any recoveries from third parties, which would normally be shared by co-insurers according to the proportion of loss borne by each, are not so shared with the assured in respect of the deductible. Such recoveries are payable in full to the insurer up to the amount paid as the claim.

Underinsurance

When a person does not insure for a sufficient amount to cover the total loss which he might suffer he is said to be underinsured. In non marine insurance the principle of "average" is applied to determine underinsurance for a person who insures for less than he has at risk. This use of the word "average" does not apply in marine insurance but it is as well to know of the manner in which it is used in non marine insurance. Let us assume the assured has ten items of property of equal value totalling £100. He insures the whole for £90. One item is lost by reason of an insured peril, its value being £10. By applying the principle of "average" it can be shown that if the whole property valued £100 is insured for £90 the item lost, valued £10, is insured for £9. Thus there is underinsurance of £1 for which the assured is deemed to be his own insurer.

In non marine insurance it is not an easy matter to avoid the terms of the "average" principle by obtaining agreed values but in marine insurance it is customary for all policies on ship or cargo to be on an agreed value basis, so the terms of the "average" principle cannot be applied in practice. The Marine Insurance Act, 1906, therefore, has little to say on the subject.

It would be difficult to understand the provisions of the Marine Insurance Act, 1906, in relation to underinsurance without knowing something about "valued" and "unvalued" policies.

A "valued" policy is one which *specifies* the agreed value of the subject matter insured. It can usually be recognized by the use of the term "so valued" after the details of the subject matter insured or the term "valued at" preceding the specified value. The value in the policy is deemed to be conclusive of the insurable value, as between the insurer and the assured, where there is no fraud, whether or not it is the true value (M.I.A. 1906 Sect. 27—Sub 3).

One must not confuse "Insured Value" with "Sum Insured". The "Insured Value" is the amount specified in the policy as the value of the insured property, whereas the "Sum Insured" is the total amount of the subscriptions of the insurers in the policy. Where the property is insured for its full value both the sum insured and the insured value will be identical. This is usually the case in cargo insurance so that the policy will show for example,

"£2,000 on merchandise so valued."

It is not compulsory for the assured to insure for the full value and in some cases he prefers to be his own insurer for part of the risk but still to have an agreed value. Section 81 of the Act provides that where the assured on a valued policy insures for less than the insured value he is deemed to be his own insurer for the balance. This sometimes happens in an insurance on a ship, as for example,

"£40,000 on Hull and Machinery valued at £50,000."

Here the assured is his own insurer for 1/5th of the risk. The sum insured is £40,000, which is the maximum recoverable on the policy, while the insured value is £50,000. The assured must bear 1/5th of all losses himself, being underinsured by 1/5th.

An "unvalued policy" is one which does not specify any "value" but leaves this to be determined if and when a claim arises. The Act makes provisions for establishing the value for the purposes of an unvalued policy but it is not necessary to study these at this point. The chapter on "valued and unvalued policies" goes into this in more detail later.

In practice, all hull and cargo policies have an agreed value but the Act must consider the possibility of an unvalued policy being used. If this circumstance should arise the same principle of "average" will apply as it does in non marine insurance. The policy will simply state the "Sum Insured" and, in the event of any claim, a comparison will be made between the actual value and the sum insured to determine whether there is any underinsurance. If the sum insured is less than the insurable value the assured is underinsured by the difference between the two and must bear that proportion of any claim.

Assignment

Assignment means the handing over of all rights and benefits to another party. The party handing over the rights and benefits is called the "assignor" and the party receiving the rights and benefits is called the "assignee". There can be the assignment of interest or there can be the assignment of the policy. When a person assigns his interest he assigns to the assignee all his rights in that interest and has no longer any insurable interest in any policy effected by him or on his behalf. Nevertheless, the mere assignment of interest does not automatically assign the policy (M.I.A. 1906 Sect. 15) unless an agreement has already been made to that effect. Once the interest has passed the assured's policy lapses and he cannot assign it, any assignment after the passing of the interest being inoperative. In practice, where goods are concerned, there is an implied agreement that the policy be assigned when the interest passes.

From a practical point of view the cargo policy must be freely assignable so every effort is made to ease the process of assigning. All policies are effected on a "lost or not lost" basis so that proof of actual interest at the time of loss is not necessary when the final assignee makes a claim. Further, cargo policies can be assigned by "blank" endorsement, whereby the assignor simply endorses the policy and hands it over to the assignee. By assigning a marine policy the assignor passes over to the assured all rights and benefits in the policy, thus entitling the assignee to claim under the policy as though he had the insurable interest throughout the duration of the policy. Nevertheless, the assignee cannot be in a better position than the assignor. If the assignor is guilty of a breach of good faith entitling the insurer to avoid liability under the policy the insurer has the same rights against the innocent assignee. If the assignee wishes to take action against the insurer he may do so in his own name and the insurer may defend it as though he were defending against the original assignor (M.I.A. 1906 Sect. 50).

In a well known law case "Samuel—v—Dumas (1924)", known as

the "Gregorious" case, the vessel was scuttled on instructions of the owners and the innocent mortgagees were unable to recover because the cause of loss was an uninsured peril. In this case the mortgagees had their own policy so it is not really an example of the effect of assignment, but the same principle would apply if the policy had been assigned to the mortgagees. As assignees they could not have recovered under the policy a loss which the assignor could not have recovered.

In Section 50, the Marine Insurance Act, 1906, makes provision for the policy terms to prohibit assignment. This prohibition is never applied in cargo insurance but is customary in all policies insuring ships. To the prudent underwriter the ownership and management of the vessel is a major underwriting factor. It is, therefore, customary for the hull policy to contain a clause providing that the policy is automatically cancelled in event of change of ownership or management, unless the insurer agrees in writing to continue the insurance. Even if the insurer's agreement is obtained the assignment of the policy must be specific endorsement. That is, the insurer must be advised and a signed and dated notice of assignment must be attached to the policy.

Where a mortgagee is interested in a ship he does not have anything to do with the management of the vessel so instead of the policy being assigned to him it is usual to attach a clause to the hull policy stating that the mortgagee is interested in the ship.

CHAPTER VI

GOOD FAITH AND WARRANTIES

The Principle of Good Faith

WHEN a marine insurance contract is effected the insurer must base his judgement on the information given to him by the proposer or by the broker, acting on behalf of his principal, the proposer. The insurer must make up his mind, from the information presented, whether or not to accept the insurance and, if so, at what rate. If the insurer is told the goods are going to be shipped in wooden boxes it would be unreasonable to expect him to examine the goods when shipped to ensure they were so shipped. To place the onus on the insurer to check all the material facts would be to place an intolerable burden on him. The alternative is for the proposer to bear the onus of disclosing and correctly representing all the facts and circumstances material to the risk.

To be fair the Marine Insurance Act, 1906, in Section 17, places the responsibility for observing the utmost good faith squarely on both parties to the contract. The contract is based on the utmost good faith, under the legal doctrine *uberrimae fidei*, and if the utmost good faith be not observed by either party the contract may be avoided by the other party.

This is the first opportunity which we have had, so far, of discussing the term "avoid the contract". Obviously, any action to avoid the contract is, for all practical purposes, taken by the insurer for there would appear to be no point in the assured avoiding the contract. When circumstances arise that entitle the insurer to avoid the contract the contract is said to be "voidable". However, one must not imply from this that the insurer can declare the contract "void". It is only when the law, in the shape of the Marine Insurance Act, 1906, allows the insurer to avoid the contract that he is entitled to do so. By avoiding the contract the insurer does not make it *void*. The similarity of the terms "avoid" and "void" may be misleading but there is no connection between the two in fact. The insurer has no power, at any time, to make a contract void. Only the law can declare a contract void because a void contract is one which is unenforceable in a court of law. A P.P.I. policy is a void contract. When an insurer avoids the contract he steps aside and treats the insurance as though he never accepted it in the first place. Accordingly, avoidance is always ab initio (from inception) and the underwriter who takes this action must return the premium to the assured as provided in Sect. 84 (3a) of the M.I.A. Avoidance can only occur in certain circumstances : —

(1) In any policy—Breach of good faith, not amounting to fraud (Fraud vitiates the contract so avoidance is not necessary)—M.I.A. 1906, Sect. 17.

(2) In a voyage policy—Failure to commence the voyage within a reasonable time after the risk has been accepted by the insurer—M.I.A. 1906, Sect. 55.

There are circumstances that entitle the insurer to avoid the contract, as above, and other circumstances (e.g. Breach of warranty, deviation) that "discharge the insurer from liability" from a certain date or time. It is important to appreciate the difference. If the insurer is discharged from liability from a given time this is not avoidance of the contract for the insurer is still liable for properly recoverable losses which occurred prior to the time the insurer became discharged from liability. No part of the premium is returnable to the assured when the insurer is discharged from liability. The policy even in event of avoidance remains legally valid and the assured can take the insurer to court to press his claim, thereby forcing the insurer to defend his action of avoidance. Such cases, however, when pursued tend to be successfully defended by by the insurer so it would probably be useless for the assured to press the matter.

Disclosure and Non-Disclosure

The onus for disclosure must primarily rest on the proposer for only he is likely to be in a suitable position to know all the facts. Whilst one may call the person effecting the insurance "the proposer" before the contract is concluded and "the assured" after the contract is concluded, the Marine Insurance Act, 1906 refers to him as "the assured" the whole time in the relevant sections, Nos. 18 and 19.

Section 18 requires the assured to disclose to the insurer, before the contract is concluded, every material circumstance which is known to the assured. The assured is deemed to know every material circumstance which he ought to know in the ordinary course of his business, so it follows that if the assured fails to disclose a material circumstance which he ought to know it is no defence to say that he was not aware of the circumstance. If the assured fails to make such a disclosure the insurer is entitled to avoid the contract. The insurer need not avoid the contract if he does not want to. If he wishes to waive the breach of good faith it is his prerogative so to do.

The same section defines a material circumstance as one which would influence the judgement of a prudent insurer in fixing the premium or determining whether he will take the risk. The term "circumstance" includes any communication made to, or any information received by, the assured and in determining whether a particular circumstance is material or not the facts must be taken to make a decision.

To protect the assured where it is not reasonable to place the onus of disclosure on him Section 18 goes on to detail circumstances which need not be disclosed by the assured unless the insurer requests such information. If the insurer asks for any information, failure to disclose such information is non-disclosure even if it falls within the excused circumstances detailed in the Act. The Act provides that the assured need not disclose, in the absence of enquiry, "any circumstance which diminishes the risk". There would appear to be no benefit to the assured to withhold information which diminishes the risk for the information can only put the risk in a more favourable light to the insurer, but it would be unfair to the assured to leave a loophole for avoidance merely because the assured failed to disclose something which it would have been to his advantage to disclose.

It would not be fair to penalize the assured for non-disclosure of something already known to the insurer or which the insurer ought to know. Therefore, in the absence of enquiry, the assured need not disclose "any circumstance which is known or presumed to be known to the insurer. The insurer is presumed to know matters of common notoriety or knowledge, and matters which an insurer in the ordinary course of his business, as such, ought to know." If any circumstance is published in the national press or is available in one of the publications with which the insurer is familiar it is reasonable to expect the insurer to be aware of this circumstance.

The insurer may waive certain information and once he has done so he cannot expect to retain the right to avoid liability if this information is not disclosed to him. The Act, therefore, excuses the assured from disclosing "any circumstance as to which information is waived by the insurer".

Warranties are contained in an insurance contract to improve or maintain the risk. Where a circumstance "is superfluous to disclose by reason of a warranty" the assured is excused from disclosing it.

It is most likely that the assured will use the services of a broker in effecting the insurance and he may feel that he can avoid his obligations of disclosure because he is not personally conducting the negotiations. The Marine Insurance Act, 1906 prevents the assured from thus avoiding his obligations by imposing the same obligations on the broker in Section 19. Because the broker should be more widely versed in matters of marine insurance than the assured, Section 19 places an additional obligation on the broker. Not only must the broker disclose all that the assured must disclose but he must also disclose "every material circumstance which is known to himself, and an agent (the broker) to insure is deemed to know every circumstance which in the ordinary course of business ought to be known by, or to have been communicated to him". Further, the relevant section states that the broker must disclose "every material circumstance which the assured is bound to disclose, unless it comes to his knowledge too late to communicate it to the agent".

Obviously, the assured who uses the services of a broker is in a more vulnerable position than the assured who does not when it comes to non-disclosure. If the broker fails to disclose a material circumstance which he should disclose the insurer is entitled to avoid the contract in the same way as he could if the assured failed to make the disclosure. Therefore, it is not the broker who suffers but the assured. If the broker was aware, or should have been aware, of the material circumstance, either because the assured told him or because he should have been aware of it in the ordinary course of business, and the insurer avoided the contract because the broker failed to make the disclosure it is probable the assured would have grounds to sue the broker for damages due to the broker's negligence. Nevertheless, if the broker failed to disclose a material circumstance which the assured should have disclosed, but which the assured did not disclose to the broker and which the broker could not have known in the ordinary course of business, the assured would have no grounds to sue the broker for damages due to negligence when the insurer avoided the contract.

It may happen that the assured is not aware of a material circumstance and there is reason to believe that he could not be aware of it in the ordinary course of business. The assured may become aware of that circumstance before the contract is concluded and, if so, he must disclose it to the insurer or his broker, if he uses a broker, so that the broker can disclose it to the insurer. But, if the assured does not become aware of the circumstance until it is too late to communicate it to the broker before the contract is concluded this is not deemed to be non-disclosure.

It is important to note that the insurer can avoid the contract in the event of non-disclosure whether or not the non-disclosure affected the risk and even when it is inadvertent.

Representation and Misrepresentation

In the same manner that the principle of good faith requires the assured and his broker to disclose every material circumstance to the insurer before the contract is concluded it equally requires that disclosures be truly represented. If goods are normally carried in wooden cases and the assured, or his broker, did not disclose that on this occasion the goods were to be carried in cardboard cartons this would be non-disclosure. If the assured, or his broker did disclose that the goods were to be carried in cardboard cartons and qualified this by saying they were extra strong export cartons this would be a representation. If the goods were in fact carried in weaker cardboard cartons the statement regarding extra strong cartons would be a misrepresentation and the insurer could avoid the contract if the misrepresentation was material. A representation is material if it "would influence the judgement of a prudent insurer in fixing the premium or determining whether he will take the risk" (M.I.A. 1906 Sect. 20—Sub 2).

Therefore, a representation is a statement of fact, that is a truthful statement, and if it be untruthful it is a misrepresentation. Even though it is essential that statements to the insurer should be truthful there are occasions when the assured, or broker, thinks he is telling the truth but it turns out later that, in fact, the statement was untrue. Provided the assured, or broker, acts in good faith whatever he *believes* to be true is deemed to be true even if it subsequently proves not to be true and there is no case for misrepresentation (M.I.A. 1906 Sect. 20—Sub 3).

To ensure fairness, the assured and his broker are not committed to the representations made until the contract is concluded and up to that time they can withdraw or correct any representations already made (M.I.A. 1906 Sect. 20—Sub 2).

It is customary for the insurer to enquire into past claims experience when he is offered a large contract but, in the absence of such enquiry, the non-disclosure of past claims experience does *not* give the insurer the right to avoid the contract. If the insurer requests the information the disclosure becomes material and the information must be accurate. Brokers keep records, of the experience of open covers and similar continuous contracts, from which statistics are prepared for presentation to new insurers or, on renewal, to existing insurers.

Warranties

The Marine Insurance Act, 1906, in Section 33, Sub 1 defines a warranty. It "means a promissory warranty, that is to say a warranty by which the assured undertakes that some particular thing shall or shall not be done, or that some condition shall be fulfilled, or whereby he affirms or negatives the existence of a particular state of facts."

There seems to be little one can add to clarify this definition and the student would do well to make himself fully conversant with the definition as stated in the Act. It should be emphasized, however, that it is the *assured* who makes the undertaking in a marine insurance warranty.

Whether or not it is material to the risk the assured must comply exactly with the terms of the warranty. The warranty must be taken literally and if the assured fails to comply exactly with the warranty there is said to be a breach of warranty. In the event of a breach of warranty the insurer is *discharged from liability as from the date of the breach*. This must not be confused with "deviation" in which case the insurer is also discharged from liability but from the *time* of the deviation. Although the insurer is discharged from liability as from the date of the breach, when there is a breach of warranty he, nevertheless, remains liable for insured losses which occurred before the date of the breach (M.I.A. 1906 Sect. 33—Sub 3). It is important to note that when the assured fails to comply with a warranty and the insurer is discharged from liability the assured cannot avail himself of the defence that the breach was repaired before a loss occurred.

There is a popular misconception in the marine insurance market that in event of breach of warranty the insurer is entitled to avoid the contract. This is probably because "a breach of warranty may be waived by the insurer" (M.I.A. 1906 Sect. 34—Sub 3). Nevertheless, the Act states quite clearly in Section 33 subsection 3, that the insurer is "discharged from liability as from the date of the breach of warranty". No doubt legal opinion would find little difference between the ultimate effect of the insurer avoiding liability and his being discharged from liability. A closer study of the Marine Insurance, Act, 1906 will reveal that in all cases of avoidance the contract is avoided entirely, that is, from inception and the insurer is relieved from *all* liability. Where the insurer remains liable for part of the risk he is discharged from liability from a given time or date, thus effectively leaving him liable for insured losses occurring prior to that time or date. Further, no part of the premium is returnable to the assured when the insurer has been discharged from liability.

Although a warranty must be literally complied with there are certain circumstances where non-compliance is excused. These excuses are detailed in Section 34 of the Marine Insurance Act, 1906. As well as the circumstance where the insurer waives the breach of warranty, already mentioned, the relevant section excuses a breach in the following instances:

1. Where the circumstances which led to the insurer insisting on the insertion of the warranty into the contract cease to exist it would be unreasonable to insist on the continuance of the warranty. It must be remembered that a warranty must be literally complied with whether or not it is material to the risk. Nevertheless, when the circumstances change and the warranty is no longer necessary non-compliance is excused.

2. The insurer cannot insist on a warranty which requires the assured to break the law. It follows, that where a subsequent law makes it illegal for the assured to comply with a warranty non-compliance must be excused.

Express Warranties

A warranty may be express or implied (M.I.A. 1906 Sect. 33—Sub 2).

An express warranty is one which is contained in the policy or in a document referred to by the policy. That is, the warranty must be actually written, typed, impressed or printed in the policy or document so that it can be physically read. An express warranty is a condition which overrides anything in the policy with which it is inconsistent. It does not exclude an implied warranty, except where it is inconsistent therewith (M.I.A. 1906 Sect 35—Sub 3).

In defining an express warranty it would be useful to show an example, such as "Warranted Professionally Packed" in a policy covering goods or "Warranted not north of 50° N." in a policy covering a ship.

Implied Warranties

An implied warranty does not appear in the policy. It is a warranty which is understood by law to exist in the contract without being stated. The implied warranty must be literally complied with in the same manner as an express warranty, so that in event of non-compliance the insurer is discharged from liability as from the date of the breach.

In regard to implied warranties the Act makes reference, in

Sections 36, 37 and 40, to warranties of neutrality, of nationality and to seaworthiness of goods but these points are relatively unimportant in comparison to the two major implied warranties of seaworthiness and legality as stated in Sections 39 and 41 respectively.

Seaworthiness of the Ship—(M.I.A. 1906 Sect. 39)—The purpose of a warranty is to ensure that the assured maintains the risk as it was understood to be by the insurer when he accepted the risk, or even to improve it. Whether the insurance covers the ship itself or goods thereon it is vitally important to the insurer that the ship be seaworthy so far as is possible. The shipowner cannot take many practical measures to maintain seaworthiness whilst the vessel is at sea but he can, at least, see that the vessel does not commence the voyage in an unseaworthy state.

Therefore, in all voyage policies there is an implied warranty that the vessel be seaworthy at the commencement of the voyage. That is, the vessel must be reasonably fit in all respects for the purpose of the particular adventure insured. In establishing whether a ship is reasonably fit regard must be had for the stores, bunkering, equipment, special equipment, propelling machinery, other machinery and electrical machinery and gear, as well as the general hull and fittings of the ship. Further, the vessel must have a competent master and a full complement of competent officers and crew. The ship must be reasonably fit in all respects for the contemplated voyage. If she is in port when the insurance attaches the ship must be reasonably fit to encounter the perils of the port, but she need not be seaworthy for the contemplated voyage until she commences the voyage. The same principle applies when the voyage is to be carried out in stages where each stage requires different kinds of preparation or equipment. The vessel need only be seaworthy, at the commencement of each stage, for that stage as regards the special kind of preparation or equipment.

The statement is frequently made that there is no warranty of seaworthiness in a time policy but this is only true if it is qualified. The Act most certainly states that "in a time policy there is no implied warranty that the ship shall be seaworthy at any stage of the adventure" but it does not leave the matter there for it goes on to say that "where, with the privity of the assured, the ship is sent to sea in an unseaworthy state, the insurer is not liable for any loss attributable to unseaworthiness." It will be noted that whereas under a voyage policy the insurer is discharged from liability *for all losses* from the date of the breach of warranty in event of unseaworthiness, under a time policy the insurance continues but the insurer is not liable for losses attributable to unseaworthiness. Therefore, it can be said that whilst there is no absolute warranty of seaworthiness in a time policy there is definitely an incentive for the assured not to send the ship to sea in an unseaworthy state. The term "with the privity of the assured" used in the Act means with the knowledge and consent of the insured. Although the insurer is not liable for losses attributable to unseaworthiness the onus lies on him to show that the loss was in fact attributable to unseaworthiness and it is not sufficient for him simply to show that the vessel is unseaworthy.

Looking at the matter from a practical point of view we are probably only concerned with breach of the warranty in cargo policies. There are, of course, voyage policies on hulls but by far the majority of hull policies are on a time basis.

Cargo policies are, generally, on a voyage basis but, when one considers it, it seems most unfair that the cargo owner, who has no control over the seaworthiness of the carrying vessel, should be penalized by complete loss of cover if the vessel puts to sea in an unseaworthy state, whereas the defaulting shipowner only suffers in regard to losses attributable to unseaworthiness. The insurer is aware of this unreasonable situation and it is customary for all cargo policies to contain a clause protecting the assured. Most cargo policies are subject to the terms of one of the standards sets of Institute Cargo Clauses and each of these sets of clauses contains "seaworthiness admitted clause". The relevant clause is No. 8 in all three sets of the current clauses. In studying this clause it will be seen that the insurer admits seaworthiness "between himself and the assured". This means that the insurer is not prepared to admit seaworthiness to any other person and most particularly not to the carrier. By the terms of Section 3 of the Carriage of Goods by Sea Act, 1924, the carrier is bound to exercise due diligence to make the ship seaworthy and cargoworthy before and at the beginning of the voyage. Since the Carriage of Goods by Sea Act, 1924, applies to all bills of lading on shipments from ports in Great Britain or Northern Ireland, it follows that the carrier will probably be liable for a loss due to unseaworthiness and the insurer does not wish the carrier to have the benefit of the admission of seaworthiness contained in the Institute Cargo Clauses.

The student examining clause 8 in the Institute Cargo Clauses may be intrigued as to why no mention is made here to the second part of the clause. This has not been overlooked and will be discussed later when we consider the provisions of the Marine Insurance Act in respect of "excluded losses".

CHAPTER VII

TIME AND VOYAGE INSURANCES

Attachment and Termination of Risk

WHERE a time policy is concerned the insurance attaches and terminates at the times and dates stated in the policy and the Marine Insurance Act does not apply any special rules to qualify the position. It does state in Section 25 that a policy to insure for a definite period of time is called a "time policy" and a policy to insure "from" or "at and from" one place to another is called a "voyage policy". A contract for both a voyage and a period of time can be included in one policy.

While considering Section 25 it will be noted that subsection 2 provides that a time policy for a period of time exceeding 12 months is invalid. This subsection of Section 25 was repealed by the 8th schedule of the Finance Act, 1959, and no longer applies. As stated earlier, practices in marine insurance do not change readily and, although the law no longer requires time policies to be restricted to 12 months, it remains the practice not to effect policies for longer periods than 12 months. The continuation clause, which was introduced into hull time policies because of the provisions of Section 25 of the Act, remains in such policies because the assured has become accustomed to a policy which does not automatically expire on the stated expiry date when the vessel has not completed the current voyage, and it is better for all concerned for the ship to complete her voyage under one policy.

It is customary for English time policies to attach and terminate at midnight and for American time policies to attach and terminate at noon. Nevertheless, the policy will always state the actual time of attachment and termination. Both types of policy, in common with the majority of marine time policies used in the world, have a continuation clause. This clause was mentioned above and it provides that if, on expiry of the policy, the vessel be at sea, in distress, in a port of refuge or of call she shall, subject to prior notice being given to underwriters, be held covered, at a pro rata monthly premium, until her arrival at her destination.

Because most hull policies are on a time basis and most cargo policies are on a voyage basis, it is natural that one should think of time policies as being hull interest and voyage policies as being cargo interest. Nevertheless, it must be remembered that there are instances where the ship is insured on a voyage policy, such as in the case of a delivery trip or a voyage to the breaker's yard, and also where cargo is insured on a time policy, such as for periods in warehouse. Therefore the provisions in the Marine Insurance Act, 1906 regarding the voyage could equally apply to either hull or cargo interest.

A further consideration to be taken into account is the possibility of mixed sea and land risks on the same policy. The Act in Section 2 states that a voyage may include the risks covered by the policy on inland waters or land risks which may be incidental to a sea voyage. The same section embraces a construction risk, that is the building of a ship, within the provisions of the Marine Insurance Act, 1906 so far as those provisions are applicable to that type of risk.

In practice most cargo policies are subject to the "transit clause" which extends the sea voyage to include the risks whilst the goods are transported from the inland warehouse or place of storage to the time of loading as well as the risks from the time of discharge to the delivery at the final warehouse or place of storage at the named destination. Whilst the Act recognizes the probability of the land risks in Section 2 its terms do not extend the voyage beyond the sea voyage, which is why it is necessary to attach the transit clause to the policy.

Construction risk policies are on a time basis, in practice, but usually include the period of launching as well as tests, trials and the delivery voyage.

To understand the application of the varying clauses used in voyage policies regarding attachment and termination of risk it is first necessary to know the fundamental principles of attachment and termination when no special clauses are attached to the policy.

In the first paragraph of this chapter it will be noticed that the definition of a voyage policy includes the terms "from" and "at and from". It is customary for the marine policy to be used in the form suggested in the first schedule to the Marine Insurance Act, 1906 and, if this is studied, it will be seen that the wording includes the term "at and from".

In Section 42 the Marine Insurance Act, 1906 states that where "at and from" or "from" is used in a voyage policy to denote the attachment of risk it is "not necessary for the ship to be at that place when the contract is concluded, but there is an implied condition that the adventure shall be commenced within a reasonable time, and that if the adventure be not so commenced the insurer may avoid the contract". When the insurer concludes the contract he takes into account his assessment of the risk at that time and in the near future. It would not be reasonable for the assured to expect to obtain cover at a favourable time and then to delay commencement of the adventure for several months when circumstances might not be so favourable. Therefore, the assured is required to commence the adventure within a reasonable time after the contract is concluded. This implied condition is not overridden by the attachment to the policy of any of the current cargo clauses.

If the assured can show that the insurer was aware of the circumstances, which led to the delay, at the time the contract was concluded, or that the insurer waived the condition, the implied condition that the adventure be commenced within a reasonable time becomes negatived and the insurer cannot avoid the contract.

Where a voyage policy on a ship states that the risk attaches "at and from" a particular place shown in the policy the term means that the risk attaches immediately if the ship is already at that place, in good safety, when the contract is concluded or, if she be not there, the risk attaches as soon as the ship arrives. This latter applies even if there is another policy covering the ship for a specified time after arrival, unless the attaching policy provides otherwise. Most voyage policies follow the standard form which provides that cover on the ship continues for 24 hours after the ship has moored in good safety.

The term "in good safety" does not mean the ship must not be damaged on arrival. It merely means that the ship is in a sufficiently sound condition to enter and lie in the port in safety.

Chartered freight, that is money for hire of the whole or part of the vessel for carriage of the charterer's goods or goods which the charterer contracts to carry, is subject to the same principle as a policy on the ship when the term "at and from" is used in a voyage policy. Other freight, however, is not subject to the same principle and, in the absence of any special conditions regarding payment of the freight, the risk attaches pro rata as the goods are shipped. On the other hand, if the cargo belongs to the shipowner or to some other person who has entered into a contract with the shipowner to ship the cargo, the risk attaches as soon as the ship is ready to receive the cargo.

In the first schedule to the Marine Insurance Act, 1906, there is a specimen policy form. Section 30 of the Act states that a policy may be in the form in the first schedule to the Act and it is customary for all marine policies to be based on this form. The specimen form is drafted as a voyage policy and contains the words "at and from". Although hull insurance is generally on a time basis the same basic form of voyage policy is used, in practice, with suitable wording and clauses amending it to a time policy. Most cargo today is insured within an open cover which exists for a specified period of time. It is customary for brokers to issue slip policies or other policies, on a time basis, off the open cover but all certificates issued off such policies are limited to a specified voyage for each certificate. Sometimes separate cargo policies (voyage) are issued. To such policies or certificates the conditions of the insurance are expressed in the standard cargo clauses to bring the principles of attachment and termination of risk in line with modern requirements.

In considering the cargo form without any special clauses it will be noted that the risk attaches on the goods "from the loading thereof" and terminates when the goods are "safely landed". In practice, the transit clause overrides these provisions but, when studying the principles, it is necessary to know the attachment and termination of risk when there are no special clauses attached to the policy.

Definitions of the terms "from the loading thereof" and "safely landed" can be found in the Rules for Construction of Policy in the first schedule to the Act. The risk does not attach until the goods are actually on board the vessel, so that where it is necessary to use lighters or craft to carry the goods from shore to ship there is no insurance cover whilst the goods are in the lighters or craft, nor is there any cover whilst the goods are actually *being* loaded. In practice, the "Transit Clause" and the "Craft etc. Clause" in the Institute Cargo Clauses provide that the insurance shall continue during lighterage and loading. The risk terminates when the goods are discharged and safely landed. This includes customary lighterage from ship to shore, but if the consignee uses his own craft the risk is deemed to terminate on discharge into the craft. Discharge must take place within a reasonable time after arrival of the vessel at the port of discharge otherwise the insurance will cease from the time the delay becomes unreasonable. The Act does not state what is deemed to be reasonable but it does provide, in Section 88, that what is reasonable is a question of fact. The policy form, used for hull voyage insurance provides for the insurance to continue for 24 hours after arrival in good safety so one might consider 24 hours to be a reasonable delay. Further, if a weekend or public holiday intervened this would also, no doubt, be deemed a reasonable delay.

Different Voyage (M.I.A. 1906 Sects. 43 and 44)

The insurer concludes the contract in anticipation that the adventure will commence at the place of commencement specified in the policy and will terminate at the place of destination specified in the policy. He accepts the insurance and rates the risk on this assumption.

If the ship sails from a place other than that specified in the policy or for a different destination the risk simply does not attach, that is, the insurer does not come on risk. The Act was designed with only the sea voyage in mind but modern practice also embraces the land risk period from the inland warehouse to the loading port and from discharge to the destination warehouse. When interpreting the Act in conjunction with modern insurance, commonsense must be applied so that if the transit commences from a place other than that specified in the policy or for a different destination the same principle must be applied and the risk does not attach.

Change of Voyage (M.I.A. 1906 Sect. 45)

There is a change of voyage where the destination of the ship is voluntarily changed after the voyage has commenced. In event of change of voyage the insurer is discharged from liability from the time when the determination to change is manifested. That is, as soon as the determination to change is made clear. If the policy provides for the insurance to continue the principle does not apply. If a loss occurs after the determination to change is manifested the insurer is not liable for that loss even if the ship is still on the same course of the contemplated voyage.

In practice, the standard voyage clauses for hulls and the standard cargo clauses both make provision for the insurance to continue in event of change of voyage.

Deviation (M.I.A. 1906 Sect. 46)

In the same way that the insurer is entitled to expect the adventure to commence within a reasonable time he is equally entitled to expect the vessel to proceed directly to the destination without deviating. If the policy specifically designates the course of the voyage and the vessel departs from that course there is a deviation. If the policy does not specifically designate the course of the voyage but the vessel departs from the usual and customary course there is a deviation. A deviation occurs when the vessel departs from the designated or customary course with the intention of returning to that course.

If the ship deviates, as above, without lawful excuse the insurer is *discharged from liability from the time of deviation* and it is immaterial that the ship regains the designated or customary route before a loss occurs. The moment the ship deviates the insurer comes off risk but he remains liable for insured losses which occurred before the time of deviation.

It will be remembered that in event of change of voyage the insurer is discharged from liability as soon as the determination to change is manifested, with deviation, however, the *intention* to deviate is immaterial, the ship must actually deviate before the insurer becomes discharged from liability. A further point to note is the difference between breach of warranty and deviation. In event of breach of warranty the insurer is discharged from liability from the *date* of the breach but in event of deviation the insurer is discharged from liability from the *time* of the deviation.

When the policy specifies several ports of discharge the ship must proceed to them in the order specified in the policy. If the ship does not do so there is a deviation, except where it is customary to proceed to such ports in a different order. If the policy merely states "ports of discharge" in a given area the ship must proceed to such ports in geographical order or there is a deviation, except where it can be shown that there is sufficient usage or cause for the ship to proceed to the ports in a different order. This latter could occur when one of the ports is strikebound.

It is not unusual for a time policy covering a ship to incorporate geographical warranties restricting the navigation of the vessel. If the vessel goes outside permitted waters or enters restricted waters this is not a deviation within the meaning of the M.I.A. 1906 but is a breach of warranty and, except where the policy conditions "hold covered" the breach of warranty, the insurer would be discharged from liability as from the *date* of the breach.

In modern practice it is fairly common for the ship to be held covered at an additional premium in the event of a deviation. In the case of goods in transit, the Institute Cargo Clauses provide that the insurance will continue in the event of deviation; it being assumed that the goods are outside the control of the cargo assured whilst they are in the hands of the carrier.

Delay in Prosecution of the Voyage (M.I.A. 1906 Sect. 48)

Not only is it reasonable for the insurer to expect there to be no deviation from the contemplated voyage without reasonable excuse but he should also be able to rely on the voyage being prosecuted without unreasonable delay. The longer a voyage takes the more likelihood there is of the insured property being exposed to peril. If there is unreasonable delay the insurer is *discharged from liability from the time the delay becomes unreasonable.* Note that whereas the insurer is entitled to avoid the contract in event of delay in commencing the voyage, when there is unreasonable delay in prosecution of the voyage he is discharged from liability. The essential difference being that the insurer can avoid all liability under the contract when there is delay in commencement but he remains liable for insured losses which occur prior to his being discharged from liability in event of delay in prosecution of the voyage.

What is or is not reasonable is, in all cases, a question of fact but it was held that 10 days in port awaiting a cargo was considered unreasonable.

Since most hull insurance is effected on a "time" basis (e.g. 12 months) the matter of delay in prosecuting a voyage does not, usually, arise in the case of hull policies. Most cargo insurances are subject to the Institute Cargo Clauses or a similar set of "trade" clauses, which provide that the insurance shall continue in the event of delay in prosecution of the voyage provided such delay is beyond the control of the assured.

Excuses for Deviation and Delay (M.I.A. 1906 Sect. 49)

The insurer always expects the assured to act in a reasonable and fair manner. In return the insurer tries to be reasonable and fair also. The excuses for deviation and delay specified in the Act are based on the fair usages of the past and reflect the acceptance by the insurer of deviation and delay which the assured cannot reasonably avoid.

Before considering these excuses it would be as well to note that as soon as the excuse ceases to operate the ship must "resume her course, and prosecute the voyage, with reasonable dispatch".

The excuses for deviation or delay in prosecuting the voyage are as follows:

(a) Where authorized by any special term in the policy.
(b) Where caused by circumstances beyond the control of the master and his employer.
(c) Where reasonably necessary in order to comply with an express or implied warranty.
(d) Where reasonably necessary for the safety of the ship or subject matter insured.
(e) For the purpose of saving human life or aiding a ship in distress where human life may be in danger.
(f) Where reasonably necessary for the purpose of obtaining medical or surgical aid for any person on board the ship.
(g) Where caused by the barratrous conduct of the master or crew, if barratry be one of the perils insured against.

These excuses as detailed in the Act are perfectly clear, but the following observations might help a little in the understanding of the intentions of the excuses.

(*a*) The policy might contain a clause authorizing deviation. In fact both the hull voyage clauses and the standard cargo clauses contain a clause providing for the insurance to continue in event of deviation.

(*b*) The circumstances must be beyond the control of both the master *and* his employer.

(*c*) It would be pointless to insist on the vessel not delaying when it is necessary to delay in order to comply with a warranty which is really for the protection of the insurer. An example would be delay to make the vessel seaworthy.

(*d*) It is obviously to the insurer's advantage when delay is for the safety of the subject matter of the insurance, such as a deviation to reach a port of refuge and a delay in that port.

(*e*) It is in the public interest to encourage the saving of life but the excuse does not include salvage of a derelict, being a vessel which has been abandoned.

(*f*) This excuse is also in the public interest but is limited to helping only those on board the ship. Deviation to bring medical or surgical aid to a person on another ship is not deemed to be reasonably excused.

(*g*) All marine policies cover barratry so the rule requires no further explanation, except to define barratry as the wilful act of the master or crew to the detriment of the shipowner.

Transhipment (M.I.A. 1906 Sect. 59)

Transhipment is the act of transferring goods from one means of conveyance to another. Generally, the term is applied to transference of the goods from one overseas vessel to another overseas vessel for onward carriage. The Act only refers to transhipment made necessary because the carrying vessel's voyage is interrupted at an intermediate port or place by an insured peril and, in so doing, provides that the insurance shall continue in this event. Other than in these circumstances and, in the absence of any special agreement in the policy, transhipment which is not customary, or of which the insurer has not been advised when concluding the contract, would be considered an unreasonable delay in prosecution of the voyage. Because this could have a serious effect on the assured's cover and because the assured cannot always control the method of carriage the standard cargo clauses contain a clause providing that the insurance shall continue during any reshipment or transhipment.

CHAPTER VIII

PROXIMATE CAUSE AND MARINE PERILS

Proximate Cause

THE Marine Insurance Act, 1906, in Section 55, provides that the insurer is liable for any loss proximately caused by a peril insured against but he is not liable for any loss not proximately caused by a peril insured against. It is, therefore, essential to determine the proximate cause of a loss to ascertain whether it is to be recoverable under the policy.

The term "proximate cause" is sometimes referred to as "causa proxima". This is derived from the legal dictum "causa proxima non remota spectatur" which can be translated to mean "the proximate and not the remote cause is to be considered".

In determining the proximate cause of loss one must consider only the most dominant and effective cause of loss. This is not necessarily the nearest cause in time to the actual loss. For example, where a ship is scuttled the proximate cause of loss is the action of scuttling, because this is the dominant and effective cause, although the nearest cause to the loss is the actual entry of seawater into the ship. The simplicity of determining the proximate cause of loss in this example is so obvious that one wonders what would prompt a lawyer to use the latter argument in an attempt to prove a claim against underwriters, as happened in the case of "P. Samuel & Co.—v—Dumas (1924)". Needless to say, the argument was not accepted by the Court.

Few cases of proximate cause are simple to determine. In nearly every circumstance leading to a loss there are a number of remote causes which contribute indirectly towards the loss. Once the proximate cause has been established, however, the remote causes can be ignored.

If a ship strands because the light in a lighthouse or on a buoy is extinguished the proximate cause of loss is the accidental stranding. The extinguished light is a remote cause. This decision was held in the case of "Ionides—v—Universal Marine Insurance Assocn. (1863)".

A ship is in collision and puts into port for repairs. She carries a cargo of fruit which is unloaded, to facilitate repairs, then reloaded. This action results in damage to the fruit from deterioration caused by the delay. The proximate cause of loss is the delay. The collision which led to the delay and the actions of unloading and reloading, are all remote causes. This was the decision in the case of "Pink—v—Fleming (1890)".

On occasions it is extremely difficult to determine the proximate cause of a loss. So difficult, in fact, that even authorities on the subject hold completely differing views. An illustration of this occurred when the well known "Coxwold" case went before the Courts in 1942. For the record, this was the case of "Yorkshire Dale S.S. Co. Ltd.—v—Minister of War Transport (1942)". The "Coxwold" was a tanker carrying a cargo of petrol to the naval base at Narvik. The vessel had been chartered by the Government and there is no doubt that she was on a warlike operation. The ship was in a convoy which was ordered to disperse due to information that a danger from submarines lay in the path of the convoy. The "Coxwold" set a course via the Isle of Skye but, due to an unexpected tidal set and heavy mist, she ran aground on the Isle of Skye. Subsequently, the vessel became a total loss as a result of the strand.

It was not disputed that there was a recoverable claim for total loss. There were, however, two separate policies involved. One of these policies excluded war risks while the other policy covered the war perils excluded by the ordinary policy. The case was a test case to determine on which policy the loss should fall. One facet of the argument was that, since the vessel was on a warlike operation, chartered by the Government in furtherance of the war effort and in a convoy which dispersed due to fear of submarines the loss must be a war loss and fall on the war policy underwriters. On the other hand, it was argued that the proximate cause of loss was simply "stranding" and since stranding is a peril of the sea the loss should fall on the marine policy underwriters.

In due course the Court found that, because the vessel was on a warlike operation, the loss should fall on the war policy underwriters. On the face of it, this decision was accepted and the claim was paid by the underwriters subscribing to the war policy. Notwithstanding this, a large section of the marine insurance market disagreed with the decision and argued that the loss was proximately caused by stranding, all the rest being remote causes. So strongly was this felt in the market that steps were taken to amend the war exclusion clause in all marine policies so that any similar losses in the future must fall on the marine, rather than the war, underwriters.

Marine Perils

Having determined the proximate cause of the loss the policy must be examined to see if the proximate cause is indeed one of the perils covered by the policy. From time to time, students of the basic "S.G." policy form have objected to the use of so antiquated a document and have advocated the drafting of a more modern form of policy. Marine underwriting is based on years of experience of the present practitioners and their predecessors. Since the policy form was first drafted many law cases have taken place to establish the precise meanings of the words and phraseology used. Practically every one of the perils has been subjected to a severe legal test at some time so that insurers are loathe to make any change to the basic policy which might result in a different interpretation of the wording in the policy. Of course, where it is necessary to add certain perils to those already in the policy this can be done by adding amending clauses, or exclusions can be inserted into the policy to delete any of the items not required. To understand the effect of such amendments it is first necessary to understand the meaning of the perils in the basic form. The perils can be found approximately two thirds down the face of the policy form and commence with "Touching the adventures and perils which we the assurers are contented to bear and do take upon us in this voyage." Each of these perils will now be taken and listed below with comments to assist interpretation.

"They are of the seas"—According to Rule for Construction 7 in the first schedule to the Act the term "perils of the seas" refers only to fortuitous accidents or casualties of the seas. It does not include the ordinary action of the winds and waves. Therefore the term includes only accidental losses. Two of the major perils covered by the policy are collision and stranding. Neither of these is specifically mentioned in the policy because they are both perils of the sea and are accordingly embraced in the general term "perils of the seas".

"Men of war" and "enemies"—When the policy form was drafted the term "men of war" was used to describe naval vessels of a considerable size. At that time communication at sea was so difficult that one was never certain whether one was at war with another nation. Peaceful merchantmen were frequently subject to attack from naval vessels whether or not a war actually existed so that the peril was inserted in the policy form as well as the peril "enemies". The latter peril is self explanatory and means enemies of the country under whose flag the insured vessel sails. In modern practice the two terms together are meant to incorporate war risks into the policy whether or not there is an outbreak of war or whether or not the loss is caused by an enemy. It is the practice, however, to clarify the cover afforded by the war section of the policy by adding special war clauses, whether the interest be hull or cargo.

The cargo war clauses are simply called the "Institute War Clauses" and extend the policy perils to include hostilities, warlike operations, civil war, revolution, rebellion, insurrection or civil strife arising therefrom, also mines, torpedoes bombs or other engines of war. Due to a market understanding not to cover war risks on land, the cargo clauses also make the insurance subject to the waterborne agreement which provides that the war cover only applies whilst the goods are on the overseas vessel and ceases on discharge, or if the cargo is not discharged, on the expiry of 15 days from midnight on the day the vessel arrives at the destination port.

A similar (15 day) limit applies whilst the goods are at an intermediate port during transhipment; if the time limit expires before the goods are loaded onto the on-carrying overseas vessel, cover is suspended until such loading takes place. This extension includes a period on land but only whilst the goods remain within the area of the intermediate port.

The peril "strikes" is not included in the policy perils but is customarily added to the cargo policy by a standard set of clauses in addition to war perils if it is proposed to cover war risks. That is, the assured usually requires cover for both types of peril although there is no reason why he could not have just one of them added to the policy without the other if he so wishes. The "Strikes" cover is limited to damage to the insured property caused by strikers, locked out workmen, persons taking part in labour disturbances, riots, civil commotions or persons acting maliciously. The cargo strikes clauses are headed: "Institute Strikes Riots and Civil Commotions Clauses". It is customary in cargo insurance to increase the perils in the marine policy by simply attaching the current war clauses and strikes clauses to the same policy as is used to cover the ordinary marine risks. A special scale of premiums is agreed in the market for the addition of war and strikes risks to the cargo policy. There is no reason why the assured should not accept insurance on war risks without strikes risks or vice versa, but it has become the practice for most assureds to accept both together or neither.

In hull insurance the clauses used to cover war and strikes risks are not separate as in cargo insurance. Instead, both are included in the same set of clauses, headed the "Institute War and Strikes Clauses". The cover afforded by these hull clauses is identical to that afforded by the cargo clauses, with a few exceptions. Obviously there is no point in a waterborne clause appearing in the hull clauses. The hull clauses, however, contain a number of important exclusions and special cancellation clauses. It is not proposed to go into these clauses in detail at this stage although the student may derive some benefit and a better understanding if he reads the clauses in question. In the absence of the war clauses it is the practice for all marine policies to contain a clause excluding war risks.

Fire—this is one of the major perils in the policy. An outbreak of fire on board ship is a serious matter at any time for once it gets a grip it is very difficult to extinguish. Whilst the ship is in port there is, at least, the land fire fighting service available to assist but when the ship is at sea the fire usually has to be tackled by those on board without outside assistance. A laden ship is like a floating warehouse and is equally vulnerable to fire. Imagine a group of people *inside* a blazing warehouse attempting to extinguish the fire from within with no chance of going outside to approach the problem from relative safety and it is possible to get some idea of the situation when a ship takes fire at sea. There can be a number of causes to initiate the fire, including spontaneous combustion in a cargo loaded damp as well as negligence of crew or passengers. Where the fire overwhelms the ship the evidence is usually destroyed and. in many cases, it is practically impossible to discover the true cause of the fire. Generally the actual cause of the fire can be treated as a remote cause except where it occurs as inherent vice in the subject matter insured. For example, when spontaneous combustion sets off a fire in a cargo of soft coal, which was loaded in a damp condition, the spontaneous combustion is the proximate cause of the loss of the coal, but the proximate cause of the damage to the ship and other cargo is "fire", the spontaneous combustion being only a remote cause. However, where the cause of the fire is an excluded peril (e.g. a hostile act) then the loss is excluded.

"Pirates" and "Rovers"—The Act, in Rule for Construction 8, does not define the term "pirates" but merely states that it includes passengers who mutiny and rioters who attack the ship from the shore. This is probably because there was no doubt in people's minds in the nineteenth century and prior to that period as to the meaning of the word. Today one hears little of the activities of pirates although there are pirates still operating in Far Eastern waters, mainly from motorized junks. Large vessels are relatively safe from attacks from these modern pirates for the practice is for members of the pirate band to board a ship as passengers in order to overpower the crew and it is not easy to arrange passage on larger ships at short notice in intermediate ports. A pirate is a person who owns no allegiance to any recognized flag and who carries out a piratical act for his own personal gain. At the time of the drafting of the policy form the peril "pirates" was a real possibility and one of the main risks which a merchant vessel might encounter. The policy form in use today contains a clause excluding war perils and amongst the exclusions is the peril "piracy". The war clauses reinstate the peril "piracy" into the policy so it can be seen that, from a practical point of view, the insurer looks upon "piracy" as a war peril. The term "rover" applies to a person who roves the seas in search of the opportunity to carry out a piratical act.

"Thieves"—To understand the intention of the drafter of the policy form in the use of the word "thieves" one must consider the way in which theft was carried out in the seventeenth and eighteenth centuries. Houses would have shuttered windows and heavy doors to keep out thieves. The porch would have a permanent night light and a small heavy glass window in the door would enable the householder to identify a caller before unbarring the door. Thieves roamed in bands and would not hesitate to break in on a careless householder if given the slightest opportunity. Similar bands of these assailing thieves would roam the docks and wharves with the intention of overpowering any careless watchman in order to ransack a ship. It is this sort of thief which the policy contemplates, but alert dock police and other precautions have removed the peril almost entirely today. Therefore, it can be seen that the peril "thieves" in the policies does not include clandestine theft or a theft committed by any one of the ship's company, whether crew or passengers. This view is stated in Rule for Construction 9 in the first schedule to the Act. To cover theft as we know it today it is necessary to add the peril to the policy and, for this purpose there are standard clauses available covering theft, pilferage and non-delivery. In the absence of such specific inclusion theft and pilferage are not covered, nor is non-delivery unless it can be shown that the non-delivery was proximately caused by a peril shown in the policy.

"Jettisons"—This is the casting overboard of goods or property to lighten a vessel thereby preventing the sinking of the ship and total loss of the entire adventure. It is the primary form of "general average" which subject will be discussed in more detail later. Because, in general, an action of sacrificing one interest to benefit the majority is in insurers' interests as a whole such action is encouraged by the insurers who cover the insured value of the sacrificed property. The standard clauses used in practice for both hull and cargo make provision to cover all forms of general average, including jettisons.

"Letters of mart and countermart"—Today these expressions are only of academic interest. At one time they were called "letters of marque and counter marque". According to the dictionary the word "marque" means "reprisals—a privateer" and "letters of marque" means "a privateer's licence to commit acts of hostility." These terms are relics from the sixteenth and seventeenth centuries when private persons would apply to the Crown for letters of authority to act as privateers in order to carry out reprisal attacks on vessels sailing under the flag of another country which was considered to be hostile to the Crown. Many people called this "sailing on the edge of piracy" because the privateer tended to take advantage of his authority.

Many privateers were, in fact, tried and executed as pirates. The insurance policy drafters included these perils with the same idea as piracy.

"Surprisals and Takings at Sea"—Surprisal is the act of surprising. The peril in the policy form refers to an act of surprise in overwhelming a ship. In the sixteenth and seventeenth centuries merchant ships, in fear of pirates and privateers, would be armed. An attacking vessel suffered less risk of damage if it could surprise its victims, which was usually done by approaching a becalmed ship by rowboat under cover of mist or darkness. "Takings at Sea" does not require explanation.

"Arrests, Restraints, and Detainments of all Kings, Princes and People of what Nation, Condition, or Quality soever."—The term, lengthy though it is, embraces one specific peril. Rule for Construction 10 provides that the term "refers to political or executive acts, and does not include a loss caused by riot or ordinary judicial process". There are many infringements of law which can result in the arrest of a ship whilst in port and, whilst the shipowner may consider the arrest unfair, the policy does not contemplate such arrests. The peril in the policy is intended to cover arrests and restraints by the Government of the Country responsible for the arrest or restraint. Suppose, due to the application of sanctions, a Country decided to arrest all vessels within its jurisdiction belonging to the nation with which it had a difference this would be an arrest within the meaning of the policy. It must be remembered that the cover is for physical loss of the vessel insured not for expenses incurred pursuant to the arrest or detainment. Hence, if the vessel is released there is no claim under the policy provided none has already been met. If the vessel is released after a claim has been paid for total loss due to arrest or detainment the vessel becomes the property of the insurer.

"Barratry"—The term derives from the word "Barrat" or "Barat" which meant deceit, strife or trouble but which has become obsolete. "Barratry" is a fraudulent practice or practices by the master or crew of a ship to the prejudice of the owner. If the owner is party to the act there is no barratry. The master or crew who scuttle a ship without instructions to do so from the owner commit an act of barratry and the loss is recoverable under the policy. Where the master or crew scuttle the ship on instructions from the owner it would amount to wilful misconduct on the part of the assured and the claim would not be recoverable under the policy. Even the innocent cargo owner could suffer under this principle except that in practice he is protected by the terms of the standard cargo clauses in the event of misconduct by the shipowner or his servants, committed without the privity of the assured.

"All Other Perils, Loss or Misfortunes"—Rule for Construction 12 in the Act provides that "the term 'all other perils' includes only perils similar in kind to the perils specifically mentioned in the policy." The legal dictum "Ejusdem Generis" (of a like kind) must be applied. For example, smoke is a peril which is *ejusdem generis* with "fire", so smoke damage is recoverable as a loss by fire. Seawater damage, usually termed "heavy weather", is a peril of the sea and ice formed from seawater is *ejusdem generis* with seawater so that damage caused by contact with ice is recoverable under the policy. Freshwater is not *ejusdem generis* with seawater so neither rain nor condensation as a proximate cause of loss are perils embraced within the terms of the policy and are not covered unless specifically mentioned, or included in a term such as "all risks". However when condensation results from closing ventilators in heavy weather the proximate cause of loss is the heavy weather so the loss is recoverable.

Extraneous Risks

A "risk" is defined as something which *might* happen but does not include something which *must* happen. Therefore, something which is inevitable is not a "risk" but a certainty. The term "all risks" means all fortuities. The plain marine policy, that is a policy with no special clauses or conditions, specifies the perils previously mentioned. These perils are the risks covered by the plain form of policy but there are many other risks which might occur to any particular insured property for which the assured may require cover. These additional risks are called "extraneous risks" because they are extraneous to those risks specified in the plain policy form. There are so many of these extraneous risks which might affect a particular interest that the assured and his broker are loathe to accept an insurance which attempts to specify them all. Hence, the practice is to use the all embracing term "all risks", but it must be emphasized that this term only covers fortuities not inevitabilities. Generally, the term is only used properly in cargo insurance and a special set of cargo clauses covering "All Risks" has been in use for many years in the cargo insurance market. The term is misused in hull practice when it customarily is used to describe a hull policy effected on the widest conditions acceptable in the market, thereby differentiating from a policy on more restricted conditions.

A few examples of extraneous risks will assist one in a better understanding of the term. Hook damage caused in loading or discharging cargo, freshwater damage, oil damage to cargo from the ship's machinery or fuel or damage caused by contact with other cargo are all extraneous risks. It is probable that the insurer paying claims for such losses could recover his loss, in some degree, from the party whose negligence resulted in the loss, say from faulty handling or stowage. If the insurer pays the claim these rights of recovery automatically go to the insurer under his subrogation rights.

Statutory Exclusions

It was previously mentioned that Section 55 of the Marine Insurance Act, 1906, states that the insurer is liable for any loss proximately caused by a peril insured against but is not liable for any loss not proximately caused by a peril insured against. This provision is made in subsection 1 of the section, but a number of important losses are excluded from the policy by subsection 2 of the same section. These exclusions will now be discussed in detail.

"Wilful Misconduct of the Assured"—If the assured is guilty of wilful misconduct he cannot reasonably expect the insurer to pay for a loss resulting from such misconduct. The loss does not have to be proximately caused by the misconduct to be excluded. Any loss *attributable* to the assured's wilful misconduct is excluded whatever the proximate cause of the loss. It is the wilful misconduct of the *assured himself* which the Act will not tolerate. Technically, when the servant of the master is guilty of misconduct this is the misconduct of the master so that, since the shipmaster and crew are technically servants of the assured whether the assured be the shipowner or cargo owner the misconduct of the shipmaster and crew would be the misconduct of the assured. This is obviously unfair to the innocent assured so the Act further provides that the insurer *is* liable for a loss proximately caused by an insured peril even though the loss would not have happened but for the misconduct or negligence of the master or crew. It should be particularly noted that this section does not incorporate negligence as a peril into the policy. It merely considers that negligence as a remote cause should not defeat a claim proximately caused by a peril insured against.

Examination of the section reveals that the innocent assured is only protected in event of misconduct or negligence of the master or crew. The innocent shipowner is happy about this for he is not penalized because of the faults of his servants but the innocent cargo owner is not so fortunate for *his* servant is the shipowner and the Act does not protect the innocent cargo owner in event of misconduct or negligence of the shipowner. As the Act seeks to be fair to the innocent assured so the insurer seeks to be fair to the innocent cargo owner and the standard cargo clauses contain a clause part of which serves the purpose. The clause appears in the Institute Cargo Clauses. It is the "seaworthiness admitted" clause and is number eight in each of the current sets of clauses. The second part of the clause provides that the assured's right of recovery for loss shall not be prejudiced by the fact that the loss may have been attributable to the wrongful act or misconduct of the shipowners or their servants, committed without the actual privity of the assured. Hence, all assureds are protected from being penalized where a loss is attributable to misconduct or wrongful act except when the assured himself is a party to such misconduct or wrongful act.

"Delay"—When considering the effect of delay in commencement and prosecution of the voyage in Chapter 7, it was noted that the contract may be avoided by the insurer or the insurer is discharged from liability depending on when the delay occurs. The standard cargo clauses provide, nevertheless, for the insurance to continue *during* such delay so that, for practical purposes one may consider the provisions of the Act to be almost academic. However, this only considers the continuation of the insurance. It does not impart delay as a *peril* into the policy. The Act provides that the insurer is not liable for any loss *proximately caused by* delay and it is immaterial that the delay may be caused by a peril insured against. Let us suppose a ship carrying a perishable cargo puts into port for repairs consequent upon collision. As a result of the delay the cargo deteriorates. The proximate cause of loss is delay so the loss is not covered by the policy even though the delay was caused by collision, a peril of the sea and therefore a peril insured against. Of course, if the policy states specifically that it covers delay, or uses words implying such cover, the loss is not excluded. The insurer, in practice, does not intend to cover losses proximately caused by delay when insuring against "all risks" so the standard "All Risks" cargo clauses specifically *exclude* losses proximately caused by delay to ensure no misunderstanding.

"Wear and Tear"—This is not a risk but an inevitability and is, therefore, excluded. The Act excludes the peril unless the policy otherwise provides, but one finds it difficult to imagine that an insurer would deliberately agree to cover wear and tear which is, so obviously, not an insurance risk. Nevertheless, in the practice of hull insurance the insurer usually does cover wear and tear to some extent. When the cost of repairs is assessed for a damaged ship the insurer is entitled to deduct a percentage for the depreciation, of the part repaired, by reason of wear and tear. In some Countries this practice is still followed but when the Institute Hull Clauses are attached to a policy the insurer's right to such deductions, called "thirds" or "new for old", is waived. The same type of clause waiving such rights also appears in the "Standard Dutch Hull Form", the "American

Institute Hull Clauses" and the "Lake Time Clauses".

Incidentally, the correct titles for these clauses are "Institute Time Clauses—Hulls", "Standard Dutch Hull Form" and "American Institute Time Clauses—Hulls". A set of clauses for voyage insurance on hulls is also published by the Institute of London Underwriters. The "Lake Time Clauses" are American Institute Clauses.

"Ordinary Leakage and Breakage"—Most liquid cargoes are subject to a natural loss of quantity during the voyage without the operation of any peril. This is, generally, due to evaporation and the amount can be readily assessed as being customary. It is usually about 1% in most cases although this varies with different types of cargo. The loss is inevitable and, therefore, is not a risk. This is called "ordinary leakage" and is excluded by the Act. The loss is frequently called "natural loss" in practice and insurers sometimes insert a percentage in the policy to be deducted from all claims to ensure that they do not pay for natural loss.

"Ordinary breakage" falls in a similar category and is also excluded by the Act unless the policy specifically provides otherwise. It is breakage caused by negligence and since negligence is not a peril covered by the policy it follows that such breakage is not covered. In some cases the insurer may agree to include "breakage" as an additional peril in the policy wording. The peril is embraced as an extraneous risk within the term "All Risks" and in policies subject to the other sets of cargo clauses it is included when it occurs during discharge at a port of distress, otherwise the peril is not covered.

"Inherent Vice"—This exclusion only applies when the "inherent vice or nature" is in the subject matter insured. Inherent vice or nature is a peril which occurs due to an action set up in the property itself without the assistance of an outside agency. Examples include spontaneous combustion and deterioration. When soft coal is loaded in a damp condition it tends to overheat if not adequately ventilated. This overheating leads to spontaneous combustion and the resultant damage to the cargo by fire is not covered by the policy. If the fire causes damage to the ship or to other cargo the proximate cause is "fire" not "inherent vice" so the loss to ship and the other cargo is recoverable. When fruit deteriorates due to delay this is a combination of inherent vice and delay but there is no need to differentiate because both are excluded perils. As the "All Risks" cargo policy excludes losses proximately caused by delay, so it also excludes losses proximately caused by inherent vice or nature in the subject matter insured. This provision, contained in Clause 5 of the Institute Cargo Clauses (All Risks) is inserted to prevent arguments as to whether such losses would be embraced within the term "All Risks".

"Rats or Vermin"—Although these days the risk of damage by rats has been largely exterminated the Act excludes any loss proximately caused by rats for, at one time, rats were known to cause extensive damage to cargo and even to certain parts of the ship. Vermin occur in certain types of cargo and loss proximately caused by vermin is equally excluded. Examples of such vermin are bolweevil in cotton and weevils in flour. It is interesting to note that the Act does not limit the exclusion to vermin *in the subject matter insured* as it does with inherent vice. Therefore, if vermin from one cargo damaged another the damage would be equally excluded from the plain form of policy. Where the policy is extended by the additional peril "damage by other cargo" the damage caused by vermin from the other cargo is covered.

"Injury to Machinery"—The machinery referred to by the Act is the propelling and other machinery in use in the ship and the intention of the exclusion is to make it clear that the insurer does not intend to cover a simple breakdown of machinery. If the damage is proximately caused by a maritime peril it is not excluded by the Act but if the machinery breaks down the repair is not covered by the policy. If part of the machinery breaks causing damage to another part this other part is not covered either because the damage has not been proximately caused by a maritime peril, except where the policy makes special provision to cover such damage as in clause 7 of the Institute Time Clauses.

Customary Policy Exclusions

By market practice all marine policies and Institute clauses contain a clause excluding War Risks. This is called the F.C. & S. clause and the exclusion is incorporated so that insurers can rate the insurance without taking into account war risks. If war risks cover is required it must be specifically requested by the assured and the appropriate war rate is then charged. The books in this series on hull and cargo practice contain details of the F.C. & S. clause and of war risks insurance. It is also the practice in cargo policies to incorporate a clause excluding the risks of Strikes, Riots and Civil Commotions. The abbreviation used in the standard cargo clauses to identify the exclusion is "F.S.R. & C.C.", the "F" standing for "Free of". Actually the perils excluded do not appear in the policy perils so the exclusion is not really necessary but it has become the practice to state the exclusion in cargo policies, probably, partly to make it clear to the cargo assured that the strikes risks are *not* covered and partly to emphasize the point so that he may request the cover, which is available, if he so desires.

Hull policies do not contain the exclusion but it must not be implied that the perils are covered because there is no exclusion specified. It is probably assumed that the ship owner is aware of the fact that the policy does not cover these perils and it is not necessary, therefore, to draw the matter to his attention.

It is customary to ally war risks with strikes risks when applying cover for these perils to attach to the cargo policy or when taking out a separate insurance to cover the perils in hull insurance.

Perils not Covered

It must be emphasized that the policy covers only those perils specified therein and that in all cases these are fortuities. If an exclusion is specified in the policy removing cover for any of the perils mentioned in the policy the deletion of that exclusion reverts the policy to what is covered before the exclusion was specified, that is, as though the exclusion had never been there. If the exclusion does not remove any cover, that is it excludes something *not* already covered by the policy as in the case of the strikes exclusion, the deletion of the exclusion *must not imply* that the peril which was excluded is then incorporated into the policy.

"Sentimental Loss"—This is best illustrated with an example. Let us suppose a cargo of tea is carried on a vessel which is known to have suffered an accident. Some of the tea is damaged but the remainder is not. It is probable that the sound tea will receive a lower price because of its known proximity to damaged tea although no damage is apparent to it. This is a market loss not contemplated by the insurer and is called a "sentimental loss". Such loss is not covered by the policy.

"Sympathetic Damage"—Sometimes when a cargo is damaged, say by seawater, it causes a loss to some other cargo, possibly due to taint from odour, which other cargo was not in actual contact with the peril insured against. This is called a sympathetic damage. It is often difficult to establish the actual cause of the sympathetic damage but if it can be proved that it was due to an insured peril it can be recovered as a loss by that peril. If, however, no such proof can be found the loss is not recoverable under the policy unless the policy makes special provision to cover the loss.

CHAPTER IX

PARTIAL AND TOTAL LOSS

Particular Average

THE word "average" when used in non-marine insurance is applied in its ordinary sense of comparison between the value of that which is insured and the sum stated in the policy thereby determining underinsurance. To illustrate this, the householder's contents policy is designed to cover all the property, belonging to the assured, contained within the house stated in the policy. The assured is permitted to decide his own sum insured but there is no agreed value. Since the whole of the property in the house is insured the insurer may insert an "average clause" in the policy whereby he is entitled to value the insured property as a whole to determine whether the sum insured is adequate. If it transpires that the sum insured is less than the total insurable value the insurer is entitled to apply the principle of "average" and, thereby, to reduce the claim for partial loss by the difference, in proportion, between the insured and insurable values.

In marine insurance the word "average" has a completely different meaning. It simply means "partial loss". There are two types of average in marine insurance being "general average" and "particular average". General average is a matter of major interest to the shipping community and marine insurers so will be discussed in two separate chapters, devoted entirely to the subject, later in this book. The Marine Insurance Act, 1906, does not have a lot to say about particular average but in Section 64 it defines particular average as "a partial loss of the subject matter insured, caused by a peril insured against, and which is not a general average loss". In the same section it is stated that "particular charges" are not to be included within the term "particular average".

Apart from the F.P.A. clauses, the standard cargo clauses do not use the words "particular average" but simply refer to "average unless general". This latter expression can be said to mean particular average and, in any case, is defined in Rule for Construction 13 as "a partial loss of the subject matter insured other than a general average loss, and does not include particular charges". This is much the same as the definition for "particular average" contained in Section 64 of the Act, except that the rule omits the reference to "caused by a peril insured against". It is doubtful whether the omission has any special significance, however.

Leaving aside the technical definitions, particular average means, simply, a partial loss of the subject matter insured, caused by a fortuity which is a peril covered by the policy. There are only two basic types of loss under the policy. These are "partial loss" and "total loss". Any loss which is not a total loss *must* be a partial loss. When a loss occurs it is first necessary to establish whether it is a total loss. If it is not, then it must be a partial loss. If it is a fortuitous partial loss it is particular, not general, average. It only remains to establish whether the fortuity was a peril covered by the policy to determine whether the loss is recoverable from the insurer.

There are certain expenses which are insured pursuant to a particular average loss. These expenses which are called "particular charges", include survey fees and sale charges on cargo sold for the insurer's account. These particular charges do not come within the category of particular average but are recoverable from the insurer if there is a recoverable claim for particular average. Some cargo policies contain a provision that particular average losses are only recoverable if a specified percentage is reached. The percentage is applied to the insurable value in cargo insurance in order to assess whether a claim is recoverable. In assessing the amount of loss in order to obtain the percentage Section 76 (4) of the Act states that regard shall be had only for the physical damage to the insured property and particular charges must not be added to reach the specified percentage.

Since 1969 hull policies on full conditions have incorporated a deductible in place of the franchise provision which still applies to cargo insurance. The hull policy deductible is determined at the time of placing and is inserted in the appropriate space in clause 12 of the Institute Time Clauses. The application of this deductible is not limited to particular average, but is applied to *all* partial losses (including sue and labour charges, general average, salvage charges and collision liability claims).

When goods arrive at their destination in a sound condition but it is impossible to identify the different varieties of the goods because the marks have been obliterated the assured cannot claim a total loss. If any loss has occurred at all it must be a partial loss (M.I.A. 1906 Sect. 56—Sub 5). An example of the application of this rule occurs when a consignment of several varieties of canned goods suffers loss of labels. It may be impossible to identify the contents of the cans and the assured could consider that he has grounds to claim a total loss. The Act is concerned only with actual physical loss, in this respect, and states that there can be no claim for total loss. If the consignment has been damaged by an insured peril there is a claim for partial loss. The insurer usually makes special provisions in the policy regarding loss of labels, when such goods are insured thereby avoiding arguments over a recovery under the policy in respect of the lost labels.

The right to claim a partial loss is not defeated because the insured unsuccessfully claimed for a total loss (M.I.A. 1906 Sect. 56—Sub 4).

Total Loss (M.I.A. 1906 Sects. 56, 57 and 58)

A loss may be total or partial. Any loss which is not a total loss is a partial loss. A total loss may be either an actual total loss or a constructive total loss. A deductible is not applied to a total loss claim.

Actual Total Loss

There are three ways in which an actual total loss can occur.

a. There is an actual total loss where the subject matter insured is destroyed. Therefore, there is an actual total loss where a ship is completely destroyed by fire. Cargo destroyed by fire would equally be an actual total loss. It would be misleading, however, to give as an example ship *and* cargo destroyed by fire because the statement implies that the cargo must also be destroyed to establish a claim for actual total loss on the ship. This is not so, of course, because each interest is treated separately in considering whether it is an actual total loss.

b. There is an actual total loss where the subject matter insured is so damaged that it ceases to be a thing of the kind insured. This is called "loss of specie". The word "specie" used here means "kind" and not gold or money for which the same word is used as a noun for the purposes of insurable interest. An example of "loss of specie" would be cement which, when immersed in seawater, becomes concrete.

c. There is an actual total loss when the assured is *irretrievably* deprived of the subject matter insured. It must be emphasized that it must be apparently absolutely impossible to recover the property lost. Obviously, in this instance, the property is not destroyed, or it would be within (a) above, and it has not changed its specie, or it would be within (b) above. Therefore, to summarize, the property is not destroyed and it has not changed its specie but the assured is irretrievably deprived of the insured property. An example would be gold bars which are sunk so deep in the ocean that it is impossible to recover them. Being a natural metal gold does not corrode, so cannot be destroyed, and it does not change its specie. Even when submitted to heat the gold merely melts and eventually returns to solid gold when it has cooled.

Missing Ship (M.I.A. 1906 Sect. 58)

One further example of actual total loss occurs when a ship is deemed "missing". When a ship appears to be missing the owners usually advise Lloyd's who contact their agents in all likely localities to obtain possible news of the whereabouts of the vessel. If, after a reasonable time has elapsed, no news is received of the ship she is posted as missing and an actual total loss may be presumed. The Act makes this provision but does *not* state that the insurer is liable for the loss. This means that the proximate cause of loss must be established to decide whether the loss is recoverable under the policy. Obviously, if the ship is simply "missing" it will be extremely difficult, if not impossible, to establish the proximate cause of loss. Because of this difficulty it is always the practice to consider the loss to be proximately caused by war perils in wartime and by perils insured by the marine policy in peacetime. Of course, if the insurer can show that the ship put to sea in an unseaworthy state the insurer may insist on the assured proving that the loss was proximately caused by an insured peril, for the onus is on the assured to prove that the loss was proximately caused by a peril insured against. Nevertheless, an anomaly might occur in this hypothetical situation for, in event of the insurer repudiating liability on the ship on the grounds of unseaworthiness the onus is upon the insurer to prove that the loss was proximately caused by unseaworthiness, further, seaworthiness is admitted on the cargo policy so the insurer on a cargo policy is unlikely to find any grounds for not following market practice and paying for the loss. Incidentally, it should be noted that an actual total loss may be presumed also on the cargo carried on a "missing ship".

Constructive Total Loss (M.I.A. 1906 Sects. 60-62)

It sometimes happens that the subject matter insured, whether ship or goods, is placed in a position by an insured peril where it has not actually suffered a total loss as defined above but where the expenditure to prevent such a loss would be greater than the value of the property when saved. A prudent uninsured person, in such a situation, would simply accept the loss and abandon the property rather than incur a greater loss to recover the property. The same principle can be applied when the property is insured. The assured is entitled to abandon the property to the insurer and to claim a total loss. However, no claim for constructive total loss is valid unless notice of abandonment is given. The only exceptions to this rule are set out in the M.I.A. 1906 (see later in this chapter).

Section 60 of the Act specifies the circumstances which entitle the assured to a claim based on constructive total loss and the student is advised to study this section closely for future reference. The provisions of the section can be overridden or modified by any special condition in the policy and, in fact, it is customary for hull policies to contain such a qualification. Before considering this, however, we will first examine the provisions of the Act itself.

M.I.A. 1906—Section 60

1. Subject to any express provision in the policy, there is a constructive total loss where the subject matter insured is reasonably abandoned on account of its actual total loss appearing to be unavoidable, or because it could not be preserved from actual total loss without an expenditure which would exceed its value when the expenditure had been incurred.

2. In particular, there is a constructive total loss:

   (i) Where the assured is deprived of the possession of his ship or goods by a peril insured against, and (a) it is unlikely that he can recover the ship or goods, as the case may be, or (b) the cost of recovering the ship or goods, as the case may be, would exceed their value when recovered; or
   (ii) In the case of damage to a ship, where she is so damaged by a peril insured against that the cost of repairing the damage would exceed the value of the ship when repaired.

In estimating the cost of repairs, no deduction is to be made in respect of general average contributions to those repairs payable by other interests, but account is to be taken of future salvage operations and of any future general average contributions to which the ship would be liable if repaired; or

   (iii) In the case of damage to goods, where the cost of repairing the damage and forwarding the goods to their destination would exceed their value on arrival (M.I.A. 1906 Sect. 60).

Having studied the specific wording of the Act we will now consider the *meaning* of Section 60.

Bearing in mind that the assured must reasonably abandon the subject matter insured to the insurer it is necessary to examine the circumstances which *entitle* the assured to claim a constructive total loss. The assured cannot simply decide that he would prefer to abandon the property and claim a total loss. His entitlement to do so only exists in certain circumstances which are:

(*a*) The assured is deprived of the ship or goods, as the case may be, by an insured peril, and it is *unlikely* he will recover the insured property. The emphasis is on the word *unlikely* because if it is established that the property is irretrievably lost to the assured it is an actual total loss and there is no need to attempt to establish a constructive total loss.

An example would be where a ship is in an alien port at the outbreak of war between the Country under whose flag the ship sails and the Country in whose port the master finds his ship. Undoubtedly the alien Government would give an order for all enemy ships to be seized. The shipowner is deprived of his vessel and it is unlikely he will recover it. It is not an actual total loss because the property is not destroyed and has not changed its specie, nor is it necessarily irretrievable. The assured can abandon the property and claim a constructive total loss. Once the insurer pays the claim he has proprietary rights in the ship should it eventually be recovered by which right he may take over the ship when recovered and dispose of it as he thinks fit, retaining the whole of the proceeds even if these amount to more than the claim paid.

(*b*) The assured is deprived of his ship by an insured peril and the cost of recovering the ship would exceed its value when recovered or, in the case of damage, the cost of repairing the damage would exceed the value of the ship when repaired.

This section calls for three examples:

1. A ship is on a strand, that is it has run aground, and is so hard and fast that the operation to move and refloat it will be very expensive. By use of modern methods salvors can refloat a vessel in most stranding cases but often the expense of the operation is very high. It can even exceed the value of the ship so that a prudent uninsured person would cut his losses and abandon the property. In these circumstances the assured can claim a constructive total loss caused by stranding, a peril of the seas.

2. The expenditure in example (1) may be less than the ship's value but if the vessel is so damaged that the cost of repairs added to the salvage expenditure exceeds the repaired value of the ship the assured can still claim a constructive total loss.

3. A ship is damaged by fire, a peril covered by the policy, to such an extent that the cost of repairing the ship will exceed her value when repaired.

It should be emphasized, here, that the assured is not *obliged* to claim a constructive total loss but is *entitled* so to do in the specified circumstances. He can elect to have the repairs carried out and to claim a partial loss, even a hundred per cent partial loss, thus retaining the property.

Since the Act requires that the cost of repairs must exceed the repaired value to establish a claim for constructive total loss on the ship the assured with a badly damaged ship finds himself in a difficult position if the cost of repairs is a little less than the repaired value. He cannot claim a constructive total loss and any claim for partial loss can be made only if the ship is actually repaired. In such circumstances it would appear to be ridiculous to repair the ship merely to establish a partial loss claim under the policy so the insurers do not insist on repairs being carried out but pay a compromised settlement, which amount is agreed with the assured, and do not take over the wreck.

In practice, the hull policy provides that the *insured value* shall be taken as the repaired value for the purpose of determining whether there is a constructive total loss.

(c) The assured is deprived of the goods by an insured peril and the cost of recovery would exceed the value of the goods when recovered or, in the case of damage the cost of repairing the damage and forwarding the goods to their destination would exceed the value of the goods on arrival at the destination.

Different circumstances give rise to the right to claim a constructive total loss of cargo, as opposed to the circumstances for establishing constructive total loss of ship. The contract of carriage will allow the shipowner to terminate the voyage short of destination in event of an accident and to discharge the goods at the intermediate port without any liability for the cost of forwarding the goods to destination. If the goods are damaged and the cost of reconditioning them *plus* the forwarding expense exceeds the estimated value of the goods on arrival at destination it would be uneconomic for the uninsured cargo owner to recondition and forward the goods, hence he would not forward them but instead would either abandon the goods or dispose of them at the intermediate port. The insured cargo owner, finding himself in this position, can abandon the goods to the insurer and claim a constructive total loss.

It must not be implied from this that the assured can claim for forwarding expenses as such.

The Act has nothing to say on constructive total loss of freight but this is immaterial in practice for the freight is, generally, included in the cargo policy. When freight is insured separately, that is when it is the interest of the shipowner, the policy contains a clause providing that the freight insurers will pay a total loss if it is established that the insurers on the ship have paid a total loss.

Note that abandonment is essential to a claim for constructive total loss but it must be reasonable, that is such as a prudent uninsured person would do in the same circumstances. The abandonment must be unconditional and once accepted by the insurer it is irrevocable. The insurer who accepts a valid abandonment must pay a total loss even if it proves later that the loss was proximately caused by an uninsured peril; he must, also, take over what remains of the property and any liabilities attaching thereto. When the notice of abandonment is given on information based on a mistaken fact the insurer is not bound by his acceptance. (Case of "Norwich Union—v—Price (1934)".) Acceptance of notice is acceptance of abandonment.

Remember, the assured is not *obliged* to claim a constructive total loss. If he wishes he can retain the property and claim a partial loss, even a 100% partial loss, in which case the insurer has no right to the wreck (M.I.A. 1906 Sect. 61). Where the assured elects to abandon the property and claim a constructive total loss the insurer, on paying the claim, is "entitled to take over what may remain of the subject matter insured and all proprietary rights incidental thereto" (M.I.A. 1906 Sect. 63—Sub 1). The insurer, on abandonment of ship, is also entitled to "any freight in course of being earned and which is earned by her subsequent to the casualty causing the loss, less the expenses of earning it incurred after the casualty; and where the ship is carrying the owner's goods, the insurer is entitled to a reasonable remuneration for the carriage of them subsequent to the casualty causing the loss" (M.I.A. 1906 Sect. 63—Sub 2). However, it must be emphasized that an underwriter who accepts abandonment, or notice thereof, is obliged to take over the wreck and any liabilities attaching thereto; but, if he does not accept the abandonment or notice, the insured can pursue a claim for total loss but cannot insist on the underwriter taking over the wreck or liabilities.

Hence, on payment of a total loss, the insurer may take over what remains of the insured property and dispose of it as he thinks fit, retaining the whole of the proceeds even if these amount to more than the claim paid. This was illustrated in the case of "Attorney General—v—Glen Line (1930)". In this case the war risk insurers paid a total loss on a British ship which was taken over by the Germans during the First World War. On cessation of hostilities the ship was recovered by the insurers and, since the insurers acquired proprietary rights by payment of the total loss claim, they disposed of the vessel for more than the claim paid. The action was brought to determine two points, one being whether the insurers were entitled to the difference between the proceeds of the sale and the claim paid and, two being whether the insurers were entitled to reparations recovered in respect of loss of use of the ship. We are only concerned, here, with point one, because point two is a matter regarding subrogation rights and will be referred to under that heading later. The court held that the insurers acquired complete proprietary rights in what remained of the insured property on payment of a total loss and, therefore, were entitled to retain the whole proceeds of the sale. This principle applies to claims for actual loss as well as constructive total loss.

Although Section 63—Sub 2, gives the insurer the right to take over any freight this would prove difficult to establish in practice. Therefore, the insurer always waives his right to freight in practice by the "freight abandonment clause" in the Institute Time Clauses.

It has already been emphasized that abandonment is a condition precedent to a claim for constructive total loss but, in addition, the assured must give *notice* of his *intention to abandon*. Notice of abandonment is the subject of Section 62 of the Act. The purpose of notice of abandonment is to advise the insurer of the imminence of an apparent total loss in order that he may take what steps he considers necessary to prevent the total loss. The policy always contains a "waiver clause" which states that any measures taken by the insurer to preserve the insured property from loss shall not be taken as an acceptance or waiver of abandonment. Because the purpose of notice of abandonment is to give the insurer the opportunity to prevent the loss such notice is not necessary when it can be of no benefit to the insurer (M.I.A. 1906 Sect. 62—Sub 7). This does not mean *abandonment* is not necessary; it merely means notice of intention to abandon need not be given.

Further, notice of abandonment need not be given where:

(*a*) the insurer waives notice.
(*b*) there is actual total loss.
(*c*) the policy is one of reinsurance.

If the insurer accepts a valid notice of abandonment this is deemed to be acceptance of abandonment and such acceptance is irrevocable. The insurer who accepts notice of abandonment must pay a total loss even if it is proved later that the loss was caused by an uninsured peril (M.I.A. 1906 Sect. 62—Sub 6). He must, also, take over any liabilities attaching to the property. The waiver clause provides that any action of the insurer in an attempt to prevent the loss is not to be deemed an acceptance of abandonment nor is the mere silence of the insurer an acceptance.

Notice of abandonment may be given in writing or by word of mouth or partly both. It must clearly indicate the assured's intention to abandon his insured interest unconditionally to the insurer (M.I.A.

1906 Sect. 62—Sub 2) and it must be given with reasonable diligence after receipt of reliable information of the loss, but where the information is doubtful the assured is entitled to a reasonable time to make enquiry (M.I.A. 1906 Sect. 62—Sub 3). Acceptance may be express or implied but, as stated above, mere silence on the part of the insurer is not to be deemed an acceptance (M.I.A. 1906 Sect. 62—Sub 5).

Failure to give notice of abandonment means that the loss can be treated only as a partial loss (M.I.A. 1906 Sect. 62—Sub 1).

Because acceptance of notice of abandonment by the insurer is irrevocable the insurer always automatically rejects the notice. It would be unfair if the assured was prejudiced by this action so the Act protects him in Section 62—Sub 4, which states that the rights of the assured are not prejudiced by the insurer's refusal to accept a valid notice.

It is customary for the marine assured to instruct his broker regarding claims collection and, in event of circumstances which may result in a constructive total loss, the broker anticipates the insurers refusal to accept notice of abandonment. The broker prepares two letters. The first letter gives the insurer formal notice of abandonment and states the intention of the broker's Principal to claim a total loss. This letter is signed by the broker on behalf of his Principal. The second letter is not signed by the broker but is prepared for the insurer's signature. It formally refuses to accept notice of abandonment but agrees to place the assured in the same position which he would have enjoyed had he issued a writ against the insurer. This letter is necessary because without it the assured would have to go to the expense and trouble of issuing a writ to make his claim in a court of law. In the absence of this arrangement the assured could not hesitate in issuing a writ because to establish a constructive total loss in the eyes of the law it is the circumstances prevailing at the time the writ is issued which are considered.

It has become fairly common practice for the broker to include both notice and rejection in one letter. This letter is presented to the insurer who signs thereon his rejection of the notice and returns the letter to the broker. This practice is an indication of the growth of streamlining in routine matters which is becoming commonplace in the London market in an effort to combat rising costs in administration of marine insurance affairs.

CHAPTER X

THE MARINE POLICY—FRANCHISE AND EXCESSES

The Policy Form

WHILST the Marine Insurance Act, 1906 in Section 21 states that the contract is deemed to be concluded when the insurer initials the slip, that is when he accepts the proposed insurance, it further states in Section 22 that a contract of marine insurance is inadmissible in evidence unless it is embodied in a marine policy in accordance with the Act.

The policy may be issued at the time the contract is concluded or it may be issued afterwards. Of course, in practice the policy is usually issued some time after the completion of the placing of the insurance. There have been instances when the Lloyd's underwriter has signed a policy for a small sum insured actually in the "Room", to reduce his signing costs, but most Lloyd's policies are signed by the Lloyd's Policy Signing Office some time after the placing. On rare occasions the assured may agree to waive his right to a policy, particularly in reinsurance when the sum insured is very small, thereby relying on the honour of the insurer in event of a claim. A minimum premium of £2.00 per policy is generally charged in the London market but even this does not cover the cost of policy signing and some Lloyd's underwriters have agreed to sign a monthly policy covering all small insurances placed with them during that month. In this latter practice the policy names the broker as agent for the assureds and lists the various assureds.

Most marine insurance contracts are negotiated by a marine broker and it is customary for this broker to prepare the policy for signing. Lloyd's and the Institute of London Underwriters each maintain a policy signing office where Lloyd's and Institute members' policies are checked and signed on behalf of the underwriters subscribing the various policies. When the insurance or part of it, is effected with a Company which is not a member of the Institute of London Underwriters such Company prepares and issues its own policy. The broker gives closing instructions to the Company by completing a closing slip. A closing slip is a form bearing the Company's name and headed blank spaces for the broker to insert the details of the insurance. When the closing slip is completed the broker sends it to the Company which then prepares and issues the policy. When several non-Institute Companies are concerned this would involve the broker in a great deal of unnecessary work and put the individual insurers to considerable expense to issue a separate policy for each Company. Further, the assured is content to have as few documents as possible. To overcome this difficulty a practice has evolved whereby the non-Institute Companies authorize the leading non-Institute Company to sign a policy on their behalf. The broker issues authorization forms to the following Companies who sign these and return them to the broker. The broker prepares a combined Company policy form and submits this, with the authorization forms, to the leading non-Institute Company for signing.

In all cases where a single policy form is used for several subscriptions the document is called a "combined policy form". Although several different insurers subscribe on one form to the same insurance it remains a separate contract between each insurer and the assured (M.I.A. 1906 Sect. 24—Sub 2).

To be valid the policy must be signed by, or on behalf of, the insurer. Some insurers are Corporations or members of Corporations. If there is a Corporate Seal this will generally be impressed on the policy form where the Corporation signs a policy. Both Lloyd's and the Institute of London Underwriters use seals in this way. The Act states that the impression of a seal is sufficient evidence of signature, but it is not compulsory for the seal to be used (M.I.A. 1906 Sect. 24—Sub 1). Lloyd's and Institute policies are both signed and sealed in practice.

Should the assured under a combined policy wish to take legal action it is not necessary for him to sue *all* the insurers on the policy. It is a separate contract with each named insurer and he can sue any one of these individually if he so wishes. In practice, the assured sues the leading insurer only. If he loses the case the assured does not bother to incur the expense of suing any of the others. If the assured wins his case the other underwriters follow the leader and settle the claim so further litigation is not necessary.

It is common practice for most insurers to use a marine policy form based on the S.G. form shown in the first schedule to the Marine Insurance Act, 1906. "S.G." means "ship and goods" and the S. G. form in the Act is designed to cover both interests on one policy. Today hull and cargo interests are treated separately and although the basic policy form is called the S.G. form it is customary to print a separate form for each of the main interests hull and cargo, leaving out from the basic wording irrelevant subject matter in each case. The forms still look very similar in their construction so, for ease of identification, both Lloyd's and the Institute use different coloured paper to distinguish hull from cargo. The hull form remains white and the cargo form is blue.

It would be impracticable to print a policy form to provide for every type of risk and every contingency so the practice is to use a basic policy form and to amend this to fit the requirements of any particular insurance. There are two methods of amendment, one being to delete and add wording on the form, and the other to attach over-riding clauses. This system of amendment tends to invite ambiguity in the general meaning of the policy conditions so in 1936 a set of rules was devised to control such ambiguity and to clarify the intentions of the parties to the contract. The rules are in two parts being (*a*) relating to the type of wording (i.e. printed, typed, impressed or handwritten) and (*b*) the effect of attachment of clauses. The rules, which are termed "Rules of interpretation" (or, alternatively, "Rules of precedence"), are as follows:

(*a*) 1. The basic wording is deemed to be printed.
      2. Printed wording is over-ridden by type or impressed wording ("impressed" means stamped with an inked rubber stamp).

The rules do not differentiate between typed and impressed wording.

      3. Typed or impressed wording is over-ridden by handwriting.

(*b*) 1. Often, clauses are printed or typed in the margin of a policy. The main wording in the policy form is said to be "in the body of the policy". Marginal clauses over-ride the body of the policy.
      2. The margin of a policy is not wide enough to insert much in the way of clauses so it is customary to attach clauses, either to the face of the policy or inside the folded form. In either case, attached clauses over-ride both marginal clauses and the body of the policy. All clauses attached to the policy are affixed with gum and the signing office customarily signifies approval by placing a rubber stamp impression half on the clause and half on the policy form.

It is interesting to note that the rules make no provision for differing styles of type so that there are no grounds for considering that italics or heavy type over-ride ordinary styles of type. Similarly, whilst the basic printing is customarily in black, certain clauses may be printed in red. This is done to emphasize such clauses and there is no rule which states that any particular colour of printing over-rides any other.

Once a policy has been signed nothing must be added, altered or deleted in the policy without the approval of the relevant signing authority. It is seldom that a policy is so amended. Where an alteration in policy conditions has been agreed an endorsement to the policy is prepared and the policy, with the endorsement affixed is presented to the signing authority for approval.

Stamp Duty

Prior to August 1970 any marine policy that did not bear a revenue stamp was invalid. This was provided by the Stamp Act which required that every policy should bear a 6d. stamp. However, in 1970 stamp duty on all policies of insurance other than those covering life was abolished. Thus, stamp duty is no longer necessary to establish the legal validity of the policy. The situation created thereby made many practitioners wonder whether the slip could be used in place of the policy but the Marine Insurance Act is quite clear on this point when it states

"Subject to the provisions of any statute, a contract of marine insurance is inadmissible in evidence unless it is embodied in a marine policy in accordance with this Act." (M.I.A. 1906—Sect. 22).

Of course, validity in law is one thing but the need for a policy in practice is another and it is possible that legal opinion may incline to the view that the issue of a marine policy is not compulsory so that, provided an action in law is not considered, a marine policy may not be a practical necessity. Certificates were regarded with some suspicion during the time when policies required stamp duty; the certificate being unstamped was clearly invalid in law. The abolition of stamp duty for marine policies has reduced this suspicion to some extent so that banks are far more ready to accept certificates in place of policies than was formerly the case.

Slip Policies

For many years reinsurers have used a system in reinsurance between London market insurers, whereby the formal policy form is replaced by a standard slip policy wording which is attached to the signing slip. In recent years, it has been agreed that this system could be extended to embrace certain cargo and hull insurances, in those cases where neither party requires the issue of a formal policy. Full details of this type of policy and the circumstances in which it is used are contained in Volumes 2 and 3. The slip policy is issued for convenience and it makes provision for the issue of a formal policy where required. The system can be applied to all cargo insurances placed at Lloyd's or with Institute companies, but is impracticable for use where non-Institute companies are concerned. Certain hull interests (e.g. disbursements) lend themselves to a slip policy system, but hull insurances on full conditions (mis-termed "All Risks" in practice) cannot be signed on a slip policy.

Valued and Unvalued Policies (M.I.A. 1906 Sects. 27-28)

The insurer in a non-marine contract will seldom accept an "agreed" value because annual renewal is difficult where depreciation could require a revision of values every year. The Marine insurer is not faced with the same problems because goods in transit arriving in sound condition do not depreciate in value and ship values tend to increase sufficiently to offset depreciation. Therefore, the marine insurer has no objection to an "agreed" value in the policy and all marine policies covering hull or cargo contain an agreed value. A policy which has the value specified therein as such is called a "valued policy". A policy which does not specify any value is called an "unvalued policy". It is customary to use the words "so valued" after the interest in a cargo valued policy and "valued at" before the agreed value in a hull valued policy. Hence, the valued policy is easily recognized in practice.

At this point, it would be well to clarify any confusion between the insured value in a policy and the sum insured. Every marine policy, whether valued or unvalued, specifies a sum insured. The sum insured is the total of the subscriptions of the various insurers in the contract and is the maximum amount payable for a loss under the policy. The sum insured may be the whole value or it may only be part of the whole value. If it is the whole value the valued policy will state *both* the sum insured and the value as the same amount. The insurer will then be liable for an insured loss up to the value specified. If, on the other hand, the sum insured is *less* than the specified value the insurer is liable for losses only in the proportion the sum insured bears to the insured value. The assured is in consequence deemed to be his own insurer for the difference between the insurer's liability and the actual loss. For example, if the sum insured in a valued policy is £10,000 but the value is specified as £12,000 the insurer would be responsible for ten twelfths of all insured losses and the remaining two twelfths would have to be borne by the assured.

The same principle will apply for an unvalued policy except that the comparison is between the sum insured and the "insurable" value. An unvalued policy does not specify any agreed value but leaves this to be determined subsequently. Considerable difficulty would arise if ever this assessment took place in practice, but since the problem does not arise any conjecture is purely academic. The Marine Insurance Act, 1906 (Section 16) does give some guidance on the assessment of insurable values but, as has been already stated, this is not used in practice.

The value in a valued policy is, in the absence of fraud, conclusive of the insurable value whether or not it be the true value (M.I.A. 1906 Section 27—Sub 3). This means that once an insurer agrees the value and it is specified as such in the policy he cannot dispute this value when a claim arises unless he can show there has been fraud. It is possible to reopen the value in event of gross overvaluation of cargo but not in the case of ship insurance. The reason for this is that the insurer cannot be expected to know the values of all the types of goods he is called upon to insure but he is expected to know as much about hull values as the assured.

The insurer and broker prefer valued policies for marine insurance because the value is conclusive and makes for simplicity in the operation of the settlement of claims.

The cargo owner prefers a valued policy because it gives him a more realistic indemnity in event of loss. Section 16 of the Act envisages the cargo assured, in event of loss, as being placed in the same position as he would be had he not undertaken the adventure. The assured wants to be placed in the same position he would enjoy had he successfully completed the adventure. The difference between the two is the "profit" the assured would have derived from the successful completion of the adventure. The Act does not make provision for the profit, allowing only the prime cost of the goods, the charges of insurance (premium) and the shipping charges (freight). The profit anticipated by the assured may vary but a reasonable profit may be said to be 10% so that an insurer would readily accept a value based on "Cost, insurance and freight plus 10% for profit". Apart from exceptional cases in practice, the assured does not indicate how his value is made up but simply states the value, which is seldom questioned by the insurer.

The shipowner prefers a valued policy because hull values fluctuate so much that claims on a policy covering 12 months would be difficult to assess if the ship had to be valued at the end of each voyage for claims purposes. Further, the ship value would depreciate with age of the vessel but the insurers would raise the premium rate each year to combat the loss of income resulting from a reducing value. An old ship is more expensive to repair than a relatively new ship which is why insurers are anxious at least to maintain the premium income. The assured does not appreciate a decreasing value against an increasing rate, so that both parties are happy to maintain the same value year by year, following which the premium rate tends to remain constant.

The Franchise and the Memorandum

In the eighteenth century insurers became increasingly concerned at the considerable number of trivial claims. Obviously, the assured had a right to claim if a loss was proximately caused by an insured peril no matter how small that loss might be but, to the insurer, the loss was not only the amount of the claim but also the expense of documentation and processing. Relatively it costs much the same to process a small claim as it does to process a large claim. Brokers were equally concerned because any recompense for work in collecting a claim was related to the size of the claim collected and the remuneration for collecting trivial claims made the operation uneconomic.

The market felt it was time to take definite action to cut out all small claims and the best way to achieve a general practice was to amend the wording of the S.G. policy form. As has been said previously, insurers are loath to change the actual wording of the policy so, to achieve their purpose, the insurers added a rider at the bottom of the policy form. This rider is called "the memorandum" and it was added to the S.G. policy form in 1749. The attention of the assured is drawn to the memorandum by the abbreviation "N.B." ("Nota bene"—note well) and its substance is reproduced below:

"N.B.—Corn, Fish, Salt, Fruit, Flour and Seed are warranted free from Average, unless general, or the ship be stranded; Sugar, Tobacco, Hemp, Flax, Hides and Skins are warranted free from Average under Five Pounds per cent; and all other goods, also the ship and Freight, are warranted free from Average under Three Pounds per cent, unless general, or the Ship be stranded."

Although subsequent clauses have largely moderated the effect of the memorandum in modern insurance the plain policy form always contains this wording and the student should make careful note of its provisions in order that he may relate them to the policy cover as a whole.

The memorandum introduced "the franchise" into the policy and to marine insurance. A franchise is an amount which must be *reached* before a claim becomes payable, but once the franchise amount is reached the claim is payable in full. To illustrate the point we will show three claims, A, B and C on goods with a sound arrived value of £1,000 and a 3% franchise.

Sound arrived value £1,000 Franchise 3% = £30

A. Goods are damaged by an insured peril — loss £20 (2%) No Claim.
B. Goods „   „   „ „   „   „   — loss £30 (3%) Claim 3% of
                                                insured value.
C. Goods „   „   „ „   „   „   — loss £40 (4%) Claim 4% of
                                                insured value.

The franchise as shown in the memorandum applies solely to particular average, that is, it only applies to fortuitous partial loss. Hence, it does not apply to total loss nor to general average loss.

In calculating whether the percentage, necessary to establish a claim has been reached only the actual damage must be taken into account. General average loss, particular charges and survey fees must not be added to attain the franchise amount (M.I.A. 1906 Sect. 76—Sub 3 and 4).

It will be noticed that the memorandum states "or the ship be stranded" which means that the franchise applies "unless the ship be stranded". Therefore, it follows that if the ship is stranded the franchise provisions no longer apply. This is called "opening the warranty" for the memorandum warranty ceases to be effective for the whole period of the policy once the ship is stranded. It does not matter whether the damage is actually caused by the stranding so that for all goods on board at the time of the stranding *all* damage proximately caused by the insured peril becomes payable in full without regard to the franchise once the ship has stranded. The Marine Insurance Act, 1906 gives force to this statement in Rule 14 of the "Rules for construction of the Policy".

The S.G. form used in practice today extends the provision for "opening the warranty" to include "sunk" or "burnt". So, if the ship is "sunk" or if she be "burnt" the same principle applies regarding the franchise as it does when the ship is stranded.

This would appear to be a convenient point at which to define the three perils mentioned in the previous paragraph:

Stranding—A ship is deemed to be stranded when she is held aground hard and fast for an appreciable period of time. Ninety seconds was held not to be long enough to establish a strand. Bumping over a harbour bar or a mere touch and go are not strands, nor is resting on the sea or river bed with the normal rise and fall of the tide.

Sunk—A ship is deemed to be sunk when she is submerged or when she can sink no further.

Burnt—A ship is deemed to be burnt when she is substantially burnt not just "on fire". A fire of minor proportion in the galley or one of the cabins would not open the warranty.

The Marine Insurance Act, 1906 (Section 76), states that where a particular average warranty, the memorandum is such a warranty, is contained in a policy which is apportionable the warranty shall apply to each apportionable part separately. There may be some difficulty in establishing what is or is not apportionable but, undoubtedly, in a cargo policy the period during which goods are being carried to or from the ship by craft may be deemed an apportionable part. Hence it follows that the franchise can be applied to each craft load separately. In the event of loss whilst the goods are on the craft if it can be shown that the loss attains the franchise percentage by applying it to the sound arrived value of the craft load the warranty is opened for that craft load; further, if the craft strands the warranty is opened for that craft load. The standard cargo clauses give emphasis to this point by specifying that each craft load shall be deemed to be a separate insurance.

In practice the memorandum applies only to cargo insurance and the standard W.A. and F.P.A. Clauses, whilst upholding the conditions of the memorandum regarding claims under the policy, modify its application by providing that not only shall the warranty be opened if the ship is burnt or sunk, as well as being opened if the ship strands, but also loss reasonably *attributable to* (note, the loss need not be proximately caused by the perils) four specified perils shall be payable irrespective of the policy franchise provisions. These four specified perils are fire, explosion, collision or contact of the vessel and/or craft and/or conveyance with any external substance, ice included, other than water. Thus, in the case of these four perils only, the principle of proximate cause is ignored; it being necessary for the loss to be only attributable to one of these perils for the claim to be recoverable. If damage is caused to the goods by discharge at a port of distress this is also covered irrespective of 'the warranty and, to further emphasize the principle of apportionable parts, if a *whole* package is totally lost in loading, transhipment or discharge, the insurers are liable for the insured value of such package.

Because the memorandum is printed in the policy form there must be a simple acceptable way of making it clear in the contract that claims shall not be subject to its terms when the parties so agree. The term used for this purpose is "irrespective of percentage" (abbreviation I.O.P.) which is used in all policies where the insurer agrees to waive the franchise provisions. The standard cargo "All Risks" clauses and the various sets of clauses covering war risks and strikes risks are all "irrespective of percentage". In fact, in modern practice it is commonplace to see the cargo slip with "i.o.p." overriding the memorandum.

Whereas the average clause in the Institute Cargo Clauses W.A.

and F.P.A. modifies the terms of the memorandum the standard hull clauses serve to strengthen underwriters' position by applying a deductible in place of the franchise expressed by the memorandum. The deductible is not a fixed percentage but is an amount agreed between the assured and the underwriter when the contract is negotiated and is entered in the space provided for this purpose in clause 12 of the standard hull clauses. When considering claims under a hull policy the deductible must be applied to *all* partial loss claims arising out of each separate accident or occurrence. This means that not only particular average claims are subject to the deductible but also general average sacrifice and contribution, sue and labour charges, salvage charges and claims under the running down clause. The ITC also contain a further deductible of 10% to be applied to machinery damage claims arising from negligence of master, officers or crew.

In cargo insurance the policy may provide for the franchise to be applied to each package or to each series of packages. The average clause wording would state something like "To pay particular average if amounting to £x on each series of 10 packages or on the whole" thus giving the cargo assured the option of applying the franchise in series or over the whole whichever is to his advantage. In order to clarify how series shall be established the insurers may insert the abbreviation "R.L.N." in the slip; meaning "running landing numbers" so that each 10 packages unloaded forms a series as it is discharged. If the final series comprises less than 10 packages it is called a "tail series". The series system is seldom used today.

Excesses and Deductibles

Whereas a franchise has only to be *attained* to make a claim payable under the policy an excess amount must be *exceeded* and not only this but only the excess balance of the claim becomes payable. Therefore a claim of 4% under a policy with a 3% franchise would be met in full by the insurer but had the franchise been an excess the insurer's liability would have been only for 1%, being the outstanding balance after applying the excess of 3% to the 4% claim. In other words 3% is deducted from 4% when calculating the claim. It is for this reason that the term "deductible" or "excess" makes no difference to the practical application for both mean the same thing.

The following three examples of claims applied to two different policies will illustrate the difference between the application of a franchise as opposed to an excess. Policy A has a 3% franchise whilst policy B has a 3% excess. Each policy is on goods for £1,000, so valued, and each of the three losses is a percentage of depreciation, proximately caused by insured perils, assessed by a surveyor.

		Policy A. Franchise 3% (£30)	Policy B. Excess 3% (£30)
Example 1 Loss £20 (2%)	No Claim	No Claim
„ 2 „ £30 (3%)	Claim £30	„ „
„ 3 „ £40 (4%)	„ £40	Claim £10

In example 1 the franchise was not attained under Policy A nor was the loss more than the excess shown in policy B, hence no claim would be recoverable under either type of policy.

In example 2 the franchise *was* attained so the claim would be recoverable *in full* under Policy A but the loss was still not more than the excess in Policy B so no claim would be recoverable under Policy B. In example 3 the franchise was attained and the claim would be recoverable *in full* under Policy A and the loss was more than the excess in policy B so the claim would be recoverable under policy B, but the 3% must be deducted from the loss under policy B so that the insurer would be liable only for £10 not £40 in this case.

Various types of clauses are used in practice to apply an excess or deductible to the policy. Sometimes the clause is entitled "deductible average clause", in other cases the words "subject to an excess of" or "subject to a deductible of" are used and no special clause is added.

In cargo insurance there are various reasons for inserting an excess or deductible in the policy, the most prominent being to encourage the assured to take greater care of particularly vulnerable goods by ensuring that he bears part of the loss himself. Some cargoes are so susceptible to loss or damage that insurers consider a certain percentage of loss to be inevitable. In principle, the insurer is not liable for inevitable loss (M.I.A. 1906 Sect. 55) but it is not always easy to prove the point in practice. To avoid argument in the insurance of such cargoes the insurer will insert on an excess in the policy of the percentage generally agreed in the market to be, what might be called, normal loss. This particularly applies where the insurance covers the breakage risk on fragile goods or loss of quantity (weight) on bulk or liquid cargoes.

In long term cargo covers an "aggregate deductible" may be included in the conditions of the contract. This means that the deductible is applied to the aggregate value of all shipments covered over a specified period. All claims over that period are totalled and the deductible applied. This is to the benefit of the insurer because the value of shipments without loss would be included in the aggregate and the deductible amount raised correspondingly. This system has its practical problems, however, for the insurer cannot withhold claim payment until expiry of the specified period and if there are no claims on the final shipments he is dependent on the assured to give a refund on claims overpaid.

Prior to the introduction of the hull policy deductible (1969) the Institute Time Clauses incorporated a franchise provision of 3% which applied to all particular average claims occurring in one round voyage. The franchise was not applied to general average losses, sue and labour charges, salvage charges, claims under the collision clause or a total loss. Underwriters' attitude hardened in 1968 so that the current deductible, which is inserted in the Institute Time Clauses applies to all partial losses occurring in each accident; only a total loss escapes the deductible. An additional deductible of 10% is applied to machinery damage where this is attributable wholly or in part to negligence of the master, officers or crew.

CHAPTER XI

MEASURE OF INDEMNITY

THE term "measure of indemnity" is in common use in the practice of marine insurance. It means "The extent of the liability of the insurer for loss", that is the maximum amount which the insurer must pay in event of a claim under the policy.

Sections 67 to 78 of the Marine Insurance Act, 1906 are embraced in the term but several of these sections have already been considered in earlier subject matter or will be discussed later. Here we shall confine ourselves to Sections 67, 69, 70, 71, 75 and 77.

Subject always to the adequacy of the sum insured the maximum amount recoverable under an unvalued policy is the insurable value and the maximum amount recoverable under a valued policy is the insured value. Obviously where the loss is a proportion of the whole only a proportion of the above limit is recoverable under the policy. It may be that the M.I.A. makes no provision for the measure of indemnity to be calculated for a particular interest, and, if this be so, Section 75 states that the provisions of the Act shall be applied as nearly as possible. In such cases it is customary for the policy to clearly specify the way in which a claim shall be paid. Usually the words "To pay £x in the event of" are used and examples where this occurs are "Ice deviation risk" and "Loss of hire" insurances.

The measure of indemnity for total loss requires only plain commonsense to understand. It is the sum insured by the policy. For total loss of part, that is where the risk is apportionable such as each craft load of goods, the measure of indemnity is the sum insured of the part totally lost. The Act actually states "the *insured value* of the part lost" assuming that the sum insured for the whole is equal to the insured value of the whole. Once again commonsense must be applied and where the sum insured for the whole is *less* than the insured value for the whole, in event of total loss of part, the calculation must be based on the lower figure. Apart from these simple points there is no need to make any special rules for dealing with total loss. The difficulties which, in the absence of guidance, would be experienced in establishing measure of indemnity occur when one considers partial loss. Many customs and practices have grown over the years in the settlement of partial loss claims but

110

certain basic rules are laid down by the Marine Insurance Act, 1906, and these should always be borne in mind.

Partial Loss of Ship (M.I.A. 1906 Sects. 69 and 77)

It would create many difficulties if partial loss of ship were related to the insured value so neither practice nor principle seeks to do this. After all, the intention of the shipowner is to obtain insurance to cover the cost of repairs to the ship and this is precisely what the insurance policy covers.

Therefore, in event of damage to the ship, proximately caused by an insured peril, the measure of indemnity is the *reasonable cost of repairs*. It is important to note that it is immaterial that the ship is or is not insured for her full insurable value whether the policy be an unvalued or a valued policy. It is only necessary for the assured to show that the cost of repairs is reasonable for the insurer to be liable for that amount. Even though the Act protects the insurer by insisting that the cost of repairs be reasonable it is notoriously difficult to establish what is or is not reasonable in practice. It is customary, therefore, for the hull policy to contain a clause, called the "tender clause" (I.T.C. No. 19), which imposes a condition on the assured in event of an accident occurring whereby a claim may become payable under the policy. The clause requires the assured to give notice to underwriters, prior to survey, and to the nearest Lloyd's agent if the vessel is abroad at the time. The insurers reserve the right to appoint a surveyor and to decide the port to which the vessel shall proceed for dry docking and repairs. (Insurers bear the expense of sending the ship to such port.) The insurers also reserve the right to veto the repairing firm and expect the assured to invite tenders for the repair contract. The underwriters are entitled to require the assured to invite further tenders and in such circumstances are prepared to compensate the assured for loss of use whilst awaiting such further tenders. There is a penalty of 15% deduction from the claim for non-compliance with the terms of the clause.

It will be noted that the measure of indemnity allows for *customary deductions*. The term is somewhat of a mis-nomer for such deductions are no longer customary. The deductions were allowed for wear and tear at one time, and were deducted from each claim which necessitated replacing damaged old parts of a ship with new material. These deductions, which, apart from general average, are now only of academic interest, related to the replacing of worn plates, ship's rigging etc. and were either $\frac{1}{3}$rd or 1/6th of the claim. For this reason the deductions became known as "thirds". Although by the

Act the insurer is entitled to make such deductions, in practice he waives this right by a clause in the standard hull clauses with the words "without deduction, new for old" (I.T.C. Clause 10).

As has been said previously, the measure of indemnity for partial loss of ship is the reasonable cost of repairs irrespective of whether or not the ship has an insured value equal to her insurable value, the only limit being the sum insured *in respect of any one accident*. It follows, that if there are several accidents during the period of the policy the insurer is liable for the reasonable cost of repairs in *each* case up to the sum insured so that in the aggregate the claims could exceed the sum insured during the policy period. In a marine insurance policy the sum insured does not reduce with the payment of a claim so there is no need for the amount to be reinstated, hence no reinstatement additional premium is payable in marine insurance such as is paid in other branches of insurance following a claim.

Nevertheless, it must be emphasized that the insurer is only liable for a loss actually suffered by the assured so if no repairs are carried out there is no "cost of repairs" and the insurer cannot be liable for such repairs. If the ship is totally lost following unrepaired damage the insurer's liability can be for the total loss only, the claim for repairs being extinguished by the total loss (M.I.A. 1906 Sect. 77—Sub 2).

An unrepaired ship is of less value than a ship in its sound condition and if the ship does not become a total loss the assured has a ship depreciated in value when the policy expires. The insurers' period of risk has ended and if the assured wishes to take out a further insurance he has a ship of lower value. It follows that even though he has not incurred the cost of repairs he has lost the amount of depreciation. So the Act provides that where a ship has not been repaired and has not been sold in her damaged state the assured is entitled to be indemnified by a reasonable amount in respect of the depreciation, but not exceeding the reasonable cost of repairing the damage. In practice, the depreciation is equally paid if the vessel is sold but here there is some guidance as to the amount of depreciation suffered by comparing the sound value of the ship with the amount realized. In the case of "Pitman—v—Universal Marine Ins. Co. Ltd. (1822)" it was held that the amount allowed for depreciation for a vessel sold unrepaired should not exceed the loss ascertained in the sale. If the vessel is not sold the depreciation amount is settled by compromise between the assured and the underwriters.

If a ship is only partially repaired the same principle is used in respect of depreciation as for an unrepaired ship.

Since the insurer is not liable for unrepaired damage in event of the vessel becoming a total loss during the period of insurance, whether or not the loss is caused by an insured peril, neither is he liable for depreciation. Hence depreciation is not payable until the policy expires and subject to the vessel being safe upon such expiry. Once this occurs the insurer is liable for the depreciation even if a total loss takes place on the subsequent policy.

The insurer is entitled by the terms of the Institute Clauses to decide the repair port but the ship may not be in a fit state to proceed to that port. In this event temporary repairs are carried out to enable the ship to proceed to the repair port and the cost is added to the permanent repairs and treated as part of the reasonable cost of repairs. The insurer then becomes liable for both temporary and permanent repairs.

Repairs are sometimes deferred by the assured because they do not affect the seaworthiness of the vessel and because, usually, the shipowner wants to keep his ship in commission during the busy season and carry out repairs when the ship is "laid up" out of season. This does not basically affect the insurer's liability for the repairs except that the delay may enhance the cost. Adjusters generally take this into account when assessing the "reasonable" cost of repairs. Some underwriters insist on a "cut off" clause in the policy. Such a clause provides that repairs must be carried out within a specified period (usually 18 or 22 months from the date of the accident).

Before we leave this subject it would be well to emphasize that the insurer is liable for partial losses up to the full sum insured for each accident and may pay for several lots of repaired damage each of which does not exceed the sum insured but which, in the aggregate, do exceed the sum insured. This is called the principle of "successive losses" and can be found in Section 77 in the Marine Insurance Act, 1906.

Partial Loss of Freight (M.I.A. 1906 Sect. 70)

Freight is the remuneration paid to a carrier for the hire of his ship, or space in his ship or for carrying the goods of the shipper. It also includes profit derivable from carrying his own goods but does not include passage money. In theory, freight is paid against safe delivery of the goods by the carrier at the destination but much freight is demanded in advance by the shipowner and it is agreed in the contract of affreightment that such freight is non-returnable even in event of non-delivery of the whole or part of the cargo. In such circumstances the freight is included in the insured value of the goods and a claim for partial loss of goods automatically includes a proportion for the freight paid for carriage of the goods.

Where freight is not paid in advance or is returnable it is at the risk of the shipowner and it is up to him to arrange his own insurance. The policy may make special provision regarding the payment of partial loss claims, such as the 3% franchise which appears in the standard freight clauses, but subject to any such special provisions the Marine Insurance Act, 1906 (Section 70) states that the proportion of loss shall be ascertained by comparing the actual freight lost with the whole freight at risk. The simplest way of doing this is to deduct the freight paid from the freight at risk and to compare the difference with the gross freight at risk. This proportion is then applied to the sum insured by the policy. The Act refers to both valued and unvalued policies but, in practice, valued policies are not used for the insurance of freight.

Partial Loss of Goods (M.I.A. 1906 Sect. 71)

There are many systems used in cargo claims practice with regard to particular types of cargo insured under particular conditions but it is not the intention, at this point, to go into such details. Instead, we will confine ourselves to the measure of indemnity as provided by the Marine Insurance Act, 1906 which assumes the goods have been sold damaged at destination and that the application of the formula laid down by the Act is simple. In practice, it is not always so easy to ascertain a percentage of depreciation and the insurer is very often dependent upon the skill of a cargo surveyor to assess the amount of loss. Nevertheless the formula provided by the Act gives a good basis for an understanding of the measure of indemnity for partial loss of goods.

Although the Act refers to both valued and unvalued policies it is the practice for all cargo policies to be valued so we will concentrate on the effect of the formula on a valued policy and leave the commonsense of the student to appreciate that references to "insured value" would be replaced with "insurable value" if an unvalued policy were used.

We already know that if the goods are totally lost the insured value becomes payable by the insurer so it follows, logically, that where an apportionable part of the goods is totally lost the insurer is liable for the insured value of the part lost. Thus if single packages have an ascertainable insured value individually and one package is totally lost by an insured peril the insurer is liable for the insured value of that package. In fact, the standard cargo clauses, both W.A. and F.P.A., make it perfectly clear that the insurer will pay the insured value of any package or packages totally lost in loading, transhipment or discharge whatever the actual cause of loss. In ascertaining the value of an apportionable part, say one package, the Act states that the insurable value of the package must be compared with the insurable value of the whole cargo insured and the proportion thus established be applied to the insured value in the policy to determine the claim.

In the following example it must be remembered that the insurer's interest in the *actual* value is only insofar as this is necessary to determine the percentage of depreciation. The claim is based on the *insured* value which is conclusively accepted as the value for insurance purposes.

Example:

10 packages insured value £1,000. Actual value £900
One package totally lost in discharge
Conditions of policy—I.C.C. (W.A.)
Estimated value of package at destination, based on value of packages which arrived safely, £90
Percentage of depreciation 90/900=1/10th or 10%
Claim 10% of £1,000=£100 (insured value of one package).

A similar principle is applied when goods arrive damaged at destination. The first thing to ascertain in determining the claim is the percentage of depreciation and if the goods are sold this is simply done by drawing a comparison between estimated arrived sound values and actual arrived damaged values. If the goods are not sold the surveyor assesses the percentage of depreciation by estimating the damaged and sound arrived values based on the current market values. It is essential that the percentage of depreciation must remain constant whether the market is stable, falling or rising. For this reason net values are not used, unless the policy makes special provision for the use of net values. The "net" value is the gross value less destination charges. "Gross" value is the value on which a sale could be based whereby the seller would be reimbursed for all expenses of landing the goods which he has incurred including freight payable at destination in addition to the actual value of the goods themselves. Hence "Gross" value means the wholesale price of the goods at destination, or, if sold short of destination, the place where the goods are sold. If there is no sale it is the estimated price with freight, landing charges and duty paid beforehand.

The reason why gross values must be used is because the destination charges tend to remain constant whether the goods are sound or damaged. Freight is generally payable in full on both sound and damaged goods. Landing charges between sound and damaged goods only vary insomuch as "dirty" handling of damaged goods may increase, rather than reduce, the cost of landing and duty based on weight is much the same for both sound and damaged goods although there may be some variation if the duty is based on the value. Since the destination charges remain constant whilst the market rises or falls this is bound to affect the difference between sound and damaged values.

Example:

The goods are insured for £100 which was the estimated gross value at destination when the insurance was effected. Half the goods are damaged so that the true percentage of depreciation should be 50% but if the landing charges remain constant at £20 the percentage of depreciation will only be constant at 50%, whether the market rises or falls or remains stable, if gross values are used.

Example 1
(Stable market)

		Sound Value	Dmgd. Value	Loss
	Gross	£100	£50	£50 (or 50% of £100)
Destination charges		£20	£20	
	Nett	£80	£30	£50 (or 62·5% of £80)

Here although the actual loss in each is still £50 the percentage of depreciation increases by the use of net values even though the market remains stable.

Example 2
(Rising market)

		Sound Value	Dmgd. Value	Loss
	Gross	£120	£60	£60 (or 50% of £120)
Destination charges		£20	£20	
	Nett	£100	£40	£60 (or 60% of £100)

Here, again, the percentage of depreciation increases by the use of net values.

Example 3
(Falling market)

		Sound Value	Dmgd. Value	Loss
	Gross	£80	£40	£40 (or 50% of £80)
Destination charges		£20	£20	
	Nett	£60	£20	£40 (or 66⅔% of £60)

An interior view of the reconstruction of Edward Lloyd's coffee house showing the rostrum from which the "Kidney" made announcements.

The "Lutine Bell" which hangs in the underwriting room at Lloyd's

The Underwriting Room at Lloyd's where insurance of every description, except long term life cover, is transacted by Lloyd's underwriters; each day, through Lloyd's brokers, they accept insurance business worth over a million pounds in premium income, two-thirds of which comes from overseas.

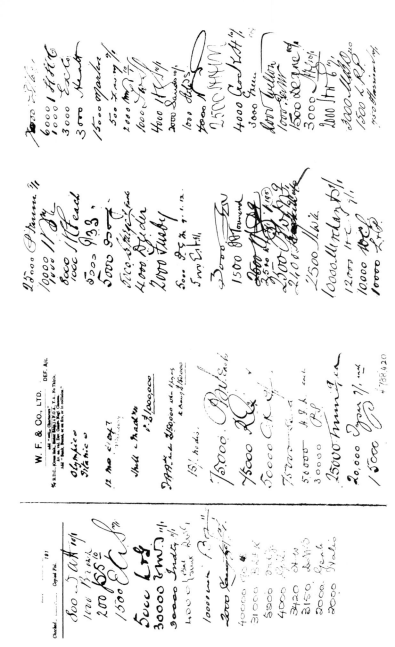

The Broker's Slip for the Insurance on the Olympic and the Titanic.

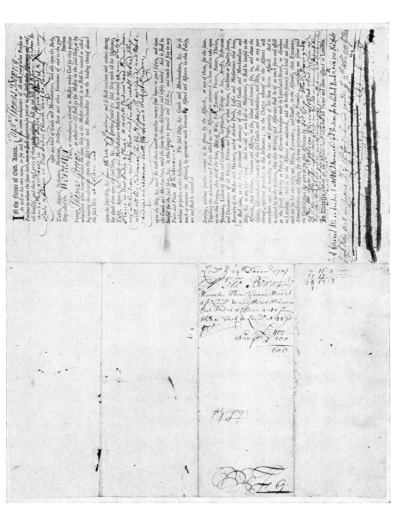

An early Lloyd's policy, dated 11 October 1701.

This last example illustrates that not only does the percentage of depreciation increase by the use of net values but also it increases by more, as the market falls than it does if the market rises in the same degree. Thus insurers would be bearing part of the loss of market which risk is not intended to be covered by the policy since it is not caused by any accident to the goods.

In all three examples it can be clearly seen that the use of gross values gives a constant 50% as the percentage of depreciation. It will be noticed that the calculation is made by comparing the difference, that is the loss, with the sound value and that the insured value is ignored at this point. Nevertheless, once the percentage of depreciation has been established this percentage is applied to the insured value to ascertain the claim.

Thus the formula for establishing the claim is as follows:

$$\frac{G\,S\,A\,V \text{ less } G\,D\,A\,V}{G\,S\,A\,V} \times \quad \text{Insured Value}$$

G S A V = Gross sound arrived value.
G D A V = Gross damaged arrived value.

Using the figures in the above example No. 1 the claim would be

$$\frac{\pounds100 - \pounds50 = \pounds50}{\pounds100} \times \frac{\pounds100}{1} = \pounds50$$

or expressed as a percentage of depreciation

$$50\% \times \pounds100 = \pounds50.$$

Using the same formula for example No. 2 the claim would remain the same

$$\frac{\pounds120 - \pounds60 = \pounds60}{\pounds120} \times \frac{\pounds100}{1} = \pounds50$$

The result is exactly the same for example No. 3.

Where goods are customarily sold "in bond", and those goods are damaged the bonded value shall replace the gross value for the purpose of calculating the claim on the policy. When certain types of goods, such as alcoholic spirits, are subject to heavy duty the importer pays the duty and, therefore, buys the goods at the price before duty is paid. The goods are placed in a bonded warehouse under customs control, pending payment of the duty, and are said to be "in bond". The value before duty is paid is called the "bonded value". Dutiable goods are only subject to duty if imported. If they are merely passing through, that is awaiting transhipment, duty is not payable but so that they are not released into the domestic market, thus avoiding duty payment, such goods are customarily held "in bond" until released for onward carriage. This latter point is only of passing interest for the insurance would be effected for the whole voyage and any claim would not be calculated until the goods arrived at their destination.

Many an assured feels that the above formula is not advantageous to him and in the event of damaged goods being sold he should receive the insured value less the gross proceeds. "Gross proceeds" means the actual price received at the sale with all charges paid by the sellers (M.I.A. 1906 Sect. 71—Sub 4). Let us consider the effect of this by using the earlier examples.

Example No. 1 (Stable market)	Insured value	£100
	Gross Proceeds	50
	Claim	£50
Example No. 2 (Rising market)	Insured value	£100
	Gross Proceeds	60
	Claim	£40
Example No. 3 (Falling market)	Insured value	£100
	Gross Proceeds	40
	Claim	£60

This illustrates where the assured's reasoning is at fault. Admitted, in example No. 1, with a stable market, the method of calculation makes no difference to the claim, and where the market falls the assured benefits, but in a rising market the assured clearly loses. It is more equitable all round to use a system which maintains the same percentage of depreciation whatever the state of the market, so gross values with the formula as shown previously are always used for partial loss of goods delivered damaged at destination. Where, however, goods are landed short of destination in a damaged state but the loss plus forwarding charges are insufficient to establish a constructive total loss a compromised settlement is often arranged. This compromise is called a "salvage loss" and is operated in the manner discussed above, that is the goods are sold. The assured retains the proceeds and receives from insurers the insured value less the amount of the proceeds.

Two important points must be remembered in considering a claim for partial loss of goods. The survey, if any, is primarily the responsibility of the consignee (the person who receives the goods) and the expense thereof is borne by the assured, in the first instance. If there is a claim under the policy the assured can add the survey fee to form part of the claim but if there is no claim the survey fee cannot be recovered from the insurer. The second point concerns sale charges. When goods are sold certain charges are incurred pursuant to the sale. Where goods are sent "on consignment", that is with the intention of selling them at destination, whether sound or damaged, one cannot argue that the sale in a damaged condition was a forced sale. Hence the assured is responsible for the sale charges whether or not there is a claim. Where the goods were not intended for sale at destination and are sold in their damaged state the same principle applies as for survey fees. The sale charges may then be added to form part of a claim on the policy.

Although the principle for calculating partial loss implies that the goods are sold to determine the percentage of depreciation, this is not always practicable so that where the consignee takes delivery of the goods with no intention of selling them, it is customary for a surveyor to estimate the percentage of depreciation which is then applied to the sum insured to determine the claim.

When goods are sold it has been suggested that a proper indemnity would be the difference between the insured value and the amount realized. There is no precedent in law to establish this form of calculation, which, in effect, would make the underwriter responsible for any diminution of value by reason of a falling market; a risk not contemplated by the cargo policy so, except where specially agreed by the underwriter, cargo claims are never settled on this basis. If the underwriter does agree to settle a claim on this basis it is termed a "salvage loss".

CHAPTER XII

SUE AND LABOUR, SALVAGE AND SUBROGATION

Sue and Labour (M.I.A. 1906 Sect. 78)

A N uninsured person who sent goods in transit would take reasonable precautions to prevent damage to, or loss of, the goods whilst in transit. If the goods were exposed to danger and damage or loss could be reduced or prevented, by some act by the owner, the owner would have no hesitation in carrying out the preventive measures necessary. Equally the uninsured owner would incur reasonable expenditure to prevent or reduce damage or loss, provided the expenditure was not large enough to warrant a constructive total loss. An uninsured shipowner would act in the same way.

Because goods or a ship are insured there is no reason why the owner should relax his efforts to prevent or reduce damage or loss. Nevertheless, it is human nature for a person to feel less responsibility for the safekeeping of his property when it is insured than he would feel if it was not insured. It is not suggested that the owner of insured property is going to deliberately expose his property to damage or that he adopts an irresponsible attitude but, simply, that he is less likely to be worried about the safety of his property.

However, the matter is not left to the conscience of the assured to decide but a common law duty is placed upon him to exercise proper care of his property during the period of the insurance. Section 78 (Sub 4) of the Marine Insurance Act, 1906 states that "It is the duty of the assured and his agents, in all cases to take such measures as may be reasonable for the purpose of averting or minimizing a loss". In practice, the cargo assured might argue that it is not reasonable to expect him to know the provisions of the Marine Insurance Act so, although ignorance of law is no excuse, the insurers make the duty clear to the assured by inserting the wording of the Act in Clause 9 of the Institute Cargo Clauses (the "Bailee Clause").

Any measure thus taken and expenditure so incurred is for the insurer's benefit, not for the benefit of the assured. It is only reasonable, therefore, that the insurers should, at least, bear the expenditure. The taking of action for the purpose of averting or minimizing loss is called "suing and labouring in and about the defence of the

120

property" which property is the subject matter insured. To "sue and labour", then, means to take measures to prevent loss for which the insurer would be liable. Because suing and labouring is for the insurer's benefit all hull and cargo policies contain a "suing and labouring clause" (sometimes called "the sue and labour clause") by which the insurer states that any action so taken by the assured shall not prejudice his right to claim and if he incurs expenditure pursuant to the clause the insurers agree to reimburse the assured.

There are certain well defined essential features regarding sue and labour expenses which help to avoid confusion of these expenses with those incurred in a general average or salvage act. These essential features, set out below, should be carefully studied and remembered.

1. Sue and labour expenses are for the sole benefit of the subject matter insured, thus effectively excluding general average which is for the common benefit.
2. Sue and labour expenses are incurred by the assured, his servants or assigns, thus excluding salvage charges which are incurred by a third party.
3. Sue and labour charges are particular charges but not all particular charges are sue and labour. Expenses incurred at destination to assess the claim, such as survey fees and sale charges are particular charges but are certainly not sue and labour. Such expenses are not recoverable from insurers when there is no claim under the policy but where properly incurred, with insurers' consent, they may be added to a recoverable claim. The same principle must be applied to costs of reconditioning or repacking damaged cargo at destination.

To be recoverable under the policy the sue and labour expense must be incurred for the purpose of preventing or minimizing a loss which would be recoverable under the policy, that is a loss proximately caused by a peril insured against. If this were not so the insurer would be paying for sue and labour charge incurred to prevent or reduce a loss in which he had no interest and, therefore, had derived no benefit from the sue and labour act.

Examples of sue and labour expenses are as follows:

1. Hull—A ship loses an anchor and cable by the operation of an insured peril. Services are carried out under contract to recover the anchor and cable. Such services are for the sole benefit of the ship underwriters and are carried out by the servants of the assured. The expense of the services is, therefore, not general average nor salvage. That part of the expense which exceeds the policy deductible is recoverable from the ship underwriters under the suing and labouring clause.

2. Cargo—The cargo on a ship was cattle (livestock) and due to heavy weather the vessel put into a port of refuge and waited for the weather to improve. Fodder had to be purchased for the feeding of the cattle during the delay. The policy covered mortality from any cause (with a few specified exceptions, none of which was "delay"). The expense was for the sole benefit of the cargo so could not be called general average. The master of the vessel was servant of the shipowner and, therefore was acting as bailee for the cargo owner, the assured. Hence, the expense was a sue and labour charge.

It can be seen from these two examples that a useful rule of thumb is to eliminate the possibility of general average or salvage first and, provided the peril involved is a peril insured against and the expense is incurred short of destination it is most probably sue and labour. General Average losses and contributions as well as salvage charges are not recoverable under the sue and labour clause (M.I.A. 1906 Sect. 78—Sub 2).

A sue and labour clause is a supplementary contract (M.I.A. 1906 Sect. 78—Sub 1). This means that the policy is a separate insurance so far as recovery of a sue and labour expense is concerned and none of the restrictions imposed by the policy apply to the sue and labour clause except where they specifically refer to the clause. Obviously, there is a limit to the amount recoverable under the clause, this limit being the sum insured, but, because the clause is a supplementary contract, the assured could claim sue and labour charges in full, up to the amount of the sum insured, even following a total loss. Further, the sue and labour act need not be successful. Provided it is a genuine attempt to save the property or to minimize loss, and the expense is reasonable, the assured can claim the expense incurred directly from his insurer even if a loss still occurs despite his efforts. The M.I.A. 1906 (Sect. 78 Sub 1) provides that sue and labour charges are not subject to the franchise in the policy. In practice, this applies to cargo policies on W.A. terms but does not apply to hull policies because these contain a deductible in place of the memorandum franchise expressed in the policy and such deductible applies also to sue and labour charges. It is important to bear in mind that a particular charge is only recoverable from underwriters when it arises from an insured peril thus an expense which might otherwise be recoverable as sue and labour would not be recoverable under a "total loss only" policy if it were incurred to prevent or minimise a partial loss. Similarly a sue and labour expense to prevent a loss recoverable under a W.A. policy but not recoverable under an F.P.A. policy would not be payable by the underwriters on the F.P.A. policy. This is, however, so difficult to establish in practice that the Institute Cargo Clauses F.P.A. state that insurers will pay "special charges" (sue and labour charges) as though the policy covered partial loss.

Except where the policy provides otherwise, sue and labour expenses are payable in full by the insurer irrespective of the insured value, subject only to the limit of the sum insured. Cargo policies make no variation to this rule but hull insurers are concerned at the possibility of paying more than they feel justified when the ship is overvalued or underinsured. Hence, the Institute Time Clauses provide that the insurer shall not be liable for a greater proportion of the sue and labour expense than the sum insured bears to the insured value or the sound value if the insured value is greater than the sound value at the time the expenses are incurred. The same principle is outlined in the Lloyd's Air Cushion Vehicle Policy (Hull), that is the standard policy covering hovercraft, but in the A.C.V. form the insurer's liability for sue and labour expenses is limited to 25% of the insured value of the air cushioned vehicle in respect of any one event.

Particular Charges

The term "particular charge" has never been defined in law but, from a practical point of view in cargo insurance, it is customary to relate the term to apply solely to those expenses incurred at destination. If one applies this rule a particular charge, as known in cargo practice, cannot include a sue and labour charge because the latter must be incurred short of destination. The reason for differentiating between the two forms of expense in cargo practice is that a charge at destination is generally incurred in the assessment of loss such as a survey fee or the cost of a sale. Even if the charge is to prevent further loss, such as rebagging or repacking goods which arrive in damaged containers, such expense is incurred to prevent loss from occurring *after* the insurer's risk has ceased.

Therefore, the insurer's only concern in a particular charge is if it relates to a claim under the policy. In other words, if there is a claim under the policy for damage to goods the insurer is liable not only for the percentage of depreciation but also for a particular charge incurred because of that claim, say, a survey fee to assess the cause or the amount of loss. So a particular charge cannot be added to reach a franchise (M.I.A. 1906 Sect. 76—Sub 4) but if the franchise is reached without the particular charge the charge may be added to the claim.

In hull insurance a particular charge is an expense incurred by the assured or his servants in connection with the ship such as the expense of entering a port following accidental damage. Except where the charge is part of a claim or is a sue and labour charge it is of no concern to the ship underwriters.

Salvage and Salvage Charges (M.I.A. 1906 Sect. 65)

"Salvage" is the remuneration paid or payable to a person who, acting as third party (that is, a person other than the owner, his servant, agent or assignee) independently of contract, voluntarily renders a successful service in preserving from peril property involved in a maritime adventure. Sometimes the term "salvage" is also used to describe property which has been salved, that is property saved in an act of salvage. Probably to differentiate from the use of the same word for both the remunerations and the saved property, the Marine Insurance Act, 1906 refers to the remuneration as "salvage charges".

The salvage act is generally referred to as a salvage service and, although marine insurance uses the term "salvage charge" to denote the remuneration paid or payable to the salvor the Admiralty Court or the Arbitration Committee refer to it as a "salvage award". In theory, the amount of the award is decided by the Admiralty Court convened at the place where the salvage services terminate. This would still be the practice for "pure" salvage cases, but these do not exist in practice today. To establish a case for pure salvage the salvor must act voluntarily, without entering into any form of contract with the owner of the property, and on the strict understanding that he receives no reward if his services are unsuccessful. This is the principle of "no cure—no pay". If the salvor is successful his award will be based on the degree of skill used combined with the expense of the operation, the hazards involved and the value of the property saved. No salvage award can be greater than the value of the property saved. No salvor is entitled to an award when he is responsible for the circumstances which led to the need for the salvage act.

Under English maritime law there is no award given for "life" salvage by itself. Therefore, if lives are saved but no property is involved English maritime law makes no provision for paying the salvor an award. If property is saved as well as life, maritime law, that is law between nations, awards life salvage against the owners of the salved property. Under English law, however, (Merchant Shipping Act, 1894) the owner of maritime property involved in a salvage service, whether hull or cargo, can be required to pay life salvage whether or not his property is also saved. Should it be necessary the Ministry of Transport can award life salvage out of the Mercantile Marine Fund. This protection for passengers and crew of a ship in peril is necessary because it discourages salvors from attempting to save the property before attempting to save life. As a matter of public policy, the saving of human life should be the primary consideration of would-be salvors but it is not practicable to award life salvage against the person whose life has been saved so the Court or Arbitration Committee tend to enhance the award against the saved property to embrace a sum sufficient to cover the life salvage. The insurer of ship or goods is not, strictly, liable for life salvage as such but where there is a salvage award against the insured property he becomes liable for this, subject to its being caused by an insured peril, and if it is enhanced because life was saved the insurer, in fact, pays for the life salvage but not as a separate entity. This only happens when the same salvor has a right to the award for saving both life and property. If a separate salvor saved the life the enhancing of the property salvage award would serve no purpose.

The principle of salvage applies only to maritime property except that under the Air Navigation Act, 1920 and the Civil Aviation Act, 1947 it is extended to cover aircraft over or in the sea or tidal waters or on or over the shores of the sea or tidal waters. Nor is salvage awarded for services rendered in saving a floating gas buoy, floating dock or similar (Gas Float Whitton 1897). Nor can the owners of personal effects be called upon for a salvage contribution.

Insurers do frequently make a reward in the nature of salvage to persons who assist in saving non-marine property from a loss for which the insurer would have been liable but the salvor cannot demand a salvage award from the owner of the property so the insurer is not legally liable for the reward.

A maritime salvor can enforce his right to salvage by exercising a lien on the salved property. This is a maritime lien whereby the salvor obtains no proprietary rights but can, nevertheless, prevent the owner of the salved property from occupying and/or using such property until a deposit or guarantee in respect of the probable salvage award has been made.

In most of the cases of salvage which come to the public notice it involves the saving of a ship or a ship with its cargo, but, in practice, salvage services apply not only to ship and cargo but also to freight in course of being earned. A salvor may claim an award in respect of any of these interests successfully saved. To obtain a right to claim salvage on freight it is generally necessary to save the cargo because, in such instances, freight is payable on delivery of such cargo. Nevertheless, since many owners of goods pay freight in advance which is not returnable, and the freight has been merged in the value of the goods, no separate interest of freight exists for the salvor to claim against. Where a ship is under charter and the salvage services enable the vessel to earn charter hire money, which would not have been earned without such services, the salvor has a right to claim an award in respect of the freight so earned.

Unless some sort of agreement is made before the salvage services commence it is sometimes difficult for a salvor to enforce his right to salvage. He may pursue an action *in rem*, that is an action against the property saved, in which case he exercises his "lien" on the salvaged property. Alternatively, under the Administration of Justice Act, 1956, the salvor may relinquish his right to hold the property and pursue an action *in personam*, that is against the owner of the property for the value of the salvage award.

The calculation for the award is based on the value of the property assessed at the place where the salvage services end. The value so assessed is called the "salved value". It is calculated on the actual value at the place where salvage services end. Of course, if the voyage is abandoned, as often happens, when the salvage services end the salved value and the contributory value are the same for both salvage and general average purposes. Salvage charges applicable to a hull policy must be added to any other claims in the same accident or occurrence and the deductible applied. One cannot recover salvage charges under a policy that has paid a total loss.

Lloyd's Salvage Agreement

The principles for pure salvage have already been considered but, as previously stated, in practice today a case of pure salvage never arises. Present day ships are so big and the task undertaken by a salvor of such formidable proportions that, in most cases, salvage services are carried out by professional salvage firms. The equipment and men employed by these concerns are of a high degree of efficiency, skill and competence so that the employer is reluctant to give a service where the reward is not bound by contract. To provide a suitable contract, but still preserving the essentials of an act of pure salvage, Lloyd's have made available to the shipping world a contract form called "Lloyd's Form of Salvage Agreement". One of the main essentials in this form of agreement, which was introduced by Lloyd's in 1890, is that it is on a "no cure—no pay" basis, thus preserving the main essential of pure salvage. The agreement has a blank space for the insertion of an amount agreed to be paid in event of a successful conclusion to the salvage service. The agreement is signed by a salvor, called the "contractor", or on his behalf by the master of the salvage vessel and by the shipowner, or the ship's master acting on behalf of the owner. Cargo is equally subject to pay its proportion of a salvage award but it is not practicable to expect each cargo owner to sign the agreement so it is understood that the shipowner's, or the master's, signature shall bind the cargo owner to the terms of the agreement. Where no amount is agreed the form provides for an arbitrator appointed by the Corporation of Lloyd's to decide the award to be paid. The arbitration award makes provision for appeal by either party and, further, an award can be made for partially successful services. The agreement permits a maritime lien to the salvor but allows this to be discharged by the owner of the salved property with the deposit of a sum of money or an acceptable guarantee for subsequent payment of the salvage award payable.

There is no doubt of the insurer's liability for salvage charges incurred as above provided they were incurred to prevent loss from an insured peril. "Services in the nature of salvage", that is services under a contract are not considered by the insurer as "salvage" and must be considered as sue and labour or general average, respectively, instead. Force is given to this latter point of view by Section 65 (2) of the Marine Insurance Act, 1906, which also places the services of servants or agents of the assured in the same category. From a practical standpoint, however, the Lloyd's Form of Salvage Agreement is treated as pure salvage and insurers accept liability for their proportion of the salvage amount agreed in the form or awarded by arbitration as though it was, in fact, a pure salvage award. The insurer's liability is, of course, limited to the sum insured by the policy and is subject to the loss prevented being from an insured peril and, further, is subject to adjustment in event of underinsurance.

It will be noted that the Act provides that services by the *assured* shall not be deemed to be "salvage" which means that where a sister ship renders such service it becomes a "service in the nature of salvage" and not "salvage". To avoid confusion, however, the Institute Time Clauses contain a provision (Clause 2) that salvage services rendered by a sister ship shall be treated as though the vessel was separately owned. This is because it is in the interests of the insurers to encourage salvage services by any reasonable means available. Sistership salvage can be recovered under a cargo policy without the necessity for a similar clause.

Before leaving the subject of salvage it might be worthwhile to note the following definitions:

Lagan—Such property marked for subsequent recovery. An example would be where a vessel has been sunk in shallow water and has been located but requires lifting gear to raise. A marker buoy is floated above the wreckage.

Jetsum—Derived from the word "jettison", meaning property thrown overboard in time of peril.

Flotsum—A term used to describe property found floating on the surface. Salvors can receive an award not only for services rendered in saving a ship and/or cargo therein but also for raising and recovering lagan or for salving floating cargo or other interests in a maritime adventure, such as, a ship's boat. The salved property must, of course, have some value since any award will be based on the salved value.

In practice, it is customary to deal with most salvage in the same manner as general average and to reapportion the values at destination. A salvor cannot claim an award where the circumstances leading to the salvage act were brought about by the wrongful or negligent act of the salvor.

Subrogation (M.I.A. 1906 Sects. 79-81)

At this point it would be well to reconsider Section 78 (4) of the Marine Insurance Act, 1906, whereby a duty is imposed on "the assured and his agents, in all cases, to take such measures as may be reasonable for the purpose of averting or minimizing a loss". In other words the assured must act as he would to protect his own property if it was uninsured. Both the shipowner and the cargo owner have certain rights in law against the persons causing damage to or loss of their property. For example, a shipowner whose vessel is damaged in a collision by the negligent, or partly negligent, navigation of another ship has a right to claim against the defaulting vessel in respect of the damage suffered to both ship and cargo as well as for loss of use of his ship, if any. Further, a cargo owner has a right to recover from a carrier who is at fault if his cargo is lost or damaged whilst in the care of the carrier.

Once the insurer has paid a claim in respect of the loss any rights of recovery are immediately passed to the insurer. Such transfer is called a "right of subrogation".

Rights of subrogation are not peculiar to marine insurance. Such rights also exist in non-marine insurance but there is one important difference in the application of these rights. The marine insurer does not acquire his subrogation rights until he has *paid* the claim but the non-marine insurer acquires subrogation rights immediately the assured has such rights. Therefore, technically, the insurer of a ship suffering damage in collision with a third party's ship where the third party is at fault, cannot take action to recover from the other ship's owner until he has paid the claim for the repairs to the insured ship. Nor can the cargo insurer responsible for total loss of a package of goods lost in discharge, by negligence of the carrier's servants, take action against the carrier until he has paid the claim to the assured. On the other hand, if an insured car owner has damage to his car caused by contact with a defaulting third party's vehicle the non-marine insurer of the damaged car acquires imme-diate subrogation rights and may take whatever action is necessary to recover from the defaulting third party, before the claim is paid.

This restriction on the marine insurer places him in a difficult position at times, particularly when cargo arrives damaged at destination and the insurer is liable for such damage although primary responsibility for the damage rests on the carrier. The law of carriage, in the shape of The Carriage of Goods by Sea Act, 1924, absolves the carrier from liability for damage to goods in his custody when the damage is caused by certain specified perils, which might be said to be beyond his control. At the same time, the C.G.S.A. (Carriage of Goods by Sea Act, 1924) provides that the carrier must properly stow and care for the goods in his custody. In event of damage, except when caused by the specified excepted perils, he is held responsible for such damage, subject to a limit per package of £100 (increased to £200 per package by the Gold Clause Agreement to which most carriers are signatories).

Nevertheless, whilst placing the responsibility for damage on the carrier the C.G.S.A. appreciates that, in practice, the goods are only in custody and control of the sea carrier for part, even though it be the major part, of the period of carriage and that if the goods are not inspected shortly after they leave the carrier's custody it is possible the damage may have occurred since discharge from the ship. For this reason the C.G.S.A. limits the period after discharge during which valid claims can be made against the carrier.

If any packages are missing or are discharged with apparent damage notice of intention to claim must be given in writing to the carrier or his representative, before or at the time of removal of the goods into the custody of the person entitled to take delivery under the contract of carriage. Such notice shall show the general nature of the loss. Where the goods are the subject of a "joint survey" notice need not be given. A "joint survey" is one where the inspection is carried out jointly by both the carrier's and the con-signee's surveyors.

Where the damage is not immediately apparent the consignee has three days in which to give notice of his claim against the carrier.

Failure to give notice in writing destroys the consignee's right to

N.B. A statute Carriage of Goods by Sea Act 1971 has been enacted whereby the Carrier's liability is brought more in line with modern values and circum-stances. A unit is more clearly defined bearing in mind that containerization creates a problem in this respect. The 1971 Act had not been granted force of law at the time this book was revised in 1975 and doubts have been expressed that it will ever come into effect.

claim against the carrier and, effectively, destroys the subrogation rights of the insurer in this respect. The cargo insurer is particularly concerned to protect his subrogation rights against the carrier and, therefore, usually insists on a clause to this effect appearing in the policy or certificate. The clause is printed in red to attract the attention of the assured and has become known as the "Red Line Clause". It emphasizes the duty of the assured and their agents to protect the goods and the need to preserve their rights against carriers, bailees and other third parties.

The clause goes a little further than the C.G.S.A. in its scope.

It particularly requires the assured:

1. To claim immediately on the carriers and on the Port authorities for missing packages.
2. To apply immediately for a survey by the carriers' representative in the docks, if damage be apparent.
3. Not to give "clean" receipts where goods are in doubtful condition. Where the shipowner refuses to allow delivery against a "dirty" receipt, whereby the assured is obliged to give a "clean" receipt, he must give a written letter of protest at the same time.
4. To give notice to the carriers' representative, in writing, within three days of delivery if the damage is not apparent at the time of taking delivery.

Early in 1967 the clause was amended to incorporate documentation of claims, that is, the clause now details the documents required by insurers from the consignee when the latter submits a claim.

The same legal limitations do not apply in connection with collision liability (the only form of legal liability covered by the hull policy) so a red line clause is not necessary. Nevertheless, the I.T.C. contain the "tender clause" which requires immediate notice to the underwriter in the case of an accident, thus the underwriter can take any measure necessary to protect his rights.

It is important not to confuse subrogation rights with abandonment. The right of subrogation is for the insurer to "stand in the shoes" of the assured in order to recover the whole or part of the claims paid from the party, other than the assured, responsible or partly responsible for the accident causing the loss. It does *not* confer any right whatever on the insurer to acquire proprietary rights to the property and to take over title. Such proprietary rights follow acceptance of abandonment and only exist for the insurer who has paid a *total* loss. Subrogation rights are acquired by the insurer for *all* losses paid whether they be total or partial losses but the insurer who pays a *partial* loss acquires *no* proprietary rights.

The insurer who pays a total loss may acquire, at his option, absolute title to the property, if any, which remains and may dispose of it as he thinks fit, retaining the whole of the proceeds whether or not these exceed the claim paid.

In addition, the insurer who pays a total loss acquires subrogation rights in respect of the loss and may claim from a third party accordingly. However, the amount the insurer can recover *by way of subrogation* is limited to the amount of the claim paid. If the insurer recovers more, by way of subrogation, than the claim paid he must repay the excess amount to the assured.

Whilst the insurer is entitled to recover, by way of subrogation, damages from a third party in respect of a partial loss, such subrogation rights do not extend to cover compensation for which he has not paid a claim.

A good example of the application of this principle occurred in the case of "Attorney General—v—Glen Line (1930)". The *Glenearn* was confiscated by the enemy in time of war and insurers paid a total loss by reason of a war peril. The vessel was used mainly as a hospital ship by the enemy and following cessation of hostilities she was released. Under the rights acquired by abandonment the insurers claimed the vessel and sold her realizing more in proceeds than the claim originally paid. The insurers were permitted to retain the whole proceeds because the ship became their property, if they so wished, from the moment the claim was paid. Later, a successful claim was pursued against the ex-enemy for reparations in respect of loss of use of the ship during the period she was in enemy hands and the case referred to above was brought to establish to what extent, if any, insurers were entitled to such reparations. Admitted they had paid a total loss of ship and were therefore entitled to *freight* in the course of being earned and subsequently earned by the ship, and also were entitled to recover in respect of any damage caused to the ship, but the court held that the insurers were not entitled to any of the reparations award.

For many years there was disagreement regarding the limitation of recovery applicable in the event of a total loss claim. However, in the case "Yorkshire Insurance Co. Ltd.—v—Nisbet Shipping Co. (1961)," there was a dispute regarding the disposal of £55,000; being the difference between the claim paid (£72,000) and the recovery (£127,000). In deciding for the underwriter, Mr. Justice Diplock maintained that the assured could not recover more than his actual loss and, where he is insured, it makes no difference whether he makes the recovery before or after the claim is made on the policy. However, one cannot help thinking that if such a large recovery were to be obtained before the claim is made on the policy the assured would refrain from making such claim, in practice.

The American courts do not, wholeheartedly, agree with English practice in regard to subrogation rights, particularly where a deductible appears in the policy. The Americans consider the assured to be a co-insurer in respect of the deductible and consider that the assured should be entitled to participate in a recovery relating to a partial loss. However, English hull policies require the assured to bear the deductible in full, the claim being considered to be net of such amount. Where interest is paid on the amount recovered, underwriters share this with the assured in the proportion that the time between the accident and payment of the claim bears to the time between the accident and the recovery from the third party.

The insurer who pays a claim for partial loss acquires no title (i.e. proprietary rights). He does, however, acquire subrogation rights. For example: Goods are delivered damaged by an insured peril. It can be shown that the damage would not have occurred but for the fault of the carrier, whereby the owner of the goods has a right to take action against the carrier in respect of the damage. The insurer pays the claim but, because the loss is only partial, he has no right to take over what remains of the property. Nevertheless, he has subrogation rights against the carrier.

To summarize, subrogation rights exist for both total and partial loss but proprietary rights can only follow payment of a claim for total loss. After payment of a total loss claim the insurer is entitled to proprietary rights over what remains of the property and may retain the whole proceeds whereas under subrogation rights the insurer may only retain a sum of no more than the claim paid.

Subrogation is one of the five basic principles of insurance, the other four being "insurable interest", "good faith", "indemnity" and "proximate cause". It is a legal right of the insurer but can only exist where a legally valid insurance contract is in force. Therefore, there are no subrogation rights under a P.P.I. policy. A policy by which the insurer forgoes his right to salvage is also an invalid policy (M.I.A. 1906 Sect. 4—Sub 26) so no subrogation rights exist under such a policy.

It is important to ensure that claims against carriers and others responsible for loss do not become time barred. The Carriage of Goods by Sea Act, 1924 requires suit to be served against a carrier within one year dating from the time of delivery of the goods or, if not delivered, from the time they should have been delivered. In practice, most interested parties have agreed by the terms of the Gold Clause Agreement to extend this time limit to two years. The agreement also increases the limit of liability of the carrier from £100 per package to £200 per package in view of the inadequacy of the limit of £100 in modern practice. Even this is the subject of some concern today because the development of the use of "containers" in cargo handling makes it difficult to agree on what constitutes a "package".

When considering contractual liability of carriers and the law in relation to contracts of affreightment it will probably be noticed that the application of the above principles depends on whether the particular shipment is subject to the terms of the Carriage of Goods by Sea Act, 1924 or a similar type of foreign statute. Not all contracts of affreightment are subject to the Act of 1924 which applies only to shipments under bill of lading, or a similar agreement, from ports in Great Britain or Northern Ireland. The Act does not apply to goods whilst being carried to or from the sea going vessel nor when the goods are being on carried by lighter following discharge from the overseas vessel. Insurers, then, are particularly concerned to protect their rights of recovery against such carriers and, to this end, incorporate two clauses in the Institute Cargo Clauses which emphasize the assured's duty to protect the insurers' interest in the assured's rights against the carriers. The clauses are called the "Bailee Clause" and the "Not to inure Clause". The bailee clause points out the duty of the assured, as provided in the M.I.A. 1906 Sect. 78, to ensure that reasonable measures are taken to avert or minimize loss and that all rights against carriers are properly preserved and exercised. Unfortunately, the clause has little practical effect, in cases where the assured's rights are not protected by the Carriage of Goods by Sea Act, 1924, because the carrier generally inserts a clause in the contract of affreightment relieving himself of all liability for loss of or damage to the goods in his care. Further, the carrier inserts a clause claiming benefit of the cargo owners policy which clause would be void if the contract was subject to the C.G.S.A. 1924. The "not to inure clause" is an attempt by insurers to defeat the effect of the benefit of insurance clause. Despite these two clauses in the policy claims proximately caused by an insured peril are paid by the insurer who relies on the subrogation of any rights the assured may have left to effect a recovery.

At one time the bailee clause relieved the insurer from liability in event of there being a "benefit of insurance clause" in the contract of affreightment and agreed to advance the amount of the claim as an interest free loan to the assured. The bailee clause used today does not contain this provision and the "not to inure" clause has been introduced in an attempt to prevent carriers taking advantage of the cargo owners' insurance on the goods.

Letter of Subrogation

The insurer who pays a claim will generally require the assured to furnish a "letter of subrogation". From a legal standpoint the letter of subrogation is not necessary in order to establish rights of subrogation. The insurer automatically acquires such rights once he has paid the claim. Nevertheless, it is often easier to pursue a satisfactory claim for recovery from a third party if this is done in the name of the assured, which the underwriter is entitled so to do. The letter of subrogation authorizes the insurer to use the assured's name in any proceedings to recover the loss and, at the same time, makes it clear that the insurer has no further liability to the assured. The wording of the letter shows that the assured understands that he has passed all his rights of recovery, in respect of the loss, to the insurer and, thus, the introduction of the document into the recovery proceedings indicates that the assured will not be making a separate claim. Further, the production of the letter of subrogation ensures that the recovery is paid to the right party and should a claim for the recovery be submitted by the assured directly to the third party it can be rejected on the evidence of the letter of subrogation.

Double Insurance

Generally, one tends to think of subrogation rights as a means of recovery of the whole or part of a claim paid from someone like a carrier or another shipowner but the Marine Insurance Act, 1906 also envisages the possibility of an insurer having paid a claim when there is another policy in force covering the same loss but under which no claim has been paid, that is, in cases of "double insurance". The Act provides, in Section 80, that the insurer who has paid more than his proper proportion of the loss is entitled to claim a contribution from the other insurers.

When an unvalued policy is effected for an amount less than the insurable value or a valued policy is effected for a sum insured of less than the insured value there exists underinsurance and the assured is deemed to be his own insurer for the difference between the sum insured and the insurable value or the sum insured and the insured value, as the case may be.

Example:

Unvalued policy Sum Insured £800   Insurable value £1,000
Valued policy Sum Insured £800   Insured value £1,000

In each case there is underinsurance and the assured is deemed to be his own insurer for 20% of all losses (M.I.A. 1906 Sect. 81).

Under English law so far as the right of recovery for loss is concerned the insurer, who has paid the loss, is subrogated in full "insofar as the assured has been indemnified" (M.I.A. 1906 Sect. 79—Sub 2). This means that the first right of recovery is vested with the insurer who may recover all amounts due until the amount of the claim has been reached. So that if the property is undervalued the assured receives no part of the monies received by way of subrogation until the claim has been satisfied, when he receives the balance. But, when he is underinsured he is deemed to be his own insurer for the difference as above (M.I.A. 1906 Sect. 81) so in accordance with Section 80 of the M.I.A. 1906 he is entitled to share proportionately with the insurer in respect of any recovery. There is no guarantee that other countries will follow English law and, in a relatively recent case in U.S.A. on subrogation the court held that the assured, not the insurer, was entitled to the first right of recovery. This principle of co-insurance does not apply to a deductible in the policy thus under a hull policy all amounts recovered go directly to the insurer even though the assured paid part of the cost of repairs. A clause in the ITC gives effect to this principle.

CHAPTER XIII

THIRD PARTY LIABILITY AND NEGLIGENCE

Third Party Liability

FOR insurance purposes, at least, the word "liability" means *legal* liability of the assured. We may all, at times, feel we have a moral responsibility to make amends for some loss to another, for which we feel guilty, but the insurer is not concerned to salve the assured's conscience. The purpose of the liability cover afforded by a marine insurance policy is to reimburse the assured for a sum of money which he has *paid* to another because of his *legal* responsibility for a loss suffered by that other person.

There are two broad categories of liability, contractual liability and third party liability. A contractual liability is one incurred within the terms of a contract. An example of contractual liability is the liability of the carrier for goods damaged whilst in his care, which he has contracted to carry safely. Another form of contractual liability is that of a shipowner to the crew which he employs to work his ship. A contract can be "implied" as is the contract of agency between the marine insurance broker and his Principal, the assured. Liability under an implied contract is no less powerful than it is under an expressed contract, in fact it could be more binding because without a written agreement neither party can insert a provision whereby he relieves himself of any part of his liability.

Except by special arrangement, marine insurers tend, generally, not to insure contractual liability and shipowners, who can incur large amounts in respect of contractual liability usually enter their vessels in a P & I Club which covers such liabilities. P & I Clubs are mutual societies supported by contributions from members.

Third party liability is a liability incurred as a result of some form of negligence whereby loss or damage is suffered by someone, who is not a party to a contract with the person who caused the loss or damage. The term derives from the fact that there are two parties to a contract and any person outside the contract is a third party. So, a third party liability is one incurred in the absence of a contract. To establish the extent of the liability it is usually necessary to obtain a court ruling. If the loss arises out of negligence; this is then brought as an action in "tort". The person successfully sued in the action is called the "tort feasor" (i.e. "wrong doer") and if more than one person or party is guilty of the negligence they can be sued jointly as "joint tort feasors". An example of third party liability is the liability of a shipowner arising out of collision of his ship with another ship. The other ship may suffer damage, the cargo in the other ship may suffer damage and, if it is badly damaged, the other ship may be laid up for repairs resulting in loss of use. The expression commonly used in marine insurance to define loss of use consequent upon collision is "demurrage" although, in fact, the term "demurrage" really means payment by a charterer for delaying a vessel at a port for a period longer than the number of "lay days" permitted by the charterparty. Nevertheless, the expression is so commonly used in marine insurance to define "loss of hire or use" that we shall continue to use it in that sense.

Under a contract some form of maximum liability may be agreed although this is not always possible. Where there is third party liability no prior agreement can be reached to establish the extent of recompense properly due except that in the case of loss of or damage to property the value of the property lost or damaged is, naturally, the maximum liability. But for loss of life or injury it is practically impossible to establish the value of the life lost or the injury sustained. Hence, recompense awarded by the courts for loss of life or personal injury tends to be somewhat erratic and the only financial yardstick one can apply appears to be the loss of earning power plus an allowance for pain and suffering. Nevertheless, one thing is clear so far as insurance is concerned the maximum liability of an insurer is the sum fixed by the policy.

Although it is only fair that a person suffering loss due to the fault of another should receive generous consideration as a compensation for the loss suffered, the negligent party is not always in a suitable financial position to pay a just compensation. Regrettably, one's degree of negligence is not tempered by one's ability to pay generously for the consequences of one's actions. This inequity is relieved in accidents caused by drivers of motor vehicles by the legal requirement of third party insurance, thus ensuring that any negligent driver has adequate funds available to meet his liability for loss of life, injury or damage on the roads. There is no similar law governing the liability of shipowners but lack of insurance cover does not remove the liability, so common prudence encourages the shipowner to effect insurance to protect himself from financial loss resulting from the negligence of his employees. As a general practice marine insurers are not prepared to cover all forms of third party liability but the hull marine policy is customarily extended to cover legal liability consequent upon collision.

Limitation of Liability

Concentrating on collision liability, the difficulties of relating the liability with ability to pay become even more apparent because there is not necessarily any common relationship between the values of two ships involved in a collision so that, in theory, a relatively low valued ship could be in collision with a high valued ship whereby the owners of the former incurred a liability for an amount far greater than the value of the defaulting vessel. Various rules and statutes have granted the shipowner a right to limit liability culminating in the provisions of the Merchant Shipping Act, 1894, and subsequent amendments. The right to limit liability consequent upon a collision is not automatic. Application for limitation must be made to the Courts where no limitation is granted if there is actual fault or privity on the part of the shipowner. It follows that limitation is only granted where the collision was caused by a servant or agent of the shipowner. In most cases the collision is caused by faulty navigation by an employee of the shipowner so the right to limit liability remains unimpaired. The right to limit is extended to managers, charterers or other operators of the ship and where the master or a member of the crew is guilty of negligence he shall equally have the right to limit liability notwithstanding his actual fault or privity in that capacity. The reason for this latter provision, which applies under English law but not necessarily under foreign law, is to overcome the possibility of a claimant taking action against the person actually responsible instead of the shipowner on the assumption that by so doing the claimant would not be faced with a limitation of liability.

The question arises as to what method is to be adopted to establish the maximum limitation fund payable by the defaulting party. Naturally, in the absence of insurance, this must necessarily relate to the ability to pay, otherwise the purpose of the right to limit liability becomes non-effective. So the basis must be no more than the value of the property involved and the income derivable from the adventure. Under some foreign laws the limit of liability is based on the value of the ship and the freight in course of being earned, but English law ignores the freight and concentrates on the value on the ship. There must be a common yardstick for valuation purposes since hull values fluctuate rapidly, so the calculation is made on the tonnage of the vessel which remains constant. Although the word "tonnage", being derived from "ton", implies weight it would not be practical to actually weigh a vessel to discover its tonnage. An alternative is to calculate the volume of that part of the vessel which is below the waterline and to use the weight of the quantity of water, which would fill that space, as the ship's weight on the principle that the weight of a floating object is equal to the weight of the water it displaces. The use of this method has proved unrealistic in practice and a system for tonnage calculation is laid down which involves the use of volumetric tons of 100 cub. ft. per ton. The "gross tonnage" as shown in a shipping register is the capacity of the space within the hull, and of the enclosed spaces above deck, available for cargo, stores, passengers or crew.

The tonnage to be used in the calculation for limitation purposes is the registered tonnage with the addition, in the case of a ship propelled mechanically, of any engine room space deducted from the gross tonnage when arriving at the registered tonnage. (Ref. Merchant Shipping Act (1894) which is amended from time to time in relation to Liability of Shipowners and others. Such an amending Act was published in 1958.

Most vessels today are propelled mechanically and as a rough guide one might estimate the tonnage for limitation purposes to be approximately midway between the gross and net registered tonnage.

The minimum tonnage entertained for the purposes of limitation, with regard to loss of life and personal injury, is 300 tons. This does not prevent a vessel of less than that tonnage from applying for limitation of liability but if she does the limit will be based on 300 tons.

Although laws in various countries differ on the application of the principle the right to limit liability is common so it is necessary to have a monetary unit, which is not subject to fluctuation in value, on which to base the system of calculation. The gold franc has been chosen for this purpose. The gold franc is defined as "a unit consisting of sixty five and one half milligrams of gold of millesimal fineness nine hundred".

The limit per ton for loss of life and personal injury alone is 3,100 gold francs.
The limit per ton for loss of life, personal injury and property damage *combined* is 3,100 gold francs.
The limit per ton for property damage alone is 1,000 gold francs.

These provisions are set out in the Merchant Shipping (Liability of Shipowners and Others) Act, 1958. The Act also gave powers to the Minister of Transport to establish the value of the gold franc in sterling from time to time. Continuing inflation causes frequent changes in rates of exchange. In 1974 (Statutory instrument No. 1974/536) the rates of exchange established the following equivalent:

$$3,100 \text{ gold francs} = £108.1677$$
$$100 \text{ gold francs} = £34.8928$$

For practical purposes one uses £108 and £35 in examples.

Example A.

A ship in collision has a registered tonnage of 1,000 tons. She incurs liability for damage to property amounting to £50,000. The shipowner applies for, and is granted, limitation of liability. The limit of his liability at £35.00 per ton is £35,000.

Example B.

A ship is in collision and incurs liability for £200,000 in respect of loss of life and personal injury only. The ship has a registered tonnage of 1,000 tons so the limit of liability, if limitation is granted by the court, at £108.00 per ton, is £108,000.

Example C.

A ship is in collision and incurs liabilities for the following:

Loss of life and Personal Injury	£110,000
Property damage	60,000

The registered tonnage of the ship is 1,000 tons and the shipowner is granted limitation of liability so the total limitation fund available, at £108 per ton is £108,000. The first £73,000 goes to satisfy loss of life and personal injury claims leaving £35,000. The loss of life and personal injury claims remaining unsatisfied rank with the property damage claims and the balance of the fund is apportioned "pari passu" (pro rata) between the loss of life/personal injury claims and the property damage claims.

Loss of life and personal injury claims	£110,000
Satisfied by limitation fund	73,000
Unsatisfied	£37,000

Limitation fund at £86.00* per ton	£108,000
Satisfied loss of life/personal injury claims	73,000
Outstanding balance	£35,000

Apportionment:

Unsatisfied loss of life/Personal injury claims	£37,000	receive	£13,351
Property damage claims	60,000	,,	21,649
	£97,000	,,	£35,000

Summary:

Loss of life and personal injury claims receive		£73,000
	Plus	13,351
		£86,351

being 78.50% of the total claimed, so each claimant receives 78.50% of his claim.

The property damage claims receive £21,649 being 36.08% of the total claimed. So each successful claimant for property damage receives 36.08% of the damage to his property caused by the ship at fault.

When any person enters into a "limitation suit" the costs of the suit are payable by the person who institutes the proceedings. The shipowner, therefore, pays into the court the total limitation fund plus costs of the suit and, in addition, an amount in respect of interest. The court pays out the amounts due to the parties entitled to claim as illustrated in the examples above.

The limitation laws above apply, of course, to collision liability assessed under English law. Individual Foreign Countries may vary their rules but the limitation amounts are generally accepted. An example of a variation occurs under the Louisiana Direct Action Statute which permits a damage claimant to sue a liability underwriter direct without even the necessity of joining the assured as a co-defendant.

Whether or not hull underwriters could benefit from the statutory limitation of the shipowner's (the assured's) liability where an accident occurred in Louisiana waters was left unsettled by the U.S. Supreme Court after the "Cushing" case in 1954 (Ref. 347 U.S. 409 1954 A.M.C. 837).

However, in 1965 the U.S. District Court in New Orleans gave a judgement which appears to hold that insurers of vessels cannot benefit from the shipowner's statutory rights to limit liability and can be *directly* liable to third parties to the full extent of the insurance coverage.

These cases are mentioned only to illustrate the variations which may occur and conflicts which may arise where the law may be interpreted by different courts even in the same Country.

Collision Liability

The Marine Insurance Act, 1906 (Section 5) states that where a person may incur a liability in respect of a marine adventure he has an insurable interest. He may, therefore, insure his potential liability and Section 74 of the Act provides that where third party liability is insured the measure of indemnity is the amount paid or payable to the third party but subject to any limit expressed in the policy.

The plain marine policy form was designed to cover physical damage to the insured property. It makes no mention of cover for liabilities and in the case of "De Vaux—v—Salvador (1836)" it was held that the plain policy form does not extend to cover third party liability. Later, when the Marine Insurance Act, 1906, was drafted no action was taken to over-ride the decision of the 1836 case but Sections 5 and 74 were worded to provide a basis for third party liability insurance cover if it was effected. The Institute Time Clauses, in common with similar hull clauses, have been designed to *extend* the marine policy to cover legal liability consequent upon *collision only*. Certain types of hull clauses, such as Port Risks clauses and Builder's Risks clauses, have been extended to cover other forms of legal liability but the ordinary hull clauses restrict cover to apply to collision cases only.

It becomes necessary, therefore, to establish exactly what the term "collision with a ship or vessel" embraces for insurance purposes. Obviously, when one ship strikes another this is collision but when a ship's "wash" causes damage to another ship this is *not* collision nor is damage to fishing nets of a trawler, but striking the anchor or mooring chain of another ship *does* constitute collision. A "ship" in this context is any "vessel used in navigation". The ship need not be navigating at the time of the contact but she must be a vessel within the definition above. So not only are ocean liners embraced but also lighters, tugs, and even dumb barges, that is barges without means of self propulsion. Buoys, wharves, piers, floating landing stages and similar are outside the scope of the term "collision" within the meaning of the Institute Hull Clauses so that if a ship strikes one of these it is not to be construed as collision and the Institute Hull Clauses emphasize this by a specific exclusion. A floating crane, not permanently moored, is a ship for collision purposes, so presumably the same principle would be applied to a floating oil drilling rig in law. It has been established that a flying boat is not a ship. An unsalvable wreck is not a ship but the point is academic since, presumably, the ship striking the wreck would be solely at fault and it does not appear logical that further damage caused to a wreck would incur any liability.

Although vessels may be in collision where both are blameless (force majeure) if there is to be legal liability there must be negligence on the part of one or both parties. Thus where two ships A and B are in collision any one of three circumstances may apply. A may be solely to blame, B may be solely to blame or both A and

B may be partly to blame. Where only one of the ships is to blame there is no question as to which vessel incurs the legal liability. Where two or more ships are to blame the degree of fault must be assessed in order to establish the proportion of liability which attaches to each defaulting vessel. Before the Maritime Conventions Act, 1911 came into force whatever the degree of fault both negligent ships were deemed equally to blame, but since 1911 English law provides for the degree of liability to be the same as the degree of fault. Thus, today, if two vessels A and B are equally at fault each is liable for 50% of the other's damage but where vessel A is 60% to blame A is liable for 60% of B's damage whilst B is liable for 40% of A's damage. U.S.A. and many other countries still maintain the principle of equal fault if both are to blame but attempts are being made to introduce the proportionate principle into the U.S.A.

A manned ship which is being towed by a tug is deemed to be controlling the tug's movements so liability in event of collision lies with the shipowner. On the other hand, when the tug is towing an unmanned ship or dumb barges the tug is in control so liability in event of collision lies with the tugowner.

The Running Down Clause (I.T.C. No. 1)

In practice, all hull policies are extended to cover legal liability consequent upon collision by the use of the "running down clause". In the Institute Time Clauses this is clause number one which commences with the words "And it is further agreed". This preliminary wording is important because it has been established that by the wording the clause becomes a supplementary contract. Whether or not this was the insurers' intention when drafting the clause no steps have been taken to amend the wording so it follows that insurers are quite prepared to accept that the collision liability is a separate contract. This means that the sum insured is in effect repeated for collision liability so that if the insured ship became a total loss in the collision the insurer would pay the collision liability claim *in addition* to the full sum insured for the total loss. Prior to 1969 the ITC contained no provision that the franchise should apply to the R.D.C., thus claims under the R.D.C. were paid irrespective of percentage; nor were such claims subject to the F.C. & S. Clause. Following a tightening of hull underwriters' attitude the ITC were amended in 1969; one of the amendments being to embrace claims under the R.D.C. within the policy deductible. Thus, R.D.C. claims must be added to other partial loss claims arising out of the same accident or occurrence and the deductible expressed in clause 12 be applied. Further, the

ITC were amended to make the F.C. & S. Clause a paramount clause, thereby making its provisions applicable to R.D.C. claims.

To establish a claim under the collision clause the assured must *have paid* an amount in respect of legal liability consequent upon collision. If he has not paid he cannot claim. If this were strictly applied in practice few claims would ever be paid by the insurer for collision liability where the degree of fault is shared by both ships for the basis of calculation of liability adopted by the law is one of "single liability". Under the principle of single liability only the ship with the greater liability pays and then only the difference between the two liabilities is paid. Simply, it is like saying A owes B £1 and B owes A £3, so if B gives A £2 the matter is settled but only B has actually paid anything.

Example:

A and B are in collision
A suffers £20,000 damage
B   ,,   £10,000 damage
Each vessel held equally to blame
B is liable for 50% of £20,000 = £10,000
A is liable for 50% of £10,000 = £5,000

B pays A on balance   £5,000

It will be noted that the only money to have changed hands is a payment from B to A of £5,000 although in theory A is deemed to have recovered from B 50% of £20,000 whilst B is deemed to have recovered from A 50% of £10,000.

The principle of single liability settlement outlined above can lead to inequity and to illustrate this let us suppose that ship A was not insured for collision damage in which case her owners would have to bear the whole loss of £20,000 recovering only £5,000 from B although, in theory, 50% of A's damage has been recovered from B. Further, suppose B's claim of £10,000 is only £1,000 physical damage, fully insured, and £9,000 loss of hire, uninsured. Then B may recover from his insurers the £1,000 physical damage and £5,000 collision liability (assuming this is fully insured) but he is left to bear £9,000 himself despite the theoretical recovery of 50% of £10,000 from A.

To avoid these inequities, which arise only through the application of the principle of single liability, the running down clause provides that claims thereunder shall be settled on the principle of cross liabilities except where there is limitation of liability. That is, A would have been deemed to have paid B 50% of £10,000 and B would have been deemed to have paid A 50% of £20,000. On the assumption that, in the above example, A's claim is for £15,000 physical damage and £5,000 loss of hire whilst B's claim is for £1,000 physical damage and £9,000 loss of hire, also that both vessels are fully insured for collision damage and liability, the settlement would be as follows:

Ship A	Ship Insurer	Ship Owner
Pays for collision repairs	£15,000	
„ damage done to B		
50% of £10,000	5,000	
	£20,000	
Recoveries		
Recovery from B		
50% of physical damage £15,000	7,500	
„ „ loss of hire £5,000		£2,500
Underwriters pay to A	£12,500	
A's owners retain		£2,500
Ship B	Ship Insurer	Ship Owner
Pays for collision repairs	£1,000	
„ damage done to A		
50% of £20,000	10,000	
	£11,000	
Recoveries		
Recovery From A		
50% of physical damage £1,000	500	
„ „ loss of hire £9,000		£4,500
Underwriters pay to B	£10,500	
B's owners retain		£4,500

There are no restrictions in the Marine Insurance Act, 1906 regarding the type of legal liability envisaged by the insurance contract but insurers wish to restrict their responsibility to make good only liability which is incurred directly consequent upon collision between two ships. Therefore, in 1971, underwriters introduced an "amended" R.D.C. for attachment to all hull policies subject to the ITC. This clause clearly sets out the extent to which hull underwriters are prepared to cover amounts paid as legal liability by the assured, consequent upon collision. The cover is limited to

(i) loss of or damage to any other vessel or property on any other vessel
(ii) delay to or loss of use of any other such vessel or property thereon

(iii) general average of, salvage of, or salvage under contract
of, any such other vessel or property thereon

It is very important to appreciate that the cover is so limited
because there are other liabilities in respect of which the shipowner
may incur expense but which are not covered by the clause.
Particularly, underwriters are conscious of the very real risk of
very large amounts being required from the assured in connection
with containerization or pollution; such incidents following a
collision in which the insured ship is concerned. In the amended
R.D.C. the underwriters make it abundantly clear that the policy
shall not extend to cover amounts that the assured is called
upon to pay for removal of wreck, removal of oil from beaches
or elsewhere and removal of obstructions of any kind. The clause
further makes it clear that liability for loss of life, personal injury
or illness is not the concern of underwriters. Liability for damage
to the insured ship's cargo and loss of use of the insured ship is
also excluded. (Further details of this clause can be found in
Vol. 3—Hull Practice.)

The Marine Insurance Act, 1906 states that the measure of
indemnity for liability is the amount paid or payable by the assured
but it qualifies this by the words "subject to any express provision
in the policy". The hull insurer, realizing that collision liability
arises from negligence, feels that some of the loss should be borne
by the assured. The idea is to encourage diligence on the part of the
assured so the insurer, by the terms of the Institute Time Clauses,
covers only three fourths of the liability and expenses leaving one
fourth at the risk of the assured. In practice, however, the clause
does not have this effect because the assured, generally, covers the
other fourth in a P & I Club. In any case the restriction does not
appear in many foreign policies, except where these are subject
to the Institute Time Clauses, because the American Hull Form, the
Dutch Hull Form and similar policies contain a collision clause
which covers a four fourths liability thus following the practice of
granting full cover where a P & I club is not available. English
policies extended to cover P & I risks also have a four fourths
collision clause, such policies are those used for port risks and
construction risks.

The sistership clause was mentioned earlier when dealing with
the subject of salvage. This same clause, Institute Time Clause
No. 2, is applicable to collision liability. It will be recalled that
the collision clause covers only *legal* liability. Where sister ships
are in collision there can be no legal liability for a man cannot sue
himself. By the sistership clause the insurer agrees to treat the

circumstance as though the ships were separately owned. The same principle applies for ships under the same management.

Both to Blame Collision Clause

This clause appears in cargo contracts of affreightment for goods on a voyage to or from the U.S.A. Under American law, when two ships are to blame in a collision the degree of fault is ignored and both are deemed equally to blame (see note on page 148).

The cargo owner whose goods are damaged in the collision may follow any one of the following three courses in sueing for damages. He may take action for

(1) 100% against the vessel carrying his cargo (called the carrying vessel).
(2) 100% against the other vessel involved in the collision (called the non-carrying vessel).
(3) 50% against each vessel.

The carrying vessel's owner effectively defeats (1) and (3) above by claiming exemption under the Harter Act, which allows him certain protections, leaving only course (2) open to the cargo owner. Because there is no contract between the non-carrying vessel's owner and the owner of the damaged goods the non-carrying vessel cannot contract out of liability. American law, however, allows the non-carrying vessel's owner to include 50% of his liability to the carrying vessel's cargo in his claim against the carrying vessel.

Example:
Vessels A & B in collision, both to blame, so each assumes a 50% liability for all losses.

Damage to ship B $2,000.   Damage to A's cargo $1,000.
A's cargo sues B for $1,000
B sues A for 50% of $2,000   = $1,000
Plus   „   „ $1,000   500
                                 ‾‾‾‾‾‾
                                 $1,500

The carrying vessel (A in the example) cannot avoid his liability to B, for in the absence of contract, he cannot contract out of liability so he takes the only course of action open to him by inserting the "both to blame" collision clause in his contract of affreightment. By this clause A requires his cargo to reimburse him with the amount he has paid to B in respect of the damage to the goods on board "A".

This puts the cargo owner in an inequitable situation. He has lost $1,000 through no fault of his own and can recover only $500 from the parties at fault which is payable to his insurer. Admitted he can recover $1,000 from his insurer for the damage caused by collision (a peril of the sea) but his policy covers neither contractual nor third party liability so he cannot, on the face of it, recover from his insurer the $500, paid to his carrier. Insurers, however, in practice insert a clause in the policy (Clause 11 Institute Cargo Clauses) whereby they agree to reimburse the assured for the $500.

Finally, on the subject of collision, collision is a "peril of the sea" and damage, proximately caused thereby to the *insured* property is covered by the plain form of policy.

Note: In 1952 the Supreme Court declared the "Both to Blame Collision" clause in bills of lading invalid, but the clause has continued to appear in the I.C.C. In 1975 it was held that the 50/50 basis be replaced with a degree of fault basis (U.S. Government—v—Reliable Transfer Co. Inc.—"Mary A. Whalen").

Negligence

So far, we have considered negligence
(*a*) giving rise to collision liability
(*b*) giving rise to other third party liabilities, which is a matter for Protection and Indemnity Clubs.

It is now proposed to consider negligence giving rise to damage to the insured ship and to goods under a cargo policy.

There are few circumstances where losses occur of their own volition or where the cause of loss is beyond control of man. The vast majority of losses occur as a result of negligence. The negligence is not always that of the person who suffers the loss and where one's negligence causes loss to another that other person has a legal right to sue the negligent party for damages. In recognition of human failings, where the negligence is only a contributory factor it is ignored and only the proximate cause of loss is considered. (e.g. collision or fire).

Nevertheless, it is quite clear that a great many accidents or losses, for which insurers pay, indirectly result from negligence. The insurer who pays the loss is subrogated to the rights of the assured and may make a recovery, in respect of such loss from any negligent party other than the assured. In some cases a policy covers such liability and the insurer very often finds himself recovering from or paying to other insurers. In car insurance the situation could result in regular payments back and forth between insurers to the economic detriment of the industry. To counteract this a "knock for knock" system has evolved whereby motor insurers do not press their claims against other motor insurers. The system does not operate for marine insurance.

Section 55 of the Marine Insurance Act, 1906 excludes from the policy loss attributable to wilful misconduct of the assured so that if a shipowner, charterer or manager, being the assured, is guilty of misconduct the insurer is not liable for any loss attributable to such misconduct. Technically, the master and crew being servants of the shipowner are acting as the shipowner and he is responsible for their actions. Hence, if the master, is guilty of misconduct this is the misconduct of his employer, the assured. If the assured has nothing to do with the misconduct it is unfair that he should be penalized by the action of the master. The Act, however, protects the innocent shipowner in this respect when it goes on to say that the insurer *is* liable for any loss proximately caused by an insured peril even though it would not have arisen but for the misconduct or negligence of the master or crew.

It will be noted that, in the Act, the peril "negligence" is allied with "misconduct". It can be considered that negligence is a form of misconduct for, although we tend to think of misconduct as a wilful deliberate act and negligence as simply carelessness, there are varying degrees of negligence some of which undoubtedly amount to misconduct. For instance, a person may be negligent because he neglects to do something which it may reasonably be expected he ought to have done or he may do something which he ought not to have done. In the latter case, if this were a deliberate act it would clearly be misconduct, that is a deliberate act with full knowledge of the consequences of that act. On the other hand, one might reasonably expect a person to be competent in a certain sphere of activity and if that person commits an act, prejudicing the adventure thereby, which impairs that competence this could be an act of negligence.

Reading Section 55 of the Act for the first time one might readily jump to the conclusion that "negligence" is a peril covered by the policy but closer study will reveal that the Act does not say this. All it says is that if the loss is proximately caused by an insured peril negligence as a contributory cause is to be ignored. As an example of this, a vessel may strand due to negligent navigation, but the loss would be treated as "stranding damage" not as "negligence damage". This supports the findings in the case of "Hamilton, Fraser and Co—v—Thames and Mersey Marine Insurance Co. (1887)". This was the famous "Inchmaree" case in which a member of the crew of the vessel "Inchmaree" started up a donkey engine operating a pump without satisfying himself that an inlet pump valve was open. The pump was used for filling the main boilers and the valve was closed either by silting up or because one of the engineers left it closed. Damage was caused to an air chamber and insurers refused to pay on the grounds that it was proximately caused by negligence. The assured sued insurers for a loss by "peril of the sea" but the court held that the proximate cause of the loss was the negligence of the member of the crew who started the donkey engine and that negligence is *not* a peril of the sea. Since negligence is not a peril of the sea it must be specifically stated as a peril in the policy for loss *proximately caused* by negligence to be covered. It must be emphasized that negligence as a contributory cause of loss is ignored. There are many losses proximately caused by insured perils, "fire" for example, which would not have arisen but for someone's negligence, yet in all these instances negligence is only a contributory cause and is, therefore ignored.

The cargo policy is not extended, in practice, to cover losses proximately caused by negligence so breakage caused by negligent handling would not be covered unless the policy specifically stated that it covered breakage or implied it by the term "all risks". On the other hand the Institute Cargo Clauses do provide that the insurer shall pay the insured value of any package or packages totally lost in loading, transhipment or discharge also damage to the goods caused during discharge at a port of distress, both of which types of losses would probably be caused by negligent handling.

Inchmaree Clause

Following the decision of the "Inchmaree" case careful consideration was given by insurers to decide to what extent hull policies should be extended to cover losses proximately caused by negligence. It was decided to introduce the "negligence clause" (often called the "Inchmaree Clause" or "latent defects clause" or "additional peril clause" in practice) into the "Institute Time Clauses, hulls". The clause has been the subject of many amendments since it was first introduced in 1888 but we shall concentrate on the cover provided today. The clause is No. 7 in the ITC. Basically the negligence clause covers damage to the insured ship directly caused by negligence of the master, officers, crew, pilots or repairers (it does not cover damage caused by negligence of the owner or manager himself unless he also happens to be the master, an officer or a member of the crew at the time) and provided the loss was not the result of lack of due diligence on the part of the owners or managers. The clause, as it appears today, is divided into two sections, thereby isolating those perils which might result in damage to the ship's machinery attributable to negligence of the master, officers or crew. This isolation is so that a special deductible can be applied to such losses. The section that is subject to the special deductible (10%) is 7(a) which lists the perils as

Accidents in loading, discharging or shifting cargo or fuel
Explosions on shipboard or elsewhere
Breakdown of or accident to nuclear installations or reactors on shipboard or elsewhere
Bursting of boilers, breakage of shafts or any latent defect in the machinery or hull
Negligence of Master, Officers, Crew or Pilots
Negligence of repairers provided such repairers are not the Assured

Should any damage to the ship be recoverable from underwriters under this section of the ITC the claim must be added to any other partial loss claim arising out of the same accident or occurrence and the policy deductible expressed in clause 12 be applied. In addition a deductible of 10% of the net claim, after applying the policy deductible, shall be applied to any such damage to machinery which is attributable to the negligence of the master, officers or crew. (Ref. ITC No. 11). Section (b) of the clause is not subject to the special deductible but claims thereunder remain subject to the policy deductible expressed in clause 12. The perils in section (b) are

Contact with aircraft
Contact with any land conveyance, dock or harbour equipment or installation
Earthquake, volcanic eruption or lightning

It must be emphasized that claims under both sections of the clause are confined to damage caused directly to the ship so the clause does not extend to cover *liability* incurred by negligence, explosion, etc. to the cargo nor to property other than the ship insured. The words "directly caused by" obtained special significance in the case of "Oceanic Steamship Co.—v—Faber (1906)" when it was held that the clause did not cover a faulty shaft discovered in drydock and that only damage to the ship (usually the shaft tunnel) by the shaft breaking is covered. In this case no such damage had occurred so there was no claim. The same principle may be said to apply to the discovery of any latent defects. An example occurred when a stern frame cracked whilst cooling at the founders. The builders did not discover the crack and in ignorance of the fault, built the frame into the ship. The ship was insured by an ordinary hull policy by the owners. Some time later during paint stripping, for repainting, part of the steel wash covering the crack came off revealing the crack. The assured claimed against insurers but the insurers refused to pay for the mere discovery of the latent defect. The court upheld the insurer's position, and stated that a latent defect is a fault which is not apparent under ordinary survey or inspection but which comes to light subsequently and where no accident has occurred no claim is payable under the policy. It must be remembered that the insurer is liable for losses occurring *during the currency of the policy*. A latent defect may be a fault in construction, so the loss occurs before the ordinary marine policy attaches. If it is only discovered during the term of the marine policy the mere discovery is not grounds for a claim. ("Hutchings Bros.—v—Royal Exchange Assurance Corporation (1911)".)

A special clause, called the Liner Negligence Clause is sometimes used for fleet insurances. This gives a little wider cover than the ordinary "Inchmaree" clause, the intention being that when an accident occurs from the manifestation of a latent defect not only is the damage to the ship directly caused thereby covered but also the repair of the part latently defective. There are varied forms of this clause but most of them emphasize that the policy does not pay for replacing the part of the ship containing the defect except as part of a claim for damage to the ship. In other words, under neither clause can a claim be made for mere discovery of a defect. The market is attempting to discourage the use of the Liner Negligence Clause so that it will probably become obsolete in the near future.

A boiler which bursts without the operation of an outside agency is not recoverable under the "Inchmaree" Clause. Only the damage to the ship directly *caused* by the bursting boiler is covered by the "Inchmaree" clause not replacement of the boiler itself.

Damage to the ship directly caused by explosion is also covered by the "Inchmaree" clause. It does not matter whether the explosion is on the insured ship or occurs elsewhere, say in another ship or warehouse in a harbour, the effect on the policy is the same.

The remainder of the Inchmaree clause requires no explanation for the wording is clear in itself although we might do well to revert to the subject of negligence. Primarily the clause was designed, following the case of "Hamilton Fraser—v—Thames and Mersey Ins. Co. (1887)", to cover damage to the insured ship proximately caused by negligence. Nevertheless, the loss must not be the result of want of due diligence on the part of the assured, owners or managers. Remember, Section 78 of the Marine Insurance Act, 1906, imposes a duty on the assured, in all cases, to take such measures as may be necessary to avert or minimize the loss. Further details of the Inchmaree Clause can be found in Vol. 3.—Hull Practice.

CHAPTER XIV

GENERAL AVERAGE, PRINCIPLES AND THE
YORK-ANTWERP RULES 1974

FOR no apparent reason students of Marine Insurance and indeed of Shipping Law tend to be apprehensive in studying the subject of General Average, but the subject is relatively simple, and although its application may be complicated the principles are logical.

Certainly Roman Law recognized the principle and so did an earlier code. As a custom of maritime trading it almost certainly antedates the Roman Empire. In Mediaeval times a reference is made to the subject in the Rules of Oleron which attempt to codify the shipping customs of those days and thus it will be seen that the subject has great antiquity. Its origins are in Shipping not Marine Insurance (although insurers may be interested) and it exists whether or not the parties to a maritime adventure are insured.

There may be three basic interests involved in a maritime adventure, viz:

1. The ship and its appurtenances.
2. The cargo, whether in bulk or comprising many small consignments.
3. The freight.

The purpose of general average is to reimburse the owner or owners of any of these interests who have either sacrificed property or expended money for the benefit of the whole adventure at a time when that adventure was in a state of common peril thereby saving it from complete destruction. Perhaps no better definition can be quoted than that given in the English Courts in 1801—

"All loss which arises in consequence of extraordinary sacrifices made or expenses incurred for the preservation of the ship and cargo comes within General Average and must be borne proportionally by all those interested."

So, if part of a cargo were sacrificed at a time when both ship and cargo were in peril, and thereby the ship and the balance of the cargo were saved although the loss would fall primarily on the

153

cargo owner, he might seek reimbursement for part of his loss from the shipowner who also benefited by the sacrifice.

Obviously, it would not be practicable to expect the saved interests to physically replace the interest sacrificed, so the settlement between the various parties is drawn up in financial terms, by an Average Adjuster, in what is called a "General Average Adjustment".

Although the above principle is simple enough it has been necessary from time to time to test and indeed uphold its validity in the English Courts. Decisions have also been made regarding the application of that principle to particular sets of circumstances. Some of the findings in English Law are embodied in the Rules of Practice of the Association of Average Adjusters, referred to later herein by the reference A.A.A. Other maritime countries have their own general average laws, so that various different international practices have evolved.

The shipping industry is an international matter not necessarily confined to the laws of one or even two particular countries, and in the absence of any specific agreement by the separate parties to a maritime adventure it became customary to have a general average adjustment drawn up according to the law of practice prevailing at the place where the adventure ended. Needless to say, this was not always acceptable and there evolved a general demand for an international set of rules to govern the code by which a general average adjustment should be prepared. International conferences were held in the latter half of the nineteenth century at York, Antwerp and elsewhere, and agreement was eventually reached on a set of Rules called the "York-Antwerp Rules 1890". Some effort was made to have these rules adopted into the laws of the maritime nations represented, without success, but instead they were incorporated by reference into contracts of affreightment and these became agreement by contract.

Revision of the Rules was made in Stockholm in 1924 (York-Antwerp Rules 1924) and at Amsterdam in 1949 when the 1950 rules were adopted. However, these Rules, whilst accepted generally throughout the world, were frequently criticized and the International Maritime Committee adopted a new set of Rules at the Hamburg Conference in April 1974, to be termed "York-Antwerp Rules, 1974". These Rules were planned to come into force during 1974 and insurance clauses referring to general average are deemed to incorporate the 1974 Rules or the 1950 Rules as applicable to the contract of affreightment.

The York-Antwerp Rules 1974 (Appendix B herein) comprise a general "Rule of Interpretation", lettered Rules A to G, and numbered Rules I to XXII.

The Rule of Interpretation provides firstly, that the lettered and numbered Rules shall be applied to the adjustment to the exclusion of any law or practice which might be inconsistent with their specific terms. Secondly, it provides that the numbered Rules shall be applied where the circumstances are specifically mentioned notwithstanding that those circumstances might not adhere to general principles laid down in the lettered Rules.

The Rule of Interpretation is necessary to try and ensure that international uniformity of adjusting practice may be reached and, of course, because some of the numbered Rules do not appear to adhere strictly to the more vague general principles laid down in some of the lettered Rules. Some confusion has been caused in the past by attempting to apply both numbered and lettered Rules conjointly.

Although a legal definition of general average has been quoted above, perhaps the best authority for students of Marine Insurance is now embodied in Section 66 of the Marine Insurance Act, 1906 reading as follows:

1. A general average loss is a loss caused by or directly consequential to a general average act. It includes a general average expenditure as well as a general average sacrifice.
2. There is a general average act where any extraordinary sacrifice or expenditure is voluntarily and reasonably made or incurred in time of peril for the purpose of preserving the property imperilled in the common adventure.
3. Where there is a general average loss, the party on whom it falls is entitled, subject to the conditions imposed by Maritime Law, to a rateable contribution from the other parties interested, and such contribution is called a general average contribution.

It will be seen therefore that general average losses flow from the result of a general average act, and are divided into two classes —sacrifice and expenditure. Practical examples of these will be given later in this chapter.

As to the general average act, part (2) of Section 66 is largely repeated in Rule A of the York-Antwerp Rules 1974, and these definitions are short enough to be memorized by students.

Part (3) of Section 66 of the Marine Insurance Act, 1906, is self-explanatory, but will be dealt with in some detail below.

Before considering general average losses in the nature of "sacrifice" and "expenditure", it might be best to first detail the essential requirements of a general average act giving rise to those losses, and to divide Section 66 (2) into smaller subsections giving practical examples—

1. *Extraordinary Sacrifice or Expenditure*

Expenses normally incurred to implement the provisions of the contract of affreightment are not general average. If a vessel's speed is slowed by heavy weather and the voyage prolonged with resulting increased consumption of fuel, wages of crew, etc. this is not 'extraordinary" expenditure. An interesting example of the distinction between "ordinary" and "extraordinary" expenditure comes from Harrison—v—Bank of Australasia (1872), a case concerning a sailing vessel, fitted with a donkey engine, which, leaking after a severe storm, required constant pumping out. The ship's supply of coal quickly became exhausted, due to the constant use of the donkey engine, and the Master ordered certain ship's timbers to be burnt as fuel. Fresh supplies of coal were subsequently purchased and the voyage was eventually completed. The shipowners claimed general average contributions from the cargo owners in respect of value of the ship's materials burnt, the coal purchased, and for overhaul of the donkey engine, but only the cost of replacing *materials* burnt was allowed as an "extraordinary" loss, the others being of an "ordinary" nature.

2. *Voluntary*

There must be an element of deliberate choice. That the loss must be "voluntary" follows from it being intentionally made. As an illustration, the case of a vessel in grave danger at sea may be quoted (Austin Friars S.S. Co. Ltd—v—Spillers and Bakers Ltd.—1915) when the pilot decided to enter a port knowing that there was every likelihood of her striking a quay in so doing, but circumstances were such that it was necessary to take that risk. The vessel did strike the quay damaging herself and the quay, and the sum expended in repairs to the vessel and the amount paid to the Port Authority for damage to the quay were both allowed by the Court as general average.

3. *Reasonable*

Reasonableness is a requirement of all allowances in general average both in cost and in action. An unreasonable sacrifice of ship or cargo cannot be upheld, nor can unreasonable or excessive expenditure.

4. *Imperilled in the Common Adventure*

The Marine Insurance Act uses the term "in time of peril" for the purpose of preserving the property imperilled in the common adventure and it must be noted that this phrase includes two factors, firstly, "peril" and secondly "common adventure". The peril must endanger *all* the interests at risk. Expenditure for the safety of solely one interest cannot therefore be general average expenditure. "Peril" is not easily defined. There must be real peril although not necessarily actual disaster. A mistaken idea that a fire existed in the holds caused a Master to sacrifice some cargo, as he believed for the common safety, but in fact there was no fire, and the English Courts refused to allow as general average a claim for damage to cargo caused by sacrifice. (Joseph Watson and Son Ltd—v—Fireman's Fund Ins. Co. of San Francisco—1922).

In another case a tug was hired to tow a sailing vessel to its destination owing to the possibility of submarines being in the vicinity. A claim for the cost of the tug hire to be allowed in general average was defeated, since there was no evidence that the vessel and cargo were in peril. (Soc. Nouvelle d'Armement—v—Spillers and Bakers, Ltd. 1917).

As noted above a general average loss is a loss caused by, or consequential on, a general average act and having examined the necessary requirements of a general average act, let us now consider the question of the nature of the losses.

Firstly, there must be a real loss. The cost of replacing masts and spars already in a state of wreck cut away from the vessel for the common safety is not general average since they were already lost at the time of the "sacrifice" (see York-Antwerp Rules 1974, Rule IV). Similar consideration must have led to the drafts of Rule III which, whilst it allows, in general average, damage done in extinguishing a fire, specifically excludes damage by smoke and heat however caused.

Secondly, Rule C of the York-Antwerp Rules restricts the general average allowances to the direct consequences of the general average act in terms similar to Section 66 (1) of the Marine Insurance Act. Indirect losses are excluded, as are losses due to delay which are common to all parties in the adventure.

The principle of "direct consequence" is well illustrated by Rule II of the York-Antwerp Rules 1974, particularly as it refers to damage by water entering the holds during jettison for the common safety. Rule VIII also illustrates this principle by allowing in general average damage to the ship or cargo caused by discharging cargo, etc., when the discharge is necessary for the common safety.

The Marine Insurance Act in Section 66 and Rule A of the York-Antwerp Rules both distinguish between general average "sacrifice" and "expenditure", and subject to the general principles mentioned above it may now be of convenience to examine some more frequent examples of losses mentioned in the York-Antwerp

Rules 1974 which give rise to general average allowances:

Sacrifices

    (*a*) Damage to the vessel's engines in efforts to refloat from a position of danger (Rule VII).

    (*b*) Damage to ship or cargo caused by water used in fire extinguishing operations (Rule III).

    (*c*) Damage to ship and cargo caused by lightening operations whilst the vessel is ashore and in peril (Rule VIII).

    (*d*) Damage to ship and cargo caused by intentionally running ashore (Rule V).

    (*e*) Jettison of cargo for the common safety (Rule II).

In general terms where loss of cargo is allowed as general average a similar claim for loss of freight, if any, is allowed as general average (Rule XV).

Expenditure

    (*a*) Expenses of towage in time of peril. This would include expense of towage under contract and expense of towage as part of a "no-cure-no-pay" salvage operation, provided the other circumstances to establish a general average act are present.

    (*b*) Expenses of entering and leaving a port of refuge (Rule X).

    (*c*) Cost of labour and vessels engaged to lighten a vessel ashore in a position of danger (Rule VIII).

    (*d*) Cost of discharging cargo for the common safety (Rule X b).

The importance of distinguishing between "sacrifice" and "expenditure" will be appreciated later, particularly when dealing with the application of general average to insurance.

Before examining the York-Antwerp Rules 1974 in some further detail, it is necessary to consider Section 3 of the Marine Insurance Act (Section 66). General average losses by any of the parties to a maritime adventure must be contributed to by other interests in rateable proportion. As an example, suppose the expenditure (all paid by the Shipowner) be £10,000 and the values saved be, Ship £100,000 and Cargo £400,000, then the contributions will be—

Ship valued at	£100,000	pays	£2,000
Cargo valued at	400,000	pays	8,000
Total	£500,000		£10,000

According to Rules G and XVII of the York-Antwerp Rules 1974 the values on which contributions must be made are based on net values on arrival at destination. The provisions of Rule XVII regarding freight must be noted. The contributory value will be the gross freight at risk less the expenses of crew's wages, fuel and stores, etc., i.e. the expenses of earning it incurred subsequent to the general average act. It must be emphasized that the insured value of a ship has no bearing on the "market" value for general average purposes. The market value, in effect, is the value of the ship that may be obtained "as is—where is". The advice of a qualified ship valuer is usually sought to assess this value.

The contributory value for cargo is ascertained from the commercial invoice rendered to the receiver of the goods or, if there is no invoice, the shipped value. This value includes the cost of insurance and prepaid freight but any damage suffered by the cargo prior to or at the time of discharge must be deducted. If the cargo is sold short of destination the calculation is based on the actual net proceeds of the sale.

Freight however, contributes on the basis of the gross freight saved by the general average act less the expenses of crew's wages and other charges. Passenger money is treated similarly but the Rule provides that there shall be no contribution from passengers luggage and personal effects when these are not shipped under a bill of lading.

To all the contributory values must be added the "amount made good", before the contribution is assessed. This rather obscure phrase means the amount allowed as general average in respect of sacrifice of the property. A practical example may illustrate this principle. Suppose a vessel with an arrived value of £100,000 was carrying a cargo valued at £120,000. During the voyage it was necessary to jettison half the cargo for the common safety so that the nett arrived values were—

Ship	£100,000
Delivered cargo	60,000
Total	£160,000

The owners of cargo have claimed for an allowance in general average of £60,000 in respect of their cargo jettisoned.

If the provisions of Rule XVII were ignored, so far as an addition of the amount made good were concerned, the general average would be apportioned—

Ship	£100,000	pays	£37,500
Delivered cargo	60,000	pays	22,500
	£160,000	pays	£60,000

or 37½% on arrived values.

Thus the property which arrived at destination was subject to a $37\frac{1}{2}\%$ general average contribution and the position of the cargo owner would be as follows:

Amount to receive from general average funds in respect of jettisoned cargo	£60,000
Amount to pay in respect of a contribution by delivered cargo	22,500
Receives on balance	£37,500

But the essence of general average is that the loss shall be borne *equally* by all the interests which benefit from the loss and from the above illustration it will be seen that the cargo owner has received the value of the *whole* of his general average loss by jettison but has been subject, as has also the Shipowner, to a $37\frac{1}{2}\%$ contribution based only on his (the cargo owner's) *other* property. This is inequitable and in order to correct this situation the value of property sacrificed is added to the nett arrived value of the other property in arriving at the contributory value. The result would be—

Ship		£100,000	pays	£27,272
Delivered cargo	£60,000			
Value of jettisoned cargo made good	60,000	120,000	pays	32,728
		£220,000	pays	£60,000

Or 27·272%

In effect therefore the value of jettisoned cargo pays a contribution of 27·272% as do the ship and the value of delivered cargo. The ultimate position of the cargo owner would be—

Amount to receive from general average fund in respect of jettisoned cargo	£60,000
Amount to pay in respect of contributions due from cargo	32,728
Receives on balance	£27,272

(£27,272 is, of course, the amount due from the ship to the cargo)

Before turning to a short examination of general average allowances under the numbered Rules of the York-Antwerp Rules 1974, it is necessary to restate certain principles laid down by the lettered Rules, which we have not yet considered, as follows:

Rule D. The condition of peril to the adventure giving rise to general average act and loss might have arisen due to the negligence of the ship owners, or of one of the other interests in the adventure. Nevertheless, the right to ask for contributions to the loss are not affected but, of course, there might still be other rights against the owners of the interest at fault.

As an example, the shipowner might be at fault in not having fulfilled his duties to cargo by exercising due diligence to provide a seaworthy vessel at the beginning of the voyage. If, due to unseaworthiness a general average loss was sustained, then the shipowner would be entitled to ask for cargo's contribution to that loss, but these might be reclaimed from him for breach of the contract of carriage.

Rule E. This rule is self-explanatory so requires no further comment.

Rule F. This principle is simple. Any expense which saves a general average expense may be substituted for it up to the amount of the general average expense saved. A practical example is dealt with in Rule XIV. If a vessel arrives at a Port of Refuge in damaged condition requiring permanent repairs which can be effected in say 10 days, the shipowner might elect to effect temporary repairs taking only 2 days. Thus 8 days detention have been saved by such a course of action. As detention expenses, where an accident has occurred, are allowed in General Average, in terms of Rule XI(b) so far as wages and maintenance of crew, fuel and stores consumed, etc., are concerned, then the cost of the temporary repairs may be substituted for the allowances which would have been incurred for the extra eight days. *Rule G.* Contributory values have been dealt with in detail, earlier in this chapter.

Let us now consider the numbered rules, drawing distinction between these and the position under English law as reflected in the Association of Average Adjusters' Rules of Practice.

Rule 1—Jettison of Cargo:

Both the York-Antwerp Rule and the A.A.A. Rules (No. B2) provide that no general average be allowed where cargo that is jettisoned is not carried in accordance with recognized custom of trade. Accordingly, if cargo which is normally carried under deck is carried on deck jettison of such cargo would not be allowed as general average. Usually, where the shipper agrees to the cargo being carried on deck its jettison is treated as general average between the parties who have agreed the method of carriage.

Rule II—Damage by Jettison and Sacrifice for the Common Safety:

This Rule follows the "consequences" of a general average act mentioned earlier.

Rule III—Extinguishing Fire on Shipboard:

This Rule has been mentioned before and, in general, agrees with A.A.A. Rule B4, though the Y/A rule excludes all damage by smoke and heat however caused; whereas the A.A.A. Rule (B4) excludes only ship and cargo that have, actually, been on fire.

Rule IV—Cutting away Wreck:

Where part of the ship is, already, effectively lost by the accident, the deliberate cutting away of that part to save the ship should not be deemed to be general average.

Rule V—Voluntary Stranding:

Prior to the 1974 Rules no allowance was given for damage consequent upon a ship being deliberately run aground where she would have run aground inevitably without such action. Under the 1974 Rules it does not matter whether or not she might have been driven on shore and provided she is run ashore for the common safety the consequential damage is allowed in general average. The A.A.A. Rule (B5) retains the old principle.

Rule VI—Salvage Remuneration:

There was no direct reference to salvage expenditure as part of a general average act in the old Y/A Rules though this is incorporated in the A.A.A. Rules (No. C1), where it is in general average circumstances. In drafting the Y/A Rules, it was felt that the rule regarding "Press of Sails" (previously Rule No. VI) is now obsolete so, to preserve continuance of number sequence a new rule was inserted in place of the old Rule VI. This rule provides that a salvage act that has the common features of a general average act (i.e. it is for the common safety) shall be treated as general average.

Rule VII—Damage to Machinery and Boilers:

Where a ship is stranded damage caused to any machinery or boilers in getting the vessel off the strand is allowed in general average, provided such action is for the common safety. The A.A.A. Rule B8 makes the same provision, but the Y/A Rule goes on to exclude damage consequent upon working propelling machinery and boilers whilst the vessel is afloat.

Rule VIII—Expenses Lightening a Ship when ashore, and consequent damage:

This rule requires little explanation. It corresponds, in substance, with A.A.A. Rule B6 with regard to expense but goes on to make consequential loss or damage also the subject of general average, which is incorporated in A.A.A. Rule B20. However, attention is directed to the use of the word "extra"; this coming into effect when the stranding occurs near the port of discharge and the cargo is taken ashore at that port, so that no re-shipping takes place.

Rule IX—Deficiency of Fuel:

Claims for general average contributions arising from deficiency of fuel are by no means so infrequent as might be expected. However, the Rules provide that the Shipowner may only recover, subject to proof that the loss was not due to sailing with insufficient fuel in the first place, the cost of replacing materials and stores burnt as fuel after deduction of the estimated fuel saved. Attention is also drawn to the A.A.A. Rule of Practice B9, and to Rule D of the York-Antwerp Rules. It might be possible, in certain circumstances, for the cargo owners, when asked to pay a contribution to general average arising from insufficient fuel, to plead that the shipowner had failed to carry out the requirements of the contract of affreightment.

Rule IX—Ship's Materials and Stores Burnt for Fuel:

It is logical that the shipowner should be able to recover in general average materials and stores burned as fuel in a general average act but only where he had not neglected to load sufficient fuel for completing the voyage in normal circumstances. However, he must credit the fund with the equivalent price of the extra fuel he would have consumed had it been on board. Of course, in practice, with modern oil burning ships, one cannot envisage this situation being a common occurrence and, although this Y/A rule was not amended in 1974, there appears to be no equivalent rule in the Rules of Practice; except that reference is made to the adjustment in A.A.A. Rule B9 and A.A.A. Rule B31.

Rules X and XI—Port of Refuge Expenses:

Although the majority of general average adjustments are based on the York-Antwerp Rules and, in general, there is little difference between these and the Rules of Practice, when one considers port of refuge expenses there is a difference in the treatment of these which attracts the attention of examiners from time to time. Accordingly, the student is required to know this difference and the fact that it occurs only when the vessel enters a port of refuge consequent upon particular average damage.

When the ship enters the port the following expenses may be incurred, depending on the degree of damage to the vessel:

(1) Cost of bearing up to the port.
(2) Cost of entering the port.
(3) Cost of discharging the cargo for the common safety or to effect repairs to the ship.
(4) Cost of warehousing the cargo (including insurance charges).
(5) Cost of reloading the cargo.
(6) Cost of leaving the port.
(7) Cost of returning to the original route.

Incidental expenses such as wages and maintenance of crew may be allowed as general average when these arise out of action taken for the common safety and details of these are set out in Y/A Rule XI. To understand the detail regarding port of refuge expenses in English law and practice one should examine Rules of Practice B10 to B20 but it is not proposed to go into such detail here.

However, when the ship enters a port of refuge following an accident, and not as a result of a general average act, expenses in English law and practice are allowed as general average only in respect of 1-3, above; except that where cargo is discharged in consequence of its own inherent vice (e.g. spontaneous combustion in the cargo) the expense of discharging such cargo is not allowed in general average. The other costs in items 4-7, above, are charged to the interests concerned. Warehouse rent etc. is a charge on the cargo. Reloading and outward port charges are a special charge on freight.

Rule XII—Damage to Cargo in Discharge, etc.:

Although, generally, accidental damage is not allowable as general average, damage to cargo when handled is sometimes unavoidable. Both this rule and the A.A.A. Rule of Practice B20 follow the principle that the losses consequent on a general average act (i.e. the discharge for the common safety) shall also be general average.

Rule XIII—Deductions from cost of repairs:

There is a considerable difference between the provisions of this rule and the corresponding A.A.A. Rule B21. Both are concerned with deductions to be made from the cost of repairs where new material replaces old material. This is based on the principle that the shipowner is better off than before the general average act if new material or new parts replace old material or parts sacrificed in the general average act. Before the 1974 Y/A Rules, both sets of rules provided for deductions ranging from one third to one sixth, depending on the age of the vessel. However, when the new Y/A Rules were introduced these applied no such deductions except where the ship is over 15 years old; whilst the provision in A.A.A. Rule B21 remained as previously.

Rule XIV—Temporary Repairs:

The purpose of this rule is to allow temporary repairs of accidental damage necessary in order to enable the ship to complete her voyage, or where carried out for the common safety or to repair damage caused by a general average sacrifice, all as general average. It is based on the idea that the damaged vessel is unable to complete her voyage without repair but that it is impracticable to effect permanent repairs at the port of refuge. In a way, this might be construed as a substituted expense (although temporary repairs are not mentioned in the A.A.A. Rule B19 regarding substituted expenses) for cost of such repairs to enable the voyage to be completed is only up to the expense which would have been incurred and allowed in general average if such expense had not been effected at the port of refuge.

Rule XV—Loss of Freight:

Whenever a loss of cargo is allowable in general average, the loss of freight (if at risk) thereon is treated similarly. But only the nett loss of freight is allowable, i.e. the gross loss less any expenses saved such as the cost of discharging cargo. The A.A.A. Rule of Practice No. B22 is similar.

Rule XVI—Amount to be Made Good for Cargo Lost or Damaged by Sacrifice:

Prior to the 1974 amendment the amount to be made good was based on market values on the day of discharge. This gave rise to difficulties where cargo was lost by sacrifice and, often, required the sale of goods damaged by sacrifice to determine the market value. This rule now provides that the amount to be made good shall be determined by the invoice given to the receiver or by the values shipped, where there is no such invoice. This value includes prepaid freight and insurance charges but does not include freight due at destination, nor any landing charges. Accordingly, it is still, in effect, the *net* value of that which has been sacrificed. However, where cargo has been damaged by sacrifice and is sold an agreement may be reached to ascertain the amount to be made good but, if there is no such agreement, the amount to be made good is the difference between the invoice value (or shipped value), calculated as above and the net proceeds of the sale.

Rule XVII—Contributory Values:

The values used for determining the proportion each interest shall pay towards the general average fund are called contributory values. Such values are determined at the place where the adventure ends. This will be the final destination port or place if the voyage is completed; but, if the voyage is abandoned at an intermediate port or place, the values are calculated at the intermediate port or place. The reason for this is that each interest contributes solely on the value saved by the general average act and such value may be diminished by a further accident between a port of refuge and the final destination.

In the Rules of Practice (A.A.A. Rule B23) the basis for contribution is established as the net value of the property saved plus any amount made good in general average. The Y/A Rules, also, make provision for net values to be used.

Cargo: Market values at destination are no longer taken into account and the 1974 Rule XVII provides that the value shown in the commercial invoice rendered to the receiver shall be used; in the absence of such invoice the shipped value is to be used. This value includes prepaid freight and insurance charges but does not include freight at the carrier's risk nor does it include landing charges (These are referred to as *extra* charges in the Y/A Rules). Obviously, to arrive at the saved value, any damage or loss suffered prior to discharge must be deducted and any amount made good must be added.

Ship: Surprisingly, neither the Y/A Rules (XVII) nor the Rules of Practice (A.A.A. No. B24) specify exactly how the contributory value of the ship shall be calculated. In practice, the actual arrived value of the ship is used. It is sometimes convenient to use a certificate of sound value and to deduct therefrom the cost of repairing all damage. The beneficial or detrimental effect of any demise or time charterparty to which the ship is committed is not taken into account. Of course, any amount to be made good in general average (see Rule XVIII) must be added to arrive at the contributory value.

Freight: The Rules of Practice (A.A.A. No. B25) provide that the gross amount shall be used but that from this must be deducted "such charges and crew's wages as would not have been incurred in earning the freight had the ship and cargo been totally lost at the date of the general average act and have not been allowed in general average". The Y/A Rules (XV and XVII) provide for the same deductions to be made from freight and passage money; although where such charges are allowed in general average they must not be deducted. Although Rule XVII makes no direct provision for "made good" to be included in the contributory value, the implication regarding charges so allowed is clear and where loss of freight is incurred (as in Rule XV) the "made good" would be required to contribute.

Rule XVIII—Damage to Ship:

This rule should be read in conjunction with Rule XIII, which deals with "new for old" deductions. The rule follows the basic principles of indemnity whereby only that which is actually lost shall be allowed in general average. Any depreciation allowance in respect of unrepaired damage must not exceed the estimated cost of repairing such damage. Although one tends to think of a total loss destroying the principle of general average this is so only when it is total loss of the adventure. Accordingly, where the adventure is saved there can still be general average even though one or more of the interests has become a total loss. The ship may reach a port of safety but still become a total loss (e.g. an actual total loss by fire or a constructive total loss because the cost of repairs would exceed the repaired value). In such a case, one would calculate the amount to be allowed in general average by taking the estimated sound value of the ship and deducting therefrom the estimated cost of repairing damage which is not general average and deducting from this the damage value of the ship (e.g. the net proceeds from sale of the wreck).

Rule XIX—Undeclared or wrongfully declared cargo:

The provisions of this Rule are self-explanatory. The offending interest is put into the worst possible position.

Rule XX—Provision of Funds:

Where it is necessary to sell cargo to raise funds for general average disbursements the loss on sale is allowable as general average. A "bottomry bond" is a pledge of the ship or freight or cargo in time of necessity to raise money to be repaid on arrival at the discharging port. The cost of such a bond is a general average expense. Note that allowances in respect of wages and maintenance of crew, fuel and stores not replaced during the voyage do not attract the 2% commission allowable on disbursements. This allowance would not be made under English law and practice.

Rules XXI and XXII—Interest and Cash Deposits:

Interest on general average disbursements and allowances runs from the time the disbursement is made until completion of the Adjustment. English law and practice would not admit such an allowance.

It may be convenient, now that the York-Antwerp Rules 1974 have been examined, to elaborate some of the points previously made.

The well known "Makis" case heard in 1929 gave rise to the second half of the Rule of Interpretation which was first introduced in the 1950 Rules. The vessel sustained accidental damage whilst in port and was detained there, not being in a position of danger, but effecting repairs necessary before the voyage could be prosecuted safely. The Adjustment was prepared in accordance with the York-Antwerp Rules 1924 and although the detention expenses allowable as general average under Rule X(b) and XI had been incurred "to enable damage to the ships caused by ... accident to be repaired if the repairs were necessary for the safe prosecution of the voyage" (the expenses allowable under Rule XI follow the "repairs" mentioned in Rule X), there was a lack of a "common safety" factor whilst in port as required by Rule A. The Courts decided that the latter was a necessary requirement before general average allowance could be made under the numbered Rules. Accordingly Shipowners and Underwriters drew up an agreement (now followed in the Rule of Interpretation of the York-Antwerp Rules 1974) whereby the numbered rules take precedence over the lettered rules.

It will have been noticed that the general average allowances are to be apportioned on the values at destination, but supposing after general average expenditure at a port of refuge has been incurred, ship and cargo are lost due to a subsequent accident. There are no arrived values on which an apportionment can be made and therefore the party which has incurred the expenditure must bear the whole loss. To avoid loss in event of this situation arising it is customary to insure the amount of the disbursements at risk from leaving the port of refuge until completion of discharge. The cost of the insurance is allowable in general average (Rule XX—the last paragraph).

The survival of "General Average" throughout the centuries is viewed with some surprise by most people since it may be a costly and lengthy process and one requiring a great deal of detailed work by the Average Adjuster, but the only alternative view put forward is that the losses should fall where they lie, that is to say on the interest initially bearing the loss and that that interest should claim his loss in full from his insurers. This, of course, is simplicity itself providing that the ship, the various cargo interests (often exceeding 1,000 interests in a general cargo ship) and the freight are in fact insured. More frequently than is generally supposed they may not be insured. Some quite large fleets are self-insured and many large shipments of cargo, especially those made for various governments are uninsured. Even supposing a shipowner were to ask his Ship Underwriters to allow him to claim all the ship disbursements allowable to him this would not bind uninsured cargo owners seeking a contribution from the ship to losses of a general average nature sustained by their cargo.

It is suggested that to reduce the matter to settlement between insurers is too limited a view since shipping is an international business which has existed in the past and will continue to exist with or without insurance. If a movement towards reform is needed, it must come from within the Shipping Industry and Shippers of cargo rather than from an insurance market, so the student must, for the time being, continue to study the principles involved.

CHAPTER XV

GENERAL AVERAGE PRACTICE

Procedure at Port of Discharge—
Adjustment and Underwriters' Liability

THE adjustment of general average is a long and complicated procedure. It is conducted by a qualified average adjuster who must exercise skill and patience in collecting and assessing a mass of documentation. The adjustment may take many years to prepare.

When a ship has been involved in a general average act there will be a number of interested parties, which may comprise, in addition to the shipowner's interest in the ship and freight, a variety of persons with an interest in the cargo being carried. In these circumstances, the ship is said to be "under average" when she enters the port or place where the adventure is terminated. This will be either the destination of the voyage or an alternative port or place where the voyage is abandoned.

The shipowner is, naturally, interested to make good any sacrifice or expenditure that he has suffered but, in addition, he is responsible for any loss suffered by the cargo in his care and, accordingly, he must make arrangements for such loss to be made good if he is not to have to make it good himself. To this end, the shipowner appoints an average adjuster to represent his interests and the cargo owners appoint a representative of their own. The shipowner has a possessory lien on the cargo; whereby he can prevent its delivery until satisfactory security has been established in place of the lien.

General Average Security

The security required to discharge the shipowner's lien will be No. 1 in the following list plus any one of Nos. 2-4, insofar as such is acceptable to the shipowner:

1. A general average bond.
2. A bank guarantee.
3. An underwriters' guarantee.
4. A general average deposit.

General Average Bond

This is an undertaking signed by the receivers of the cargo and

169

the shipowner whereby they agree to the adjustment being carried out, and the receiver of the goods agrees to provide such security (see 2-4, above) as is required by the shipowner. The shipowner exchanges his lien on the goods for the signed average bond as soon as the security has been provided. The bond may require that a payment on account be paid towards the general average losses (e.g. general average expenditure which may be advanced) because the adjustment may take a long time to prepare. In some countries (notably the U.S.A.) the term "average bond" may be used to define a general average guarantee.

Bank Guarantee

This may be provided in place of a deposit where the standing of the cargo owner is such that the bank is prepared to give such a guarantee. It is a guarantee that the contribution assessed against the cargo owner will be paid by the bank on completion of the adjustment. It is possible in some countries for a similar guarantee to be purchased from a bonding company and it is in these circumstances that it may be termed a "general average bond".

Underwriters' Guarantee

Where it is clear that the eventual contribution will fall upon the insurance policy, the cargo underwriters will give a written guarantee to pay the contribution attaching to the insured interest on completion of the adjustment. Such guarantee is acceptable to the shipowner and his representative only when it guarantees payment of the *full* contribution assessed against the insured cargo, but it may be that the underwriters' liability is for only a proportion of the contribution. Where the contributory value, assessed to establish the assured's contribution, is more than the insured value there is underinsurance and the underwriters' liability is reduced proportionately for the contribution payable on the policy. The alternative is for the underwriters to issue an unlimited guarantee and to obtain from the assured a counter guarantee to reimburse the underwriters for any overpayment due to underinsurance. In modern practice, this situation seldom arises because it has become customary for the cargo policy or certificate to incorporate a "G.A. in full clause", whereby general average contributions attaching to the policy or certificate are paid in full without regard to any difference between the insured and contributory values.

General Average Deposit

In the absence of any acceptable form of guarantee the receiver of the cargo will be required to pay a deposit into the general average fund. This fund is administered by two trustees, the representative of the shipowner and a representative nominated by the cargo interests. The money is deposited in a joint account, in the names of the trustees, where it earns interest. The amount to be paid as a general average deposit is usually slightly higher than the estimated contribution. A deposit receipt is issued and, when the adjustment has been completed, the holder of the receipt is paid the difference between the deposit, plus accrued interest, and the contribution. There is no legal obligation on the underwriters to pay, or reimburse the assured for, a general deposit. They can wait until the actual amount due on the policy or certificate has been assessed. Nevertheless, many underwriters do, in fact, pay such deposits, particularly where a valued assured has already paid the deposit and is asking for reimbursement. There is no hard and fast rule on this, in practice, but Lloyd's have a standard form of guarantee and a system which is geared to giving a guarantee rather than paying a deposit. Of course, if the underwriters *do* reimburse a deposit paid by the assured they take over the deposit receipt and they are entitled to the interest accruing against the deposit.

Average Disbursements

Often a general average act incorporates expenditure which is incurred by the shipowner. There is no claim on the hull policy for the expenditure as such and the shipowner must turn to the general average fund to recover his loss. There may be a provision in the average bond allowing the shipowner to draw his expenditure at an early stage in the adjustment procedure as an advance, but in the absence of such agreement he must wait for the final adjustment. Whether or not he can recover early from the fund, there is no fund where the voyage is not saved. It follows, that any expenditure incurred by the shipowner (e.g. towage costs, port entry, fuel stores, wages, discharge etc.) is at risk until the voyage is terminated. The wise shipowner effects a "general average disbursements" insurance which pays 100% if the ship becomes a total loss before the voyage is terminated. The cost of such insurance is allowed in general average (Y/A Rule XX).

General Average Adjustment

In the previous chapter examples are shown to illustrate the application of certain York-Antwerp Rules. However, although a detailed statement would tend to confuse one at this stage, the following illustrations will help one to examine the basic methods used in practical adjustment of general average. To study more detail one should refer to Marine Insurance Claims (Goodacre).

Contributory Values

In order to determine the amount which each saved interest shall contribute towards the general average fund, it is necessary for the average adjuster to assess the saved value of each interest. In doing this, the following must be considered:

1. What is the *actual* value at destination of the ship, cargo and freight (if the latter is at risk)?
2. Expenses and costs incurred after the general average act must be deducted.
3. Any property that has been sacrificed will be represented in the adjustment as an amount to be "made good" to the owner of that property. Thus, the receiver of a made good amount benefits to this extent and the amount so made good must, in turn, contribute towards the fund.

It is not easy to estimate the value of property at destination; except where it is sold, in which case the net proceeds can be used. Accordingly, practical methods have evolved for this purpose where property is not sold. In the following examples, care has been taken to avoid complications; so that the principle in each case is more clearly illustrated. In practice, the calculation would be more detailed.

Cargo:

The average adjuster sends a valuation form to the consignee. When this form has been completed, showing the details to be used in assessing the contributory value, it is returned to the average adjuster. The York-Antwerp Rules—1974 (Rule XVII) provide that the contributory value shall be assessed in accordance with the commercial invoice rendered to the receiver; but where no invoice exists the "shipped" value shall be used. The value so assessed will include prepaid freight (non-returnable in event of loss of the goods) and insurance charges but, since it is the value of the cargo in a sound condition, one must deduct any damage suffered during the voyage or during discharge from the ship, except where the goods are sold after discharge and the proceeds are used. The "made good", of course, must be added to the net value if any of the damage deducted was caused by the general average act.

Examples:

A vessel encounters heavy weather during which her cargo shifts. In the interest of the common safety a hatch is opened and 30 cases are jettisoned. Water enters the open hatch and damages further cases. Three consignments are involved, each shipped under different conditions. Each consignment comprises 100 cases of equal value.

Consignment No. 1. (Invoiced at £10,000)—Freight prepaid—
    5 cases in contact with other cargo—

estimated depreciation	25%
10 cases damaged by seawater entering hold—	
estimated depreciation	10%
10 cases jettisoned	

Calculation:

	Invoice Value	£10,000
Deduct	(a) 5 cases valued £500	
	25% depreciation £125	
	(b) 10 cases valued £1,000	1,225
	10% depreciation £100	
	(c) 10 cases jettisoned £1,000	
		£8,775
Add	made good (Items b and c above)	1,100

Contributory value   £9,875

Consignment No. 2. (No Invoice)—Freight paid at destination £400
    (not payable in event of loss of goods)—

                Shipped value £10,000 gross

    5 cases in contact with other cargo—

estimated depreciation	50%
10 cases damaged by seawater entering hold	
estimated depreciation	20%
10 cases jettisoned	

Calculation:

Shipped value (including insurance charges)		£10,000
Deduct	(a) 5 cases valued £500	
	50% depreciation £250	
	(b) 10 cases valued £1,000	
	20% depreciation £200	1,850
	(c) 10 cases jettisoned £1,000	
	(d) Freight paid at destination £400	
		£8,150
Add	made good (Items b and c above) £1,200	
	less freight £80	1,120

Contributory value   £9,270

Consignment No. 3. (No Invoice)—Shipped value £12,000—freight
    prepaid—damaged goods sold by public auction

5 cases in contact with other cargo
10 cases damaged by seawater entering hold
75 cases delivered sound
10 cases jettisoned

___

100

75 cases (sound) shipped value	£9,000
5 cases (contact damage) sold—realized	300
10 cases (seawater damage) sold—realized	1,000
	10,300
Sale costs and landing charges	90
Net value	10,210

Calculation:

1. Made good—
   (a) 10 cases (jettisoned) shipped value   £1,200
   (b) 10 cases (seawater damage)

shipped value	£1,200	
Less gross proceeds	1,000	
loss		200
		£1,400
Less proportion of £90 sale charges (say)		50
		£1,350

2. Contributory Value—

Net value	£10,210	
plus make good	1,350	
		£11,560

Ship:

The market value of the ship at the destination of the voyage or the place where the adventure is terminated, is the basis on which the contributory value is calculated. The term "net" value is often used to define the value of the ship with the cost of repairs deducted from the sound value and, except where the ship is sold in its damaged state (in which case the proceeds determine the net value), it is usually convenient to use the sound value as a basis and to deduct estimated repair costs in arriving at the net value.

Example:

Sound value as per certificate issued by a ship valuer £5,000,000

Estimated cost of P.A. repairs—£35,000
Estimated cost of G.A. repairs—£50,000

	85,000
net value	£4,915,000

Add "made good"
(i.e. G. A. repairs)

	50,000
contributory value	£4,965,000

Note: Of course, this calculation can be simplified by not deducting the G.A. repairs in the first place.

Freight:
Freight payable on delivery of the cargo is at risk of the ship-owner and contributes to the general average fund as a separate interest. To arrive at the contributory value for freight one must take the gross freight earned by delivering the cargo and, from this, deduct any expenses incurred in earning the freight (e.g. fuel, seamen's wages, stores, port entry charges, discharge costs). The made good to be added is calculated in relation to the freight lost by reason of non-delivery of cargo sacrificed as part of a general average act.

Example:

Gross freight earned	£5,000
Expenses incurred subsequent to G.A. act	500
	£4,500
Made good freight on jettisoned cargo	200
Contributory value	£4,700

Contribution
In order to determine the contribution due from each interest the average adjuster must establish

(1) The aggregate amount required in the general average fund to make good the losses suffered.
(2) The relationship (as a percentage) between the fund and the total of the contributory values.
(3) The contribution each interest must pay by applying the percentage.

Example (ignoring any interest allowed—Y/A Rule XXI):
Items in G.A. fund:

Cargo interest sacrificed		£12,000
G.A. repairs to ship		£240,000
Freight lost		1,000
G.A. expenditure incurred by shipowner		2,000
	Total	£255,000

Contributory values:

Ship	£2,420,000
Cargo	120,000
Freight	10,000
Total	£2,550,000

Comparison between the total contributory value £2,550,000) and the total amount to be made good (£255,000) indicates that each risk must contribute 10% of the contributory value, e.g.

Ship	£2,420,000	contribution	£242,000
Cargo	120,000	„	12,000
Freight	10,000	„	1,000
	£2,550,000		£255,000

More than One G.A. Act:

If a further general average act occurs during the voyage this is adjusted first on the grounds that the first general average act would have been futile without the second. Accordingly, the second general average act is adjusted on the values at the destination port or place and the contribution payable is deducted from the contributory value of each interest in the adjustment for the first general average act.

Salvage Prior to the General Average Act:

A salvage award is payable on the successful completion of the salvage services so that the contributory value for salvage charges is calculated on the values at the port of refuge, not at destination. The salvage award is treated as general average expenditure where it occurs within a general average act. Where property arrives the salvage award is taken into account in the contributory value and at one time, to preserve equity, it was the practice to apply "hypothetical salvage" to contributory values on property sacrificed *before* the salvage services took place. However, average adjusters no longer apply this principle.

Underwriters' Liability in General Average

Provided the general average act was incurred to prevent loss of the insured interest from an insured peril, the underwriters covering that interest are liable for

(a) general average sacrifice of the interest or part thereof
(b) the contribution paid by the interest towards the general average fund; although underwriters' liability for this is reduced by underinsurance of the interest.

Sacrifice:

The Marine Insurance Act (1906) Section 66, sub 4, provides:
"Subject to any express provision in the policy, ... in the case of a general average sacrifice, he (the assured) may recover from the insurer in respect of the whole loss without having enforced his right of contribution from the other parties liable to contribute."

This entitles the assured to make a direct claim on the underwriters for his sacrificed property without waiting the outcome of the adjustment. Nevertheless the claim is subject to "any express provision in the policy", which, in the case of hull insurance means that the claim is subject to the deductible average clause. Claims in this respect are settled in the same manner as particular average claims, though, in the case of cargo, no franchise provision is applied. Although the true indemnity would be for the amount to be made good, such is not known at the time the claim for sacrifice is settled and, in the case of hull insurance, there are other factors which vary the comparable amounts.

Cargo Underwriters pay the insured value of any package or packages totally lost. In the case of partial loss, underwriters pay such proportion of the insured value as the difference between the gross sound value and the gross damaged value bears to the gross sound value, but ignoring any franchise in the policy.

Example:
1,000 cases insured for £10 per case, so valued.
100—jettisoned
100—sold damaged for £600
800—sold sound for £9,600

Claim:
    800 cases sound realized   £9,600
    Therefore 100 cases sound value =   £1,200
    100 cases damaged realized   600

                                        loss   £600
                                   (50% depreciation)
    Policy pays (1) partial loss 50% of £1,000 =   £500
    plus (2) total loss 100 cases =   £1,000

                                                      £1,500

Ship-Underwriters pay the cost of repairing the damage but deduct therefrom the amount specified in the deductible average clause (Note: this deductible is applied to the aggregate of *all* partial loss claims occurring in a single accident—for this purpose the G.A. sacrifice is deemed to be an "accident"). The average adjuster will deduct one third from G.A. repair costs if the vessel is over 15 years old but the underwriters do not make this deduction when paying for the repairs in the first instance, so any recovery of "made good" from the general average fund could be substantially less than the claim paid on the policy.

Freight—Where freight is insured as a separate interest (i.e. it is at the risk of the shipowner), a sacrifice of cargo constitutes a sacrifice of the freight payable on that cargo. In freight policies there will be a franchise provision of 3% to be applied to particular average claims but this does not apply to general average sacrifice so the underwriters would pay the full amount of freight lost.

Subrogation—In each of the above cases the underwriter would be subrogated to the rights of the assured in respect of "made good" and would recover the claim from the general average fund on completion of the adjustment.

List of abbreviations used in the Practice of
Marine Insurance

A

A.C.V.	Air cushion vehicle (Hovercraft)
A.F.	Advanced Freight
A.F.I.A.	American Foreign Insurance Association
A.G.W.I.	Atlantic, Gulf, West Indies limits
A/H	Antwerp-Hamburg
A.H.F.	American Hull Form of policy
A.I.T.H. Form	American Institute Time Hull Form of policy
A.O.A. *or* a.o.a.	Any one accident
A.O.B. *or* a.o.b.	Any one bottom
A.O.L. *or* a.o.l.	Any one loss
A.O.O. *or* a.o.o.	Any one occurrence
a.o.occ.	Any one occurrence
A.O.S. *or* a.o.s.	Any one steamer/Any one sending
A.O.V. *or* a.o.v.	Any one vessel
A.P.	Additional premium
A.P.L. *or* a.p.l.	As per list
A.R.A.	Antwerp/Rotterdam/Amsterdam
a/s	alongside
A.T.L.	Actual total loss
att.	attached
Aux.	Auxiliary
Av.	Average
Av. Disbts.	Average Disbursements

B

Bar.	Barrel
B.B. Clause	Both to blame collision clause
Bd.	Bond
B.D.I. *or* b.d.i.	Both days inclusive
Bdls.	Bundles
Bds.	Boards
B/E	Bill of Exchange
B.f.s.l.	Being full signed line
B.f.w.l.	Being full written line
Bkge.	Breakage (sometimes used for "brokerage")
Bls.	Bales *or* barrels
B.N.A.	British North America
Brkge.	Brokerage
Brok.	Brokerage
B/s	Bales *or* bags
Bs/L	Bills of lading

btm.	bottom
B. to blame	Both to blame
B. to B.	Both to blame
C	
C/A	Central Accounting
C.A.C.T.L.O.	Compromised and/or Arranged and/or Constructive Total Loss only
C.A.D.	Cash against documents
Canc.	Cancelled
C. & F.	Cost and Freight
C. & I.	Cost and Insurance
C.B. & H.	Continent between Bordeaux and Hamburg
C.C.	Civil Commotions *or* Cancellation Clause *or* collecting commission
C.D.	Country Damage
Cert.	Certificate
C.F.I.	Cost, Freight and Insurance
c.g.a.	Cargo's proportion of general average
Cge.	Carriage
C.G.M.E.	China, Glass, Marble, Earthenware
C.g.f. proceeds	Credit given for proceeds
Cgo.	Cargo
Chaf.	Chafage
C.I.B.	Corporation of Insurance Brokers
C.I.F.	Cost, Insurance and Freight
c.i.f.	Cost, Insurance and Freight
c.i.f. & c.	Cost, Insurance, Freight and Commission
c.i.f. & i.	Cost, Insurance, Freight and Interest
C.I.F.C.I.	Cost, Insurance, Freight, Commission and Interest
C.I.I.	Chartered Insurance Institute
C.K.D.	Completely knocked down
c.l.	Craft loss
Compl.	Completed
C.M.S.	Combined Marine Surcharge (now obsolete)
C/N	Cover Note *or* Credit Note
C.O.B.	Cargo on board
Co-Ins.	Co-insurance
C. of G.S. Act	Carriage of Goods by Sea Act, 1924
Compd.	Compromised
Consgt.	Consignment
Cont.	Continent of Europe
Cont. B/H	Continent of Europe between Bordeaux and Hamburg

Cont. H/H	Continent of Europe between Havre and Hamburg
CONV. *or* Conv.	Conveyance (Sometimes used for "converted from")
C/P	Charterparty
C.P.A.	Claims Payable Abroad
Cr.L	Craft Loss
C.R.O.	Cancelling Returns Only
c/s	Cases
CSD	Closed Shelter Deck
Csk	Cask
C.T.C.	Corn Trade Clauses
Ctge.	Cartage
C.T.L.	Constructive Total Loss
Cts.	Crates

D

D/A	Deductible Average
D/B	Double bottom
D.B.B.	Deals, battens and boards
D/C	Deviation Clause
D.D. *or* d.d.	Damage done
Dd.	Delivered
D.E.	Diesel Electric
Dec.	Declaration
Decl.	Declaration *or* declared
Ded.	Deductions
Def. a/c	Deferred Account
D.f.	Dead Freight
DF	Direction Finder
Dk.	**Deck**
Dk.L	Deck Loss
D.N.O.	Debit note only
d.p.	Direct port
d.pr.	Daily pro rata
D/R	Deposit Receipt
dt.	Deep tank
D.T.B.A. *or* d.t.b.a.	Date to be advised
D/V	Dual Valuation
D/W *or* d.w.	Deadweight
d.w.c.	Deadweight capacity

E

E.	Engine
e. & e.a.	Each and every accident
e. & e.l.	Each and every loss

e. & e.o.	Each and every occurrence
E.C.	East Coast
e.g.	Ejusdem generis
E.L.	Employer's Liability
e.o.h.p.	Except as otherwise herein provided
E.P.I.	Earned Premium Income
ESD	Echo Sounding Device
Exd.	Examined
Exs.	Expenses *or* Excesses

F

F.A.S. *or* f.a.s.	Free alongside steamer/ship
F.O.M. *or* f.o.m.	Flag, ownership or management
f.o.q.	Free on quay
f.o.r	Free on rail
f.o.s.	Free on steamer or ship
f.o.t.	Free on truck
F.P.	Floating policy
F.P.A.	Free of particular average
F.P.A. abs.	Free of particular average absolutely
F.P.A. & loss	Same as F.P.A. u.c.b.
F.P.A. u.c.b.	Free of particular average unless caused by the vessel or craft being stranded, sunk or burnt
F.P.A. unl. *or* F.P.A. unless	Free of particular average unless the vessel or craft be stranded, sunk or burnt
F.P.I.L.	Full premium if lost
F.P.I.L.I.P.	Full premium if lost by an insured peril
F.P.I.L.P.I.A.	Full premium if lost by a peril insured against
F.P.T.	Forepeak tank
F.R.C.	Free of reported casualty
F.R.C.C.	Free of riots and civil commotions
Free of	Insurer has no liability
F.R.O.	Fire risk only
Front	Fronting insurer
Frt.	Freight
f.s.l.	Full signed line
Fth.	Fathom
f.v.	Fishing vessel
f.w.d.	Freshwater Damage
f.w.l.	Full written line
F.W.T. & G.D.	Fair wear and tear and gradual deterioration

G

G/A *or* G.A.	General Average
G/A con.	General Average contribution

G.A.D.	General Average deposit
G/A dep.	General Average deposit
G.A.D.V.	Gross arrived damaged value
G.A.L.	General Average loss
GC	Gyro compass
g.f.a.	Good fair average
G.R.T.	Gross registered tonnage
Gr. wt.	Gross weight
Gr.T. *or* gro. t.	Gross tons
Gy.C.	Gyro Compass

H

H.A.D.	Havre, Antwerp, Dunkirk
H & M	Hull and machinery *or* Hull and materials
h & o	Hook and oil damage
H.B.	Houseboat
H/C *or* h/c	Held covered
H/H (Europe)	Havre to Hamburg
hk.	Hook damage
H.M. etc.	Hull and Machinery etc.
H.W.	Heavy weather
H.W.D.	Heavy weather damage
H.W.M.	High water mark
H.W.O.S.T.	High water ordinary spring tides

I

i &/or o	In and/or overdeck
I.B.	In bond
I.B.C.	Institute Builder's Risk Clauses
I/C *or* I.C. *or* i/c	In commission
I.C.C.	Institute Cargo Clauses
i.f.	In full
I.F.C.	Institute Freight Clauses
I.L.U.	Institute of London Underwriters
In &/or over	Goods carried either below or above deck
I.N.M.	Incidental non marine
Ins.	Insurance
Inst.	Institute of London Underwriters
Inst. Cls.	Institute Clauses
Inst. War etc.	War and strike clauses published by the Institute of London Underwriters
Inst. Wties.	Institute Warranties
Int.	Interest
in trans.	In transit
I/o	In and/or overdeck
i.o.p.	Irrespective of percentage

I.P.C. *or* I.P.R.C.	Institute Port Risk Clauses
I.T.C.	Institute Time Clauses (Hulls)
I.V. *or* I/V	Increased value
I.V.C.	Institute Voyage Clauses (Hulls)
I.Y.C.	Institute Yacht Clauses

J

j & l.o.	Jettison and loss overboard
j. & w.o.	Jettison and washing overboard
Jett.	Jettison

K

K.D.	Knocked down
K.D.C.	Knocked down condition
Kild.	Kilderkin

L

L/C	Label clause *or* Letter of credit
L.C.T.A.	London Corn Trade Assocation
L.d.d.	Loss during discharge
L/Def.	Latent defect
Ldg.	Loading
Ldg. & dely.	Landing and delivery
L.d.l.	Loss during loading
Lds.	Loads
L.d.t.	Loss during transhipment
Lead	Leading underwriter
Leg. Chgs.	Legal charges
L.H.A.R.	London, Hull, Antwerp, Rotterdam
Lkge.	Leakage
Lkge. & Bkge.	Leakage and breakage
Llds.	Lloyd's
L.M.C.	Lloyd's machinery certificate
L.M.C.C.S.	Lloyd's machinery certificate continuous survey
L.N.G.	Liquid natural gas carrier
L.n.y.d.	Liability not yet determined
L.P.S.O.	Lloyd's Policy Signing Office
L.R.	Lloyd's Register
L.R.M.C.	Lloyd's refrigerating machinery certificate
L.S. Cls.	Livestock Clauses
L.S.H.W. Liab.	Longshoremen's and harbour worker's liability
L.S.R.	Line, Syndicate number, pseudonym and reference
Ltr.	Lighter
L/U	Leading underwriter
l/u	Laid up *or* lying up

L.U.A.	Lloyd's Underwriters' Association
L.U.C.O.	Lloyd's Underwriters' Claims Office
L.W.	Low water
L.W.O.S.T.	Low water ordinary spring tide

M

Mal.d.	Malicious damage
M. & W.	Marine and War risks
Mar.	Marine
m.b.	Motor boat
M.B.D.	Machinery breakdown
M/c	Machinery certificate
Machy.	Ship's machinery
Machy. dge.	Machinery damage
M.D.	Malicious Damage
Mdse.	Merchandise
Med. Exps.	Medical Expenses
M.H.W.S.	Mean highwater spring tide
M.I.A. *or* M.I.Act	Marine Insurance Act, 1906
MIN/DEP	Minimum and deposit premium
M.I.P.	Marine Insurance Policy
M.L.W.S.	Mean low water spring tide
Mort.	Mortality
m. pack.	Missing package
M/R	Mate's receipt
M.S.	Machinery survey
M.S.A.	Merchant Shipping Act, 1894
M.S.C.	Manchester Ship Canal
mt.	Empty
M.T.L.	Mean tide level
M.V.	Motor vessel

N

N.A. *or* n.a.	Net absolutely
N.C.A.D.	Notice of cancellation at anniversary date
N.C.A.R.	No claim for accident reported
N.C.C.	No collecting commission
N.D.	Non delivery *or* no discount
n.d.	Non delivery
N.E.	Not entered
n.e.	Not exceeding
Neg.	Negligence
N.L.U.R.	No lying up returns
N.M.	Non marine
N.M.A.	Lloyd's Non Marine Association
N/N	Not north of

No B.N.A.	Warranted no British North America
non.d.	Non delivery
No S.I.	No short interest
N/P	Net proceeds
N.R.	No risk
n.r.a.d.	No risk after discharge
n.r.a.l.	No risk after Landing
N.R.T. *or* n.r.t.	Net registered tonnage
n.r.t.o.r.	No risk until on rail
N.S.	Nuclear ship
n.s.p.f.	Not specially provided for
Nt. wt.	Net weight
N.U.R. *or* n.u.r.	Not under repair

O

o/b	On or before
O/C *or* O.C.	Open cover *or* off cover
O.C.A.	Outstanding Claims Advance
Oc.B/L	Ocean bill of lading
o.cgo.	Damage caused by other cargo
o/d	Overdraft
O.G.P.	Original gross premium
O.G.P.I.	Original gross premium income
O.G.R.	Original gross rate
O.N.P.	Original net premium
O.N.P.I.	Original net premium income
O.N.R.	Original net rate
O.N.R.P.I.	Original net retained premium income
O.N.R. to H.O.	Original net rate to Head Office
O.R.	Original rate
O/R	Overriding commission
Ors.	Others
O/S *or* o/s	Outstanding
OSD	Open shelter deck
o.s.l.	On signed lines

P

P.A.	Particular average
P.A. & G.A.L.	Particular average and general average loss
Pac.	Pacific coast ports
P & I	Protection and Indemnity
P/C	Particular charges *or* profit commission
P.chgs.	Particular charges
Pcl.	Parcel
P.D.	Property damage *or* Port dues
Per. inj.	Personal injury

Pers. Acc.	Personal accident
P.I.	Personal injury
P.I.A.	Peril insured against
Pilf.	Pilferage
Pkg.	Package
P.L.	Public liability
P/L	Partial loss
P.L.A.	Port of London Authority
Pm.	Premium
P.M.L.	Possible maximum loss
p.o.c.	Port of call
P.O.R.	Port of Refuge
P.P.	Parcel post
ppd.	prepaid
P.P.I.	Policy Proof of Interest
P.R.	Port Risks
p.r.	pro rata
Prem. red.	Premiums reducing
Proceeds t.b.a.f.	Proceeds to be accounted for
Prop.	Propeller
P. sett.	Previous settlement
P.S.T.	Pacific standard time

R

R. & C.C. *or* r. & c.c.	Riots and civil commotions
r.d.	running days
R.D.C.	Running Down Clause
Reefer	Refrigerated vessel *or* refrigerating space
Ref.	Refrigerating machinery
Res. a/c	Reserve Account
Ret.	Return of Premium
R/I	Reinsurance
R.I.C.C.	Reinsurance for Common Account
R.L.N.	Running Landing Numbers
R.M.S.	Royal Mail Ship
R.N.R.	Renewal not required
Roads.	Roadstead
r.o.b.	Remaining on board
R.O.D.	Rust, oxidation and discolouration
R.O.J.A.	Reinsurance of Joint Account
R.P.	Return of Premium
R.T.B.A.	Rate to be agreed
Rtng.	Returning premium

S

S.A.	South America

S/A	Subject to acceptance by the assured
S/A *or* S.A.	Salvage Association
S.A. a/c	Salvage Association account
S.A L/U	Subject to acceptance by the assured, to be advised to the leading underwriter
Salv.L.	Salvage loss
S and/or N.D.	Shortage and/or Non-delivery
S.A.N.R.	Subject approval no risk
s.a.p.l.	Sailed as per List
s.b.s.	Surveyed before shipment
SBS	Submarine signalling equipment
S/C	Salvage charges
Sch.	Schooner
S.D. *or* s.d.	Steam drifter *or* short delivery
S/D	Steel diesel
S/F	Survey Fee
S/Fee	Survey Fee
S.G.	Ship and Goods
S/H.E. *or* SHEX	Sundays and holidays excepted
Shipt.	Shipment
Short.	Shortage
S.I.	Sum insured *or* short interest
Sk.	Sack
S/L	Sue and Labour charges
S.L.	Salvage loss
S.L.C.	Sue and labour clause
Sld.	Sailed
Sld. apl.	Sailed as per List
Sling L.	Sling Loss
S/N	Shipping Note
S/O	Shipowner
S.O.L.	Shipowner's Liability
S.O.S.	Service of Suit
Sp. chgs.	Special Charges
Spd.	Sparred
S.R. & C.C. *or* s.r. & c.c.	Strikes Riots and Civil Commotions
S.R.C.C. & M.D.	Strikes, Riots, Civil Commotions and Malicious Damage
S.R.L.	Shiprepairer's Liability
S.S.M.U.A.	Steamship Mutual Underwriting Association
S.S.O.	Struck submerged object
Std.	Standard
Stev. Liab.	Stevedores' Liability
Str.	Steamer

Strd.	Stranded
Sub. U/wrs. App.	Subject to Underwriters' approval
S.V.	Sailing Vessel
S.W.	Shipper's weights
S.W.D. *or* s.w.d.	Seawater damage
Syn. *or* Synd.	Syndicate
Synd. R/I	Syndicate Reinsurance
T	
T and/or C.T.L.	Total and/or Constructive Total Loss
t and s	Touch and stay
T.B.A.	"To be advised" *or* "to be agreed"
T.C.A.T.L.V.O.	Total or constructive or arranged total loss of vessel only
Tcs.	Tierces
Thirds	Deductions from a claim due to new material replacing old materials
Thro. B/L	Through Bill of Lading
T.L. *or* T/L	Total Loss
T.L.O.	Total Loss Only
T.L.O. excs.	Total Loss Only and Excess Liabilities
T.L.O. R/I Cl.	Total Loss Only Reinsurance Clause
T.L.V.O.	Total Loss of Vessel Only
T.O.R.	Time on risk
Tow. liab.	Tower's liability
T.P.	Third Party
T.P. Liab.	Third Party Liability
T.P.N.D.	Theft, Pilferage and Non Delivery
T.P.N.S.D.	Theft, Pilferage, Non and/or Short Delivery
T/S	Transhipment
T.T.	Telegraphic Transfer
T.T.F. Cls.	Timber Trade Federation Clauses
Tty	Reinsurance treaty
T.W.M.C.	Transport, wages, maintenance and care
U	
U/A	Underwriting account
U. & O.	Use and occupancy
U.C.B. *or* u.c.b.	Unless caused by
U/D *or* u/d	underdeck
U.K. Cont.	United Kingdom and/or Continent of Europe
ul. *or* unl.	Unlimited during the currency of the insurance
Ult.	Ultimate
U.N.L.	Ultimate Net Loss
U.P. Fee	Underwriters pay the C.P.A. fee
U.P.S.	Underwriters pay policy stamp duty

U.P. tax	Underwriters pay tax
U/R *or* u/r	Under repair
U.T. *or* u.t.	Unlimited transhipment
U/W *or* U/Wr. *or* U/wr	Underwriter

V

V.C.	Valuation clause
vd.	Valued
Vice Propre	Inherent vice
V.L.C.C.	Very large cargo carrier
V.O.P.	Valued as original policy or policies

W

W.A.	With average
W.A. Clauses	Institute Cargo Clauses—W.A.
W.A. Cover	Institute Cargo Clauses—W.A.
War etc.	War, strikes, riots, civil commotions and malicious damage
w.b.	Water ballast
W.B.S.	Without benefit of salvage to the insurer
W.C.	West Coast
W.C.A.	Workmen's Compensation Act
W.C.B.	With cargo on board
W.C.S.A.	West Coast South America
W/d	Warranted
WDF	Wireless Direction Finder
Whse.	Warehouse
W.M.	Weight and/or measurement *or* winter mooring
w.o. *or* w.o.b.	Washing overboard
W.O.L.	Wharfowner's Liability
W.P. *or* w.p.	Without prejudice
W.P.A.	With particular average
W.R.I.O.	War Risks Insurance Office
W.R.O.	War risks only
Wt.	Weight
Wtd.	Warranted
W.T.E. Cl.	Wartime Extension Clause (now obsolete)
W/W	Warehouse to warehouse
W.W.D.	Weather working days

X

XS	Excess
XS Loss	Excess Loss Reinsurance

Y

Y.A.R.	York-Antwerp Rules
Y/A Rules	York-Antwerp Rules

THE MARINE INSURANCE ACT, 1906

[6 Edw. 7. Ch. 41.]

ARRANGEMENT OF SECTIONS

MARINE INSURANCE ACT, 1906
An Act to codify the Law relating to Marine Insurance
(21st *December,* 1906.)

Be it enacted by the King's most Excellent Majesty, by and with the advice and consent of the Lords Spiritual and Temporal, and Commons, in this present Parliament assembled, and by the authority of the same, as follows:—

MARINE INSURANCE

Marine Insurance Defined
1.   A contract of marine insurance is a contract whereby the insurer undertakes to indemnify the assured, in manner and to the extent thereby agreed, against marine losses, that is to say, the losses incident to marine adventure.

Mixed Sea and Land Risks
2.—(1) A contract of marine insurance may, by its express terms or by usage of trade, be extended so as to protect the assured against losses on inland waters or on any land risk which may be incidental to any sea voyage.

(2) Where a ship in course of building, or the launch of a ship, or any adventure analogous to a marine adventure, is covered by a policy in the form of a marine policy, the provisions of this Act, in so far as applicable, shall apply thereto; but, except as by this section provided, nothing in this Act shall alter or affect any rule of law applicable to any contract of insurance other than a contract of marine insurance as by this Act defined.

Marine Adventure and Maritime Perils Defined
3.—(1) Subject to the provisions of this Act, every lawful marine

adventure may be the subject of a contract of marine insurance.
    (2.) In particular there is a marine adventure where—

(a) Any ship goods or other moveables are exposed to maritime perils. Such property is in this Act referred to as "insurable property";

(b) The earning or acquisition of any freight, passage money, commission, profit, or other pecuniary benefit, or the security for any advances, loan, or disbursements, is endangered by the exposure of insurable property to maritime perils;

(c) Any liability to a third party may be incurred by the owner of, or other person interested in or responsible for, insurable property, by reason of maritime perils.

"Maritime perils" means the perils consequent on, or incidental to, the navigation of the sea, that is to say, perils of the seas, fire, war perils, pirates, rovers, thieves, capture, seizures, restraints, and detainments of princes and peoples, jettisons, barratry, and any other perils, either of the like kind or which may be designated by the policy.

INSURABLE INTEREST

Avoidance of Wagering or Gaming Contracts
    4.—(1) Every contract of marine insurance by way of gaming or wagering is void.
    (2) A contract of marine insurance is deemed to be a gaming or wagering contract—

(a) Where the assured has not an insurable interest as defined by this Act, and the contract is entered into with no expectation of acquiring such an interest; or

(b) Where the policy is made "interest or no interest", or "without further proof of interest than the policy itself", or "without benefit of salvage to the insurer", or subject to any other like term:

Provided that, where there is no possibility of salvage, a policy may be effected without benefit of salvage to the insurer.

Insurable Interest Defined
    5.—(1) Subject to the provisions of this Act, every person has an insurable interest who is interested in a marine adventure.
    (2) In particular a person is interested in a marine adventure where he stands in any legal or equitable relation to the adventure or to any insurable property at risk therein, in consequence of which he may benefit by the safety or due arrival of insurable property, or may be prejudiced by its loss, or by damage thereto, or by the detention thereof, or may incur liability in respect thereof.

When Interest Must Attach

6.—(1) The assured must be interested in the subject-matter insured at the time of the loss though he need not be interested when the insurance is effected:

Provided that where the subject-matter is insured "lost or not lost", the assured may recover although he may not have acquired his interest until after the loss, unless at the time of effecting the contract of insurance the assured was aware of the loss, and the insurer was not.

(2) Where the assured has no interest at the time of the loss, he cannot acquire interest by any act or election after he is aware of the loss.

Defeasible or Contingent Interest

7.—(1) A defeasible interest is insurable, as also is a contingent interest.

(2) In particular, where the buyer of goods has insured them, he has an insurable interest, notwithstanding that he might, at his election, have rejected the goods, or have treated them as at the seller's risk, by reason of the latter's delay in making delivery or otherwise.

Partial Interest

8.   A partial interest of any nature is insurable.

Re-insurance

9.—(1) The insurer under a contract of marine insurance has an insurable interest in his risk, and may re-insure in respect of it.

(2) Unless the policy otherwise provides, the original assured has no right or interest in respect of such re-insurance.

Bottomry

10.   The lender of money on bottomry or respondentia has an insurable interest in respect of the loan.

Master's and Seamen's Wages

11.   The master or any member of the crew of a ship has an insurable interest in respect of his wages.

Advance Freight

12.   In the case of advance freight, the person advancing the freight has an insurable interest, in so far as such freight is not repayable in case of loss.

Charges of Insurance
13. The assured has an insurable interest in the charges of any insurance which he may effect.

Quantum of Interest
14.—(1) Where the subject-matter insured is mortgaged, the mortgagor has an insurable interest in the full value thereof, and the mortgagee has an insurable interest in respect of any sum due or to become due under the mortgage.

(2) A mortgagee, consignee, or other person having an interest in the subject-matter insured may insure on behalf and for the benefit of other persons interested as well as for his own benefit.

(3) The owner of insurable property has an insurable interest in respect of the full value thereof, notwithstanding that some third person may have agreed, or be liable, to indemnify him in case of loss.

Assignment of Interest
15. Where the assured assigns or otherwise parts with his interest in the subject-matter insured, he does not thereby transfer to the assignee his rights under the contract of insurance, unless there can be an express or implied agreement with the assignee to that effect.

But the provisions of this section do not affect a transmission of interest by operation of law.

INSURABLE VALUE

Measure of Insurable Value
16. Subject to any express provision or valuation in the policy, the insurable value of the subject-matter insured must be ascertained as follows:—
  (1) In insurance on ship, the insurable value is the value, at the commencement of the risk, of the ship, including her outfit, provisions and stores for the officers and crew, money advanced for seamen's wages, and other disbursements (if any) incurred to make the ship fit for the voyage or adventure contemplated by the policy, plus the charges of insurance upon the whole:
    The insurable value, in the case of a steamship, includes also the machinery, boilers, and coals and engine stores if owned by the assured, and, in the case of a ship engaged in a special trade, the ordinary fittings requisite for that trade:
  (2) In insurance on freight, whether paid in advance or otherwise, the insurable value is the gross amount of the freight at the risk of the assured, plus the charges of insurance:

(3) In insurance on goods or merchandise, the insurable value is the prime cost of the property insured, plus the expenses of and incidental to shipping and the charges of insurance upon the whole:

(4) In insurance on any other subject-matter, the insurable value is the amount at the risk of the assured when the policy attaches, plus the charges of insurance.

DISCLOSURE AND REPRESENTATIONS

Insurance is Uberrimae Fidei

17. A contract of marine insurance is a contract based upon the utmost good faith, and, if the utmost good faith be not observed by either party, the contract may be avoided by the other party.

Disclosure by Assured

18.—(1) Subject to the provisions of this section, the assured must disclose to the insurer, before the contract is concluded, every material circumstance which is known to the assured, and the assured is deemed to know every circumstance which, in the ordinary course of business, ought to be known by him. If the assured fails to make such disclosure, the insurer may avoid the contract.

(2) Every circumstance is material which would influence the judgement of a prudent insurer in fixing the premium, or determining whether he will take the risk.

(3) In the absence of enquiry the following circumstances need not be disclosed, namely:—

(a) Any circumstance which diminishes the risk;

(b) Any circumstance which is known or presumed to be known to the insurer. The insurer is presumed to know matters of common notoriety or knowledge, and matters which an insurer in the ordinary course of his business, as such, ought to know;

(c) Any circumstance as to which information is waived by the insurer;

(d) Any circumstance which it is superfluous to disclose by reason of any express or implied warranty.

(4) Whether any particular circumstance, which is not disclosed, be material or not is, in each case, a question of fact.

(5) The term "circumstance" includes any communication made to, or information received by, the assured.

Disclosure by Agent Effecting Insurance

19. Subject to the provisions of the preceding section as to

circumstances which need not be disclosed, where an insurance is effected for the assured by an agent, the agent must disclose to the insurer—

(a) Every material circumstance which is known to himself, and an agent to insure is deemed to know every circumstance which in the ordinary course of business ought to be known by, or to have communicated to, him; and

(b) Every material circumstance which the assured is bound to disclose, unless it comes to his knowledge too late to communicate it to the agent.

Representations Pending Negotiation of Contract

20.—(1) Every material representation made by the assured or his agent to the insurer during the negotiations for the contract, and before the contract is concluded, must be true. If it be untrue the insurer may avoid the contract.

(2) A representation is material which would influence the judgement of a prudent insurer in fixing the premium, or determining whether he will take the risk.

(3) A representation may be either a representation as to a matter of fact, or as to a matter of expectation or belief.

(4) A representation as to a matter of fact is true, if it be substantially correct, that is to say, if the difference between what is represented and what is actually correct would not be considered material by a prudent insurer.

(5) A representation as to a matter of expectation or belief is true if it be made in good faith.

(6) A representation may be withdrawn or corrected before the contract is concluded.

(7) Whether a particular representation be material or not is, in each case, a question of fact.

When Contract is Deemed to be Concluded

21.   A contract of marine insurance is deemed to be concluded when the proposal of the assured is accepted by the insurer, whether the policy be then issued or not; and for the purpose of showing when the proposal was accepted, reference may be made to the slip or covering note or other customary memorandum of the contract, although it be unstamped.*

THE POLICY

Contract Must be Embodied in Policy

22.   Subject to the provisions of any statute, a contract of marine

* Section 21, the last four words repealed by Finance Act, 1959.

insurance is inadmissible in evidence unless it is embodied in a marine policy in accordance with this Act. The policy may be executed and issued either at the time when the contract is concluded, or afterwards.

What Policy Must Specify

23.   A marine policy must specify—

(1) The name of the assured, or of some person who effects the insurance on his behalf:

(2) The subject-matter insured and the risk insured against:

(3) The voyage, or period of time, or both, as the case may be, covered by the insurance:

(4) The sum or sums insured:

(5) The name or names of the insurers.*

Signature of Insurer

24.—(1) A marine policy must be signed by or on behalf of the insurer, provided that in the case of a corporation the corporate seal may be sufficient, but nothing in this section shall be construed as requiring the subscription of a corporation to be under seal.

(2) Where a policy is subscribed by or on behalf of two or more insurers, each subscription, unless the contrary be expressed, constitutes a distinct contract with the assured.

Voyage and Time Policies

25.—(1) Where the contract is to insure the subject-matter at and from, or from one place to another or others, the policy is called a "voyage policy", and where the contract is to insure the subject-matter for a definite period of time the policy is called a "time policy". A contract for both voyage and time may be included in the same policy.

(2) Subject to the provisions of section eleven of the Finance Act, 1901, a time policy which is made for any time exceeding twelve months is invalid.*

Designation of subject-matter

26.—(1) The subject-matter insured must be designated in a marine policy with reasonable certainty.

(2) The nature and extent of the interest of the assured in the subject-matter insured need not be specified in the policy.

---

* Section 23, paragraphs (2) to (5) and Section 25, subsection (2) repealed by Finance Act, 1959.

(3) Where the policy designates the subject-matter insured in general terms, it shall be construed to apply to the interest intended by the assured to be covered.

(4) In the application of this section regard shall be had to any usage regulating the designation of the subject-matter insured.

Valued Policy

27.—(1) A policy may be either valued or unvalued.

(2) A valued policy is a policy which specifies the agreed value of the subject-matter insured.

(3) Subject to the provisions of this Act, and in the absence of fraud, the value fixed by the policy is, as between the insurer and assured, conclusive of the insurable value of the subject intended to be insured, whether the loss be total or partial.

(4) Unless the policy otherwise provides, the value fixed by the policy is not conclusive for the purpose of determining whether there has been a constructive total loss.

Unvalued Policy

28. An unvalued policy is a policy which does not specify the value of the subject-matter insured, but, subject to the limit of the sum insured, leaves the insurable value to be subsequently ascertained, in the manner hereinafter specified.

Floating Policy by Ship or Ships

29.—(1) A floating policy is a policy which describes the insurance in general terms, and leaves the name of the ship or ships and other particulars to be defined by subsequent declaration.

(2) The subsequent declaration or declarations may be made by indorsement on the policy, or in other customary manner.

(3) Unless the policy otherwise provides, the declarations must be made in the order of dispatch or shipment. They must, in the case of goods, comprise all consignments within the terms of the policy, and the value of the goods or other property must be honestly stated, but an omission or erroneous declaration may be rectified even after loss or arrival, provided the omission or declaration was made in good faith.

(4) Unless the policy otherwise provides, where a declaration of value is not made until after notice of loss or arrival, the policy must be treated as an unvalued policy as regards the subject-matter of that declaration.

Construction of Terms in Policy

30.—(1) A policy may be in the form in the First Schedule to this Act.

(2) Subject to the provisions of this Act, and unless the context of the policy otherwise requires, the terms and expressions mentioned in the First Schedule to this Act shall be construed as having the scope and meaning in that schedule assigned to them.

Premium to be Arranged

31.—(1) Where an insurance is effected at a premium to be arranged, and no arrangement is made, a reasonable premium is payable.

(2) Where an insurance is effected on the terms that an additional premium is to be arranged in a given event, and that event happens but no arrangement is made, then a reasonable additional premium is payable.

DOUBLE INSURANCE

Double Insurance

32.—(1) Where two or more policies are effected by or on behalf of the assured on the same adventure and interest or any part thereof, and the sums insured exceed the indemnity allowed by this Act, the assured is said to be over-insured by double insurance.

(2) Where the assured is over-insured by double insurance—

(a) The assured, unless the policy otherwise provides, may claim payment from the insurers in such order as he may think fit, provided that he is not entitled to receive any sum in excess of the indemnity allowed by this Act;

(b) Where the policy under which the assured claims is a valued policy, the assured must give credit as against the valuation for any sum received by him under any other policy without regard to the actual value of the subject-matter insured;

(c) Where the policy under which the assured claims is an unvalued policy he must give credit, as against the full insurable value, for any sum received by him under any other policy;

(d) Where the assured receives any sum in excess of the indemnity allowed by this Act, he is deemed to hold such sum in trust for the insurers, according to their right of contribution among themselves.

WARRANTIES, &c.

Nature of Warranty

33.—(1) A warranty, in the following sections relating to warranties, means a promissory warranty, that is to say, a warranty by which the assured undertakes that some particular thing shall or shall not be done, or that some condition shall be fulfilled, or whereby he affirms or negatives the existence of a particular state of facts.

(2) A warranty may be expressed or implied.

(3) A warranty, as above defined, is a condition which must be exactly complied with, whether it be material to the risk or not. If it be not so complied with, then, subject to any express provision in the policy, the insurer is discharged from liability as from the date of the breach of warranty, but without prejudice to any liability incurred by him before that date.

When Breach of Warranty Excused

34.—(1) Non-compliance with a warranty is excused when, by reason of a change of circumstances, the warranty ceases to be applicable to the circumstances of the contract, or when compliance with the warranty is rendered unlawful by any subsequent law.

(2) Where a warranty is broken, the assured cannot avail himself of the defence that the breach has been remedied, and the warranty complied with, before loss.

(3) A breach of warranty may be waived by the insurer.

Express Warranties

35.—(1) An express warranty may be in any form of words from which the intention to warrant is to be inferred.

(2) An express warranty must be included in, or written upon, the policy, or must be contained in some document incorporated by reference into the policy.

(3) An express warranty does not exclude an implied warranty, unless it be inconsistent therewith.

Warranty of Neutrality

36.—(1) Where insurable property, whether ship or goods, is expressly warranted neutral, there is an implied condition that the property shall have a neutral character at the commencement of the risk, and that, so far as the assured can control the matter, its neutral character shall be preserved during the risk.

(2) Where a ship is expressly warranted "neutral" there is also an implied condition that, so far as the assured can control the matter, she shall be properly documented, that is to say, that she shall carry the necessary papers to establish her neutrality, and that she shall not falsify or suppress her papers, or use simulated papers. If any loss occurs through breach of this condition, the insurer may avoid the contract.

No Implied Warranty of Nationality

37. There is no implied warranty as to the nationality of

a ship, or that her nationality shall not be changed during a risk.

Warranty of Good safety

38. Where the subject-matter insured is warranted "well" or "in good safety" on a particular day, it is sufficient if it be safe at any time during that day.

Warranty of Seaworthiness of Ship

39.—(1) In a voyage policy there is an implied warranty that at the commencement of the voyage the ship shall be seaworthy for the purpose of the particular adventure insured.

(2) Where the policy attaches while the ship is in port, there is also an implied warranty that she shall, at the commencement of the risk, be reasonably fit to encounter the ordinary perils of the port.

(3) Where the policy relates to a voyage which is performed in different stages, during which the ship requires different kinds of or further preparation or equipment, there is an implied warranty that at the commencement of each stage the ship is seaworthy in respect of such preparation or equipment for the purposes of that stage.

(4) A ship is deemed to be seaworthy when she is reasonably fit in all respects to encounter the ordinary perils of the seas of the adventure insured.

(5) In a time policy there is no implied warranty that the ship shall be seaworthy at any stage of the adventure, but where, with the privity of the assured, the ship is sent to sea in an unseaworthy state, the insurer is not liable for any loss attributable to unseaworthiness.

No Implied Warranty that Goods are Seaworthy

40.—(1) In a policy on goods or other moveables there is no implied warranty that the goods or moveables are seaworthy.

(2) In a voyage policy on goods or other moveables there is an implied warranty that at the commencement of the voyage the ship is not only seaworthy as a ship, but also that she is reasonably fit to carry the goods or other moveables to the destination contemplated by the policy.

Warranty of Legality

41. There is an implied warranty that the adventure insured is a lawful one, and that, so far as the assured can control the matter, the adventure shall be carried out in a lawful manner.

The Voyage

Implied Condition as to Commencement of Risk

42.—(1) Where the subject-matter is insured by a voyage policy "at and from" or "from" a particular place, it is not necessary that the ship should be at that place when the contract is concluded, but there is an implied condition that the adventure shall be commenced within a reasonable time, and that if the adventure be not so commenced the insurer may avoid the contract.

(2) The implied condition may be negatived by showing that the delay was caused by circumstances known to the insurer before the contract was concluded, or by showing that he waived the condition.

Alteration of Port of Departure

43. Where the place of departure is specified by the policy, and the ship instead of sailing from that place sails from any other place, the risk does not attach.

Sailing for Different Destination

44. Where the destination is specified in the policy, and the ship, instead of sailing for that destination, sails for any other destination, the risk does not attach.

Change of Voyage

45.—(1) Where, after the commencement of the risk, the destination of the ship is voluntarily changed from the destination contemplated by the policy, there is said to be a change of voyage.

(2) Unless the policy otherwise provides, where there is a change of voyage, the insurer is discharged from liability as from the time of change, that is to say, as from the time when the determination to change it is manifested; and it is immaterial that the ship may not in fact have left the course of voyage contemplated by the policy when the loss occurs.

Deviation

46.—(1) Where a ship, without lawful excuse, deviates from the voyage contemplated by the policy, the insurer is discharged from liability as from the time of deviation, and it is immaterial that the ship may have regained her route before any loss occurs.

(2) There is a deviation from the voyage contemplated by the policy—

    (a) where the course of the voyage is specifically designated by the policy, and that course is departed from; or

    (b) Where the course of the voyage is not specifically designated by the policy, but the usual and customary course is departed from.

(3) The intention to deviate is immaterial; there must be a deviation in fact to discharge the insurer from his liability under the contract.

Several Ports of Discharge

47.—(1) Where several ports of discharge are specified by the policy, the ship may proceed to all or any of them, but, in the absence of any usage of sufficient cause to the contrary, she must proceed to them, or such of them as she goes to, in the order designated by the policy. If she does not there is a deviation.

(2) Where the policy is to "ports of discharge", within a given area, which are not named, the ship must, in the absence of any usage or sufficient cause to the contrary, proceed to them, or such of them as she goes to, in their geographical order. If she does not there is a deviation.

Delay in Voyage

48. In the case of a voyage policy, the adventure insured must be prosecuted throughout its course with reasonable dispatch, and, if without lawful excuse it is not so prosecuted, the insurer is discharged from liability as from the time when the delay became unreasonable.

Excuses for Deviation or Delay

49.—(1) Deviation or delay in prosecuting the voyage contemplated by the policy is excused—

(a) Where authorized by any special term in the policy; or
(b) Where caused by circumstances beyond the control of the master and his employer; or
(c) Where reasonably necessary in order to comply with an express or implied warranty; or
(d) Where reasonably necessary for the safety of the ship or subject-matter insured; or
(e) For the purpose of saving human life, or aiding a ship in distress where human life may be in danger; or
(f) Where reasonably necessary for the purpose of obtaining medical or surgical aid for any person on board the ship; or
(g) Where caused by the barratrous conduct of the master or crew, if barratry be one of the perils insured against.

(2) When the cause excusing the deviation or delay ceases to operate, the ship must resume her course, and prosecute her voyage, with reasonable dispatch.

ASSIGNMENT OF POLICY

When and How Policy is Assignable

50.—(1) A marine policy is assignable unless it contains terms expressly prohibiting assignment. It may be assigned either before or after loss.

(2) Where a marine policy has been assigned so as to pass the beneficial interest in such policy, the assignee of the policy is entitled to sue thereon in his own name; and the defendant is entitled to make any defence arising out of the contract which he would have been entitled to make if the action had been brought in the name of the person by or on behalf of whom the policy was effected.

(3) A marine policy may be assigned by indorsement thereon or in other customary manner.

Assured Who Has No Interest Cannot Assign

51. Where the assured has parted with or lost his interest in the subject-matter insured, and has not, before or at the time of so doing, expressly or impliedly agreed to assign the policy, and subsequently assignment of the policy is inoperative:

Provided that nothing in this section affects the assignment of a policy after loss.

THE PREMIUM

When Premium Payable

52. Unless otherwise agreed, the duty of the assured or his agent to pay the premium, and the duty of the insurer to issue the policy to the assured or his agent, are concurrent conditions, and the insurer is not bound to issue the policy until payment or tender of the premium.

Policy Effected Through Broker

53.—(1) Unless otherwise agreed, where a marine policy is effected on behalf of the assured by a broker, the broker is directly responsible to the insurer for the premium, and the insurer is directly responsible to the assured for the amount which may be payable in respect of losses, or in respect of returnable premium.

(2) Unless otherwise agreed, the broker has, as against the assured, a lien upon the policy for the amount of the premium and his charges in respect of effecting the policy; and, where he has dealt with the person who employs him as a principal, he has also a lien on the policy in respect of any balance on any insurance account which may be due to him from such person, unless when the debt

was incurred he had reason to believe that such person was only an agent.

Effect of Receipt on Policy

54. Where a marine policy effected on behalf of the assured by a broker acknowledges the receipt of the premium, such acknowledgement is, in the absence of fraud, conclusive as between the insurer and the assured, but not as between the insurer and broker.

LOSS AND ABANDONMENT

Included and Excluded Losses

55.—(1) Subject to the provisions of this Act, and unless the policy otherwise provides, the insurer is liable for any loss proximately caused by a peril insured against, but, subject as aforesaid, he is not liable for any loss which is not proximately caused by a peril insured against.

(2) In particular—

(a) The insurer is not liable for any loss attributable to the wilful misconduct of the assured, but, unless the policy otherwise provides, he is liable for any loss proximately caused by a peril insured against, even though the loss would not have happened but for the misconduct or negligence of the master or crew;

(b) Unless the policy otherwise provides, the insurer on ship or goods is not liable for any loss proximately caused by delay, although the delay be caused by a peril insured against;

(c) Unless the policy otherwise provides, the insurer is not liable for ordinary wear and tear, ordinary leakage and breakage, inherent vice or nature of the subject-matter insured, or for any loss proximately caused by rats or vermin, or for any injury to machinery not proximately caused by maritime perils.

Partial and Total Loss

56.—(1) A loss may be either total or partial. Any loss other than a total loss, as hereinafter defined, is a partial loss.

(2) A total loss may be either an actual total loss, or a constructive total loss.

(3) Unless a different intention appears from the terms of the policy, an insurance against total loss includes a constructive, as well as an actual, total loss.

(4) Where the assured brings an action for a total loss and the

evidence proves only a partial loss, he may, unless the policy otherwise provides, recover for a partial loss.

(5) Where goods reach their destination in specie, but by reason
of obliteration of marks, or otherwise, they are incapable of identification, the loss, if any, is partial, and not total.

Actual Total Loss

57.—(1) Where the subject-matter insured is destroyed, or so
damaged as to cease to be a thing of the kind insured, or where
the assured is irretrievably deprived thereof, there is an actual total
loss.

(2) In the case of an actual total loss no notice of abandonment
need be given.

Missing Ship

58. Where the ship concerned in the adventure is missing, and
after the lapse of a reasonable time no news of her has been received,
an actual total loss may be presumed.

Effect of Transhipment, etc.

59. Where, by a peril insured against, the voyage is interrupted
at an intermediate port or place, under such circumstances as,
apart from any special stipulation in the contract of affreightment,
to justify the master in landing and re-shipping the goods or other
moveables, or in transhipping them, and sending them on to their
destination, the liability of the insurer continues, notwithstanding
the landing or transhipment.

Constructive Total Loss Defined

60.—(1) Subject to any express provision in the policy, there is
a constructive total loss where the subject-matter insured is reasonably abandoned on account of its actual total loss appearing to be
unavoidable, or because it could not be preserved from actual
total loss without an expenditure which would exceed its value when
the expenditure had been incurred.

(2) In particular, there is a constructive total loss—
  (i) Where the assured is deprived of the possession of his ship
      or goods by a peril insured against, and (a) it is unlikely
      that he can recover the ship or goods, as the case may be, or
      (b) the cost of recovering the ship or goods, as the case may
      be, would exceed their value when recovered; or
  (ii) In the case of damage to a ship, where she is so damaged
       by a peril insured against that the cost of repairing the
       damage would exceed the value of the ship when repaired.
       In estimating the cost of repairs, no deduction is to be

made in respect of general average contributions to those repairs payable by other interests, but account is to be taken of the expense of future salvage operations and of any future general average contributions to which the ship would be liable if repaired; or

(iii) In the case of damage to goods, where the cost of repairing the damage and forwarding the goods to their destination would exceed their value on arrival.

Effect of Constructive Total Loss

61. Where there is a constructive total loss the assured may either treat the loss as a partial loss, or abandon the subject-matter insured to the insurer and treat the loss as if it were an actual total loss.

Notice of Abandonment

62.—(1) Subject to the provisions of this action, where the assured elects to abandon the subject-matter insured to the insurer, he must give notice of abandonment. If he fails to do so the loss can only be treated as a partial loss.

(2) Notice of abandonment may be given in writing, or by word of mouth, or partly in writing and partly by word of month and may be given in any terms which indicate the intention of the assured to abandon his insured interest in the subject-matter unconditionally to the insurer.

(3) Notice of abandonment must be given with reasonable diligence after the receipt of reliable information of the loss, but where the information is of a doubtful character the assured is entitled to a reasonable time to make inquiry.

(4) Where notice of abandonment is properly given, the rights of the assured are not prejudiced by the fact that the insurer refuses to accept the abandonment.

(5) The acceptance of an abandonment may be either express or implied from the conduct of the insurer. The mere silence of the insurer after notice is not an acceptance.

(6) Where notice of abandonment is accepted the abandonment is irrevocable. The acceptance of the notice conclusively admits liability for the loss and the sufficiency of the notice.

(7) Notice of abandonment is unnecessary where, at the time when the assured receives information of the loss, there would be no possibility of benefit to the insurer if notice were given to him.

(8) Notice of abandonment may be waived by the insurer.

(9) Where an insurer has re-insured his risk, no notice of abandonment need be given by him.

Effect of Abandonment

63.—(1) Where there is a valid abandonment the insurer is entitled to take over the interest of the assured in whatever may remain of the subject-matter insured, and all proprietary rights incidental thereto.

(2) Upon the abandonment of a ship, the insurer thereof is entitled to any freight in course of being earned, and which is earned by her subsequent to the casualty causing the loss, less the expenses of earning it incurred after the casualty; and, where the ship is carrying the owner's goods, the insurer is entitled to a reasonable remuneration for the carriage of them subsequent to the casualty causing the loss.

PARTIAL LOSSES (INCLUDING SALVAGE AND GENERAL AVERAGE AND PARTICULAR AVERAGE)

Particular Average Loss

64.—(1) A particular average loss is a partial loss of the subject-matter insured, caused by a peril insured against, and which is not a general average loss.

(2) Expenses incurred by or on behalf of the assured for the safety of preservation of the subject-matter insured, other than general average and salvage charges, are called particular charges. Particular charges are not included in particular average.

Salvage Charges

65.—(1) Subject to any express provision in the policy, salvage charges incurred in preventing a loss by perils insured against may be recovered as a loss by those perils.

(2) "Salvage charges" means the charges recoverable under maritime law by a salvor independently of contract. They do not include the expenses of services in the nature of salvage rendered by the assured or his agents, or any person employed for hire by them, for the purpose of averting a peril insured against. Such expenses, where properly incurred, may be recovered as particular charges or as a general average loss, according to the circumstances under which they were incurred

General Average Loss

66.—(1) A general average loss is a loss caused by or directly consequential on a general average act. It includes a general average expenditure as well as a general average sacrifice.

(2) There is a general average act where any extraordinary sacrifice or expenditure is voluntarily and reasonably made or incurred in time of peril for the purpose of preserving the property imperilled in the common adventure.

(3) Where there is a general average loss, the party on whom it falls is entitled, subject to the conditions imposed by maritime law, to a rateable contribution from the other parties interested, and such contribution is called a general average contribution.

(4) Subject to any express provision in the policy, where the assured has incurred a general average expenditure, he may recover from the insurer in respect of the proportion of the loss which falls upon him; and, in the case of a general average sacrifice, he may recover from the insurer in respect of the whole loss without having enforced his right of contribution from the other parties liable to contribute.

(5) Subject to any express provision in the policy, where the assured has paid, or is liable to pay, a general average contribution in respect of the subject insured, he may recover therefor from the insurer.

(6) In the absence of express stipulation, the insurer is not liable for any general average loss or contribution where the loss was not incurred for the purpose of avoiding, or in connection with the avoidance of, a peril insured against.

(7) Where ship, freight, and cargo, or any two of those interests, are owned by the same assured, the liability of the insurer in respect of general average losses or contributions is to be determined as if those subjects were owned by different persons.

Measure of Indemnity

Extent of Liability of Insurer for Loss

67.—(1) The sum which the assured can recover in respect of a loss on a policy by which he is insured, in the case of an unvalued policy to the full extent of the insurable value, or, in the case of a valued policy to the full extent of the value fixed by the policy, is called the measure of indemnity.

(2) Where there is a loss recoverable under the policy, the insurer, or each insurer if there be more than one, is liable for such proportion of the measure of indemnity as the amount of his subscription bears to the value fixed by the policy in the case of a valued policy, or to the insurable value in the case of an unvalued policy.

Total Loss

68. Subject to the provisions of this Act and to any express provision in the policy, where there is a total loss of the subject-matter insured—

(1) If the policy be a valued policy, the measure of indemnity is the sum fixed by the policy:

(2) If the policy be an unvalued policy, the measure of indemnity is the insurable value of the subject-matter insured.

Partial Loss of Ship

69.   Where a ship is damaged, but is not totally lost, the measure of indemnity, subject to any express provision in the policy, is as follows: —

(1) Where the ship has been repaired, the assured is entitled to the reasonable cost of the repairs, less the customary deductions, but not exceeding the sum insured in respect of any one casualty:

(2) Where the ship has been only partially repaired, the assured is entitled to the reasonable cost of such repairs, computed as above, and also to be indemnified for the reasonable depreciation, if any, arising from the unrepaired damage, provided that the aggregate amount shall not exceed the cost of repairing the whole damage, computed as above:

(3) Where the ship has not been repaired, and has not been sold in her damaged state during the risk, the assured is entitled to be indemnified for the reasonable depreciation arising from the unrepaired damage, but not exceeding the reasonable cost of repairing such damage, computed as above.

Partial Loss of Freight

70.   Subject to any excess provision in the policy, where there is a partial loss of freight, the measure of indemnity is such proportion of the sum fixed by the policy in the case of a valued policy, or the insurable value in the case of an unvalued policy, as the proportion of freight lost by the assured bears to the whole freight at the risk of the assured under the policy.

Partial Loss of Goods, Merchandise, etc.

71.   Where there is a partial loss of goods, merchandise, or other moveables, the measure of indemnity, subject to any express provision in the policy, is as follows: —

(1) Where part of the goods, merchandise or other moveables insured by a valued policy is totally lost, the measure of indemnity is such proportion of the sum fixed by the policy as the insurable value of the part lost bears to the insurable value of the whole, ascertained as in the case of an unvalued policy.

(2) Where part of the goods, merchandise, or other moveables insured by an unvalued policy is totally lost, the measure of indemnity is the insurable value of the part lost, ascertained as in case of total loss.

(3) Where the whole or any part of the goods or merchandise insured has been delivered damaged at its destination, the measure of indemnity is such proportion of the sum fixed by the policy in the case of a valued policy, or of the insurable value in the case of an unvalued policy, as the difference between the gross sound and damaged values at the place of arrival bears to the gross sound value.

(4) "Gross value" means the wholesale price or, if there be no such price, the estimated value, with, in either case, freight, landing charges, and duty paid beforehand; provided that, in the case of goods or merchandise customarily sold in bond, the bonded price is deemed to be the gross value. "Gross proceeds" means the actual price obtained at a sale where all charges on sale are paid by the sellers.

Apportionment of Valuation

72.—(1) Where different species of property are insured under a single valuation, the valuation must be apportioned over the different species in proportion to their respective insurable values, as in the case of an unvalued policy. The insured value of any part of a species is such proportion of the total insured value of the same as the insurable value of the part bears to the insurable value of the whole, ascertained in both cases as provided by this Act.

(2) Where a valuation has to be apportioned, and particulars of the prime cost of each separate species, quality, or description of goods cannot be ascertained, the division of the valuation may be made over the net arrived sound values of the different species, qualities, or descriptions of goods.

General Average Contributions and Salvage Charges

73.—(1) Subject to any express provision in the policy, where the assured has paid, or is liable for, any general average contribution, the measure of indemnity is the full amount of such contribution if the subject-matter liable to contribution is insured for its full contributory value; but, if such subject-matter be not insured for its full contributory value, or if only part of it be insured, the indemnity payable by the insurer must be reduced in proportion to the under insurance, and where there has been a particular average loss which constitutes a deduction from the contributory value, and for which the insurer is liable, that amount must be deducted from the insured value in order to ascertain what the insurer is liable to contribute.

(2) Where the insurer is liable for salvage charges the extent of his liability must be determined on the like principle.

Liabilities to Third Parties

74.   Where the assured has effected an insurance in express terms against any liability to a third party, the measure of indemnity, subject to any express provision in the policy, is the amount paid or payable by him to such third party in respect of such liability.

General Provisions as to Measure of Indemnity

75.—(1) Where there has been a loss in respect of any subject-matter not expressly provided for in the foregoing provisions of this Act, the measure of indemnity shall be ascertained, as nearly as may be, in accordance with those provisions, in so far as applicable to the particular case.

(2) Nothing in the provisions of this Act relating to the measure of indemnity shall affect the rules relating to double insurance, or prohibit the insurer from disproving interest wholly or in part, or from showing that at the time of the loss the whole or any part of the subject-matter insured was not at risk under the policy.

Particular Average Warranties

76.—(1) Where the subject-matter insured is warranted free from particular average, the assured cannot recover for a loss of part, other than a loss incurred by a general average sacrifice, unless the contract contained in the policy be apportionable; but, if the contract be apportionable, the assured may recover for a total loss of any apportionable part.

(2) Where the subject-matter insured is warranted free from particular average, either wholly or under a certain percentage, the insurer is nevertheless liable for salvage charges, and for particular charges and other expenses properly incurred pursuant to the provisions of the suing and labouring clause in order to avert a loss insured against.

(3) Unless the policy otherwise provides, where the subject-matter insured is warranted free from particular average under a specified percentage, a general average loss cannot be added to a particular average loss to make up the specified percentage.

(4) For the purpose of ascertaining whether the specified percentage has been reached, regard shall be had only to the actual loss suffered by the subject-matter insured. Particular charges and the expenses of and incidental to ascertaining and proving the loss must be excluded.

Successive Losses

77.—(1) Unless the policy otherwise provides, and subject to the provisions of this Act, the insurer is liable for successive losses, even though the total amount of such losses may exceed the sum insured.

(2) Where, under the same policy, a partial loss, which has not been repaired or otherwise made good, is followed by a total loss, the assured can only recover in respect of the total loss:

Provided that nothing in this section shall affect the liability of the insurer under the suing and labouring clause.

Suing and Labouring Clause

78.—(1) Where the policy contains a suing and labouring clause, the engagement thereby entered into is deemed to be supplementary to the contract of insurance, and the assured may recover from the insurer any expenses properly incurred pursuant to the clause, notwithstanding that the insurer may have paid for a total loss, or that the subject-matter may have been warranted free from particular average, either wholly or under a certain percentage.

(2) General average losses and contributions and salvage charges, as defined by this Act, are not recoverable under the suing and labouring clause.

(3) Expenses incurred for the purpose of averting or diminishing any loss not covered by the policy are not recoverable under the suing and labouring clause.

(4) It is the duty of the assured and his agents, in all cases, to take such measures as may be reasonable for the purpose of averting or minimising a loss.

RIGHTS OF INSURER ON PAYMENT

Right of Subrogation

79.—(1) Where the insurer pays for a total loss, either of the whole, or in the case of goods of any apportionable part, of the subject-matter insured, he thereupon becomes entitled to take over the interest of the assured in whatever may remain of the subject-matter so paid for, and he is thereby subrogated to all the rights and remedies of the assured in and in respect of that subject-matter as from the time of the casualty causing the loss.

(2) Subject to the foregoing provisions, where the insurer pays for a partial loss, he acquires no title to the subject-matter insured, or such part of it as may remain, but he is thereupon subrogated to all rights and remedies of the assured in and in respect of the subject-matter insured as from the time of the casualty causing the loss, in so far as the assured has been indemnified, according to this Act, by such payment for the loss.

Right of Contribution

80.—(1) Where the assured is over-insured by double insurance, each insurer is bound, as between himself and the other insurers, to contribute rateably to the loss in proportion to the amount for which he is liable under his contract.

(2) If any insurer pays more than his proportion of the loss, he is entitled to maintain an action for contribution against the other insurers, and is entitled to the like remedies as a surety who has paid more than his proportion of the debt.

Effect of Under Insurance

81. Where the assured is insured for an amount less than the insurable value or, in the case of a valued policy, for an amount less than the policy valuation, he is deemed to be his own insurer in respect of the uninsured balance.

RETURN OF PREMIUM

Enforcement of Return

82. Where the premium, or a proportionate part thereof is, by this Act, declared to be returnable—

(a) If already paid, it may be recovered by the assured from the insurer; and,

(b) If unpaid, it may be retained by the assured or his agent.

Return by Agreement

83. Where the policy contains a stipulation for the return of the premium, or a proportionate part thereof, on the happening of a certain event, and that event happens, the premium, or, as the case may be, the proportionate part thereof, is thereupon returnable to the assured.

Return for Failure of Consideration

84.—(1) Where the consideration for the payment of the premium totally fails, and there has been no fraud or illegality on the part of the assured or his agents, the premium is thereupon returnable to the assured.

(2) Where the consideration for the payment of the premium is apportionable and there is a total failure of any apportionable part of the consideration, a proportionate part of the premium is, under the like conditions, thereupon returnable to the assured.

(3) In particular—

(a) Where the policy is void, or is avoided by the insurer as from the commencement of the risk, the premium is returnable, provided that there has been no fraud or illegality on the part of the assured; but if the risk is not apportionable, and has once attached, the premium is not returnable:

(b) Where the subject-matter insured, or part thereof, has never been imperilled, the premium, or, as the case may be, a proportionate part thereof, is returnable:

Provided that where the subject-matter has been insured "lost or not lost", and has arrived in safety at the time when the contract is concluded, the premium is not returnable unless, at such time, the insurer knew of the safe arrival.

(c) Where the assured has no insurable interest throughout the currency of the risk, the premium is returnable, provided that this rule does not apply to a policy effected by way of gaming or wagering;

(d) Where the assured has a defeasible interest which is terminated during the currency of the risk, the premium is not returnable;

(e) Where the assured has over-insured under an unvalued policy, a proportionate part of the premium is returnable;

(f) Subject to the foregoing provisions, where the assured has over-insured by double insurance, a proportionate part of the several premiums is returnable:

Provided that, if the policies are effected at different times, and any earlier policy has at any time borne the entire risk, or if a claim has been paid on the policy in respect of the full sum insured thereby, no premium is returnable in respect of that policy, and when the double insurance is effected knowingly by the assured no premium is returnable.

MUTUAL INSURANCE

Modification of Act in Case of Mutual Insurance

85.—(1) Where two or more persons mutually agree to insure each other against marine losses there is said to be a mutual insurance.

(2) The provisions of this Act relating to the premium do not apply to mutual insurance, but a guarantee, or such other arrangement as may be agreed upon, may be substituted for the premium.

(3) The provisions of this Act, in so far as they may be modified by the agreement of the parties, may in the case of mutual insurance be modified by the terms of the policies issued by the association, or by the rules and regulations of the association.

(4) Subject to the exceptions mentioned in this section, the provisions of this Act apply to a mutual insurance.

SUPPLEMENTAL

Ratification by Assured

86. Where a contract of marine insurance is in good faith

effected by one person on behalf of another, the person on whose behalf it is effected may ratify the contract even after he is aware of a loss.

Implied Obligations Varied by Agreement or Usage

87.—(1) Where any right, duty, or liability would arise under a contract of marine insurance by implication of law, it may be negatived or varied by express agreement, or by usage, if the usage be such as to bind both parties to the contract.

(2) The provisions of this section extend to any right, duty, or liability declared by this Act which may be lawfully modified by agreement.

Reasonable Time, Etc., a Question of Fact

88. Where by this Act any reference is made to reasonable time, reasonable premium, or reasonable diligence, the question what is reasonable is a question of fact.

Slip as Evidence

89. Where there is a duly stamped policy, reference may be made, as heretofore, to the slip or covering note, in any legal proceeding.

Interpretation of Terms

90. In this Act, unless the context or subject-matter otherwise requires—

"Action" includes counter-claim and set off:

"Freight" includes the profit derivable by a shipowner from the employment of his ship to carry his own goods or moveables, as well as freight payable by a third party, but does not include passage money:

"Moveables" means any moveable tangible property, other than the ship, and includes money, valuable securities, and other documents:

"Policy" means a marine policy.

Savings

91.—(1) Nothing in this Act, or any repeal effected thereby, shall affect—

(a) The provisions of the Stamp Act, 1891, or any enactment for the time being in force relating to the revenue;

(b) The provisions of the Companies Act, 1862, or any enactment amending or substituted for the same;

(c) The provisions of any statute not expressly repealed by this Act.

(2) The rules of the common law including the law merchant, save insofar as they are inconsistent with the express provisions of this Act, shall continue to apply to contracts of marine insurance.

Repeals
92.   The enactments mentioned in the Second Schedule to this Act are hereby repealed to the extent specified in that schedule.

Commencement
93.   This Act shall come into operation on the first day of January one thousand nine hundred and seven.

Short Title
94.   This Act may be cited as the Marine Insurance Act, 1906.

SCHEDULES

First Schedule

FORM OF POLICY

Lloyd's S.G. Policy
Be it known that   as well in
own name as for and in the name and names of all and every other person or persons to whom the same doth, may, or shall appertain, in part or in all doth make assurance and cause
                                            and them, and every of them, to be insured lost or not lost, at and from
                                            Upon all kind of goods and merchandises, and also upon the body, tackle, apparel, ordnance, munition, artillery, boat, and other furniture, of and in the good ship or vessel called the   whereof
is master under God, for this present voyage   or whosoever else shall go for master in the said ship, or by whatsoever other name or names the said ship, or the master thereof, is or shall be named or called; beginning the adventure upon the said goods and merchandises from the loading thereof aboard the said ship,
upon the said ship, etc.,
and so shall continue and endure, during her abode there, upon the said ship, etc. And further, until the said ship, with all her ordnance, tackle, apparel, etc., and goods and merchandises whatsoever shall be arrived at

upon the said ship, etc., until she hath moored at anchor twenty-four hours in good safety; and upon the goods and merchandises, until the same be there discharged and safely landed. And it shall be lawful for the said ship, etc., in this voyage to proceed and sail to and touch and stay at any ports or places whatsoever without prejudice to this insurance. The said ship, etc., goods and merchandises, etc., for so much as concerns the assured by agreement between the assured and assurers in this policy, are and shall be valued at

Touching the adventures and perils which we the assurers are contented to bear and do take upon us in this voyage: they are of the seas, men of war, fire, enemies, pirates, rovers, thieves, jettisons, letters of mart and countermart, surprisals, takings at sea, arrests, restraints, and detainments of all kings, princes, and people, of what nation, condition, or quality soever, barratry of the master and mariners, and of all other perils, losses, and misfortunes, that have or shall come to the hurt, detriment, or damage of the said goods and merchandises, and ship, etc., or any part thereof.

And in case of any loss or misfortune it shall be lawful to the assured, their factors, servants and assigns, to sue, labour, and travel for, in and about the defence, safeguards, and recovery of the said goods and merchandises, and ship, etc., or any part thereof without prejudice to this insurance; to the charges whereof we, the assurers, will contribute each one according to the rate and quantity of his sum herein assured.

And it is especially declared and agreed that no acts of the insurer or insured in recovering, saving, or preserving the property insured shall be considered as a waiver, or acceptance of abandonment. And it is agreed by us, the insurers, that this writing or policy of assurance shall be of as much force and effect as the surest writing of policy of assurance heretofore made in Lombard Street, or in the Royal Exchange, or elsewhere in London. And so we, the assurers, are contented, and do hereby promise and bind ourselves, each one for his own part, our heirs, executors, and goods to the assured, their executors, administrators, and assigns, for the true performance of the premises, confessing ourselves paid the consideration due unto us for this assurance by the assured, at and after the rate of

In Witness whereof we, the assurers, have subscribed our names and sums assured in London.

N.B.—Corn, fish, salt, fruit, flour, and seed are warranted free from average, unless general, or the ship be stranded—sugar, tobacco, hemp, flax, hides and skins are warranted free from average, under five pounds per cent., and all other goods, also the ship and freight, are warranted free from average, under three pounds per cent, unless general, or the ship be stranded.

RULES FOR CONSTRUCTION OF POLICY

The following are the rules referred to by this Act for the construction of a policy in the above, or other like form, where the context does not otherwise require: —

Lost or Not Lost

1. Where the subject-matter is insured "lost or not lost", and the loss has occurred before the contract is concluded, the risk attaches unless, at such time the assured was aware of the loss, and the insurer was not.

From

2. Where the subject-matter is insured "from" a particular place, the risk does not attach until the ship starts on the voyage insured.

At and From

3.—(a) Where a ship is insured "at and from" a particular place, and she is at that place in good safety when the contract is concluded, the risk attaches immediately.

(b) If she be not at the place when the contract is concluded, the risk attaches as soon as she arrives there in good safety, and, unless the policy otherwise provides, it is immaterial that she is covered by another policy for a specified time after arrival.

(c) Where chartered freight is insured "at and from" a particular place, and the ship is at that place in good safety when the contract is concluded the risk attaches immediately. If she be not there when the contract is concluded, the risk attaches as soon as she arrives there in good safety.

(d) Where freight, other than chartered freight, is payable without special conditions and is insured "at and from" a particular place, the risk attaches *pro rata* as the goods or merchandise are shipped; provided that if there be cargo in readiness which belongs to the shipowner, or which some other person has contracted with him to ship, the risk attaches as soon as the ship is ready to receive such cargo.

From the Loading Thereof

4. Where goods or other moveables are insured "from the loading thereof," the risk does not attach until such goods or

moveables are actually on board, and the insurer is not liable for them while in transit from the shore to the ship.

Safely Landed

5.   Where the risk on goods or other moveables continues until they are "safely landed," they must be landed in the customary manner and within a reasonable time after arrival at the port of discharge, and if they are not so landed the risk ceases.

Touch and Stay

6.   In the absence of any further license or usage, the liberty to touch and stay "at any port or place whatsoever" does not authorise the ship to depart from the course of her voyage from the port of departure to the port of destination.

Perils of the Seas

7.   The term "perils of the seas" refers only to fortuitous accidents or casualties of the seas. It does not include the ordinary action of the winds and waves.

Pirates

8.   The term "pirates" includes passengers who mutiny and rioters who attack the ship from the shore.

Thieves

9.   The term "thieves" does not cover clandestine theft or a theft committed by any one of the ship's company, whether crew or passengers.

Restraint of Princes

10.   The term "arrests, etc., of kings, princes, and people" refers to political or executive acts, and does not include a loss caused by riot or by ordinary judicial process.

Barratry

11.   The term "barratry" includes every wrongful act wilfully committed by the master or crew to the prejudice of the owner, or, as the case may be, the charterer.

All Other Perils

12.   The term "all other perils" includes only perils similar in kind to the perils specifically mentioned in the policy.

Average Unless General

13.   The term "average unless general" means a partial loss of

the subject-matter insured other than a general average loss, and does not include "particular charges".

Stranded

14.   Where the ship has stranded, the insurer is liable for the excepted losses, although the loss is not attributable to the stranding, provided that when the stranding takes place the risk has attached and, if the policy be on goods, that the damaged goods are on board.

Ship

15.   The term "ship" includes the hull, materials and outfit, stores and provisions for the officers and crew, and, in the case of vessels engaged in a special trade, the ordinary fittings requisite for the trade, and also, in the case of steamship, the machinery, boilers, and coals and engine stores, if owned by the assured.

Freight

16.   The term "freight" includes the profit derivable by a ship-owner from the employment of his ship to carry his own goods or moveables, as well as freight payable by a third party, but does not include passage money.

Goods

17.   The term "goods" means goods in the nature of merchandise, and does not include personal effects or provisions and stores for use on board.

In the absence of any usage to the contrary, deck cargo and living animals must be insured specifically, and not under the general denomination of goods.

Second Schedule

Enactments Repealed

Session and Chapter	Title or Short Title	Extent of Repeal
19 Geo. 2. c. 37	An Act to regulate insurance on ships belonging to the subjects of Great Britain, and on merchandises or effects laden thereon.	The whole Act.
28 Geo. 3. c. 56	An Act to repeal an Act made in the twenty-fifth year of the reign of his present Majesty, intituled "An Act for regulating Insurances on Ships, and on goods, merchandises, or effects," and for substituting other provisions for the like purpose in lieu thereof.	The whole Act so far as it relates to marine insurance.
31 & 32 Vict. c. 86	The Policies of Marine Assurance Act, 1868.	The whole Act.

THE YORK-ANTWERP RULES 1974

Rule of Interpretation

In the adjustment of general average the following lettered and numbered Rules shall apply to the exclusion of any Law and Practice inconsistent therewith.

Except as provided by the numbered Rules, general average shall be adjusted according to the lettered Rules.

Rule A

There is a general average act when, and only when, any extraordinary sacrifice or expenditure is intentionally and reasonably made or incurred for the common safety for the purpose of preserving from peril the property involved in a common maritime adventure.

Rule B

General average sacrifices and expenses shall be borne by the different contributing interests on the basis hereinafter provided.

Rule C

Only such losses, damages or expenses which are the direct consequence of the general average act shall be allowed as general average.

Loss or damage sustained by the ship or cargo through delay, whether on the voyage or subsequently, such as demurrage, and any indirect loss whatsoever, such as loss of market, shall not be admitted as general average.

Rule D

Rights to contribution in general average shall not be affected, though the event which gave rise to the sacrifice or expenditure may have been due to the fault of one of the parties to the adventure, but this shall not prejudice any remedies or defences which may be open against or to that party in respect of such fault

Rule E

The onus of proof is upon the party claiming in general average to show that the loss or expense claimed is properly allowable as general average.

RULE F

Any extra expense incurred in place of another expense which would have been allowable as general average shall be deemed to be general average and so allowed without regard to the saving, if any, to other interests, but only up to the amount of the general average expense avoided.

RULE G

General average shall be adjusted as regards both loss and contribution upon the basis of values at the time and place when and where the adventure ends.

This rule shall not affect the determination of the place at which the average statement is to be made up.

RULE I—*Jettison of Cargo*

No jettison of cargo shall be made good as general average, unless such cargo is carried in accordance with the recognized custom of the trade.

RULE II—*Damage by Jettison and Sacrifice for the Common Safety*

Damage done to a ship and cargo, or either of them, by or in consequence of a sacrifice made for the common safety, and by water which goes down a ship's hatches opened or other opening made for the purpose of making a jettison for the common safety, shall be made good as general average.

RULE III—*Extinguishing Fire on Shipboard*

Damage done to a ship and cargo, or either of them, by water or otherwise, including damage by beaching or scuttling a burning ship, in extinguishing a fire on board the ship, shall be made good as general average; except that no compensation shall be made for damage by smoke or heat however caused.

RULE IV—*Cutting away Wreck*

Loss or damage sustained by cutting away wreck or parts of the ship which have been previously carried away or are effectively lost by accident shall not be made good as general average.

RULE V—*Voluntary Stranding*

When a ship is intentionally run on shore for the common safety, whether or not she might have been driven on shore, the consequent loss or damage shall be allowed in general average.

RULE VI—*Salvage Remuneration*

Expenditure incurred by the parties to the adventure on account of salvage, whether under contract or otherwise, shall be allowed in general average to the extent that the salvage operations were undertaken for the purpose of preserving from peril the property involved in the common maritime adventure.

RULE VII—*Damage to Machinery and Boilers*

Damage caused to any machinery and boilers of a ship which is ashore and in a position of peril, in endeavouring to refloat, shall be allowed in general average when shown to have arisen from an actual intention to float the ship for the common safety at the risk of such damage; but where a ship is afloat no loss or damage caused by working the propelling machinery and boilers shall in any circumstances be made good as general average.

RULE VIII—*Expenses lightening a ship when ashore, and consequent damage*

When a ship is ashore and cargo and ship's fuel and stores or any of them are discharged as a general average act, the extra cost of lightening, lighter hire and reshipping if incurred and the loss or damage sustained thereby, shall be admitted as general average.

RULE IX—*Ship's Materials and Stores Burnt for Fuel*

Ship's materials and stores, or any of them, necessarily burnt for fuel for the common safety at a time of peril, shall be admitted as general average, when and only when an ample supply of fuel had been provided; but the estimated quantity of fuel that would have been consumed, calculated at the price current at the ship's last port of departure at the date of her leaving, shall be credited to the general average.

RULE X—*Expenses at Port of Refuge, etc.*

(a) When a ship shall have entered a port or place of refuge, or shall have returned to her port or place of loading in consequence of accident, sacrifice or other extraordinary circumstances, which render that necessary for the common safety, the expenses of entering such port or place shall be admitted as general average; and when she shall have sailed thence with her original cargo, or a part of it, the corresponding place consequent upon such entry or return shall likewise be admitted as general average.

When a ship is at any port or place of refuge and is necessarily removed to another port or place because repairs cannot be carried out in the first port or place, the provisions of this Rule shall be applied to the second port or place as if it were a port or place of refuge and the cost of such removal including temporary repairs and towage shall be admitted as general average. The provisions of Rule XI shall be applied to the prolongation of the voyage occasioned by such removal.

(b) The cost of handling on board or discharging cargo, fuel or stores whether at a port or place of loading, call or refuge shall be admitted as general average, when the handling or discharge was necessary for the common safety or to enable damage to the ship caused by sacrifice or accident to be repaired, if the repairs were necessary for the safe prosecution of the voyage, except in cases where the damage to the ship is discovered at a port or place of loading or call without any accident or other extraordinary circumstances connected with such damage having taken place during the voyage.

The cost of handling on board or discharging cargo, fuel or stores shall not be admissible as general average when incurred solely for the purpose of re-stowage due to shifting during the voyage unless such re-stowage is necessary for the common safety.

(c) Whenever the cost of handling or discharging cargo, fuel or stores is admissible as general average, the costs of storage, including insurance if reasonably incurred, reloading and stowing of such cargo, fuel or stores shall likewise be admitted as general average.

But when the ship is condemned or does not proceed on her original voyage storage expenses shall be admitted as general average only up to the date of the ship's condemnation or of the abandonment of the voyage or up to the date of completion of discharge of cargo if the condemnation or abandonment takes place before that date.

RULE XI—*Wages and Maintenance of Crew and other expenses bearing up for and in a port of Refuge, etc.*

(a) Wages and Maintenance of masters, officers and crew reasonably incurred and fuel and stores consumed during the prolongation of the voyage occasioned by a ship entering a port or place of refuge or returning to her port or place of loading shall be admitted as general average when the expenses of entering such port or place are allowable in general average in accordance with Rule X(a).

(b) When a ship shall have entered or been detained in any port or place in consequence of accident, sacrifice or other extraordinary circumstances which render that necessary for the common safety, or to enable damage to the ship caused by sacrifice or accident to be repaired, if the repairs were necessary for the safe prosecution of the voyage, the wages and maintenance of the master, officers, and crew reasonably incurred during the extra period of detention in such port or place until the ship shall or should have been made ready to proceed upon her voyage, shall be admitted in general average.

Provided that when damage to the ship is discovered at a port or place of loading or call without any accident or other extraordinary circumstance connected with such damage having taken place during the voyage, then the wages and maintenance of master, officers and crew and fuel and stores consumed during the extra detention for repairs to damages so discovered shall not be admissible as general average, even if the repairs are necessary for the safe prosecution of the voyage.

When the ship is condemned or does not proceed on her original voyage, wages and maintenance of the master, officers and crew and fuel and stores consumed shall be admitted as general average only up to the date of the ship's condemnation or of the abandonment of the voyage or up to the date of completion of discharge of cargo if the condemnation or abandonment takes place before that date.

Fuel and stores consumed during the extra period of detention shall be admitted as general average, except such fuel and stores as are consumed in effecting repairs not allowable in general average.

Port charges incurred during the extra period of detention shall likewise be admitted as general average except such charges as are incurred solely by reason of repairs not allowable in general average.

(c) For the purpose of this and the other Rules wages shall include all payments made to or for the benefit of the master, officers and crew, whether such payments be imposed by law upon the shipowners or be made under the terms or articles of employment.

(d) When overtime is paid to the master, officers or crew for maintenance of the ship or repairs, the cost of which is not allowable in general average, such overtime shall be allowed in general average only up to the saving in expense which would have been incurred and admitted as general average, had such overtime not been incurred.

RULE XII—*Damage to Cargo in discharging etc.*

Damage to or loss of cargo, fuel or stores caused in the act of handling, discharging, storing, reloading and stowing shall be made good as general average, when and only when the cost of those measures respectively is admitted as general average.

RULE XIII—*Deductions from cost of repairs*

Repairs to be allowed in general average shall not be subject to deductions in respect of "new for old" where old materials or parts are replaced by new unless the ship is over fifteen years old in which case there shall be a deduction of one third. The deductions shall be regulated by the age of the ship from the 31st December of the year of completion of construction to the date of the general average act, except for insulation, life and similar boats, communications and navigational apparatus and equipment, machinery and boilers for which deductions shall be regulated by the age of the particular parts to which they apply. The deductions shall be made only from the cost of the new material or parts when finished and ready to be installed in the ship.

No deduction shall be made in respect of provisions, stores, anchors and chain cables.

Drydock and slipway dues and costs of shifting the ship shall be allowed in full.

The costs of cleaning, painting or coating of bottom shall not be allowed in general average unless the bottom has been painted or coated within the twelve months preceding the date of the general average act in which case one half of such costs shall be allowed.

RULE XIV—*Temporary Repairs*

Where temporary repairs are effected to a ship at a port of loading, call or refuge, for the common safety, or of damage caused by general average sacrifice, the cost of such repairs shall be admitted as general average.

Where temporary repairs of accidental damage are effected in order to enable the adventure to be completed, the cost of such repairs shall be admitted as general average without regard to the saving, if any, to other interests, but only up to the saving in expense which would have been incurred and allowed in general average if such repairs had not been effected there.

No deductions "new for old" shall be made from the cost of temporary repairs allowable as general average.

RULE XV—*Loss of Freight*

Loss of Freight arising from damage to or loss of cargo shall be made good as general average, either when caused by a general average act, or when the damage to or loss of cargo is so made good.

Deduction shall be made from the amount of gross freight lost, of the charges which the owner thereof would have incurred to earn such freight, but has, in consequence of the sacrifice, not incurred.

RULE XVI—*Amount to be made good for Cargo lost or Damaged by Sacrifice*

The amount to be made good as General Average for damage to or loss of cargo sacrificed shall be the loss which has been sustained thereby based on the value at the time of discharge, ascertained from the commercial invoice rendered to the receiver or if there is no such invoice from the shipped value. The value at the time of discharge shall include the cost of insurance and freight except insofar as such freight is at the risk of interests other than the cargo.

When cargo so damaged is sold and the amount of the damage has not been otherwise agreed, the loss to be made good in general average shall be the difference between the net proceeds of sale and the net sound value as computed in the first paragraph of this Rule.

RULE XVII—*Contributory Values*

The contribution to a general average shall be made upon the actual net values of the property at the termination of the adventure except that the value of cargo shall be the value at the time of discharge ascertained from the commercial invoice rendered to the receiver or if there is no such invoice from the shipped value. The value of the cargo shall include the cost of insurance and freight unless and insofar as such freight is at the risk of interests other than the cargo, deducting therefrom any loss or damage suffered by the cargo prior to or at the time of discharge. The value of the ship shall be assessed without taking into account the beneficial or detrimental effect of any demise or time charterparty to which the ship may be committed.

To these values shall be added the amount made good as general average for property sacrificed, if not already included, deduction being made from the freight and passage money at risk of such charges and crew's wages as would not have been incurred in earning the freight had the ship and cargo been totally lost at the date of the general average act and have not been allowed as general average; deduction being also made from the value of the property of all extra charges incurred in respect thereof subsequently to the general average act, except such charges as are allowed in general average.

Where cargo is sold short of destination, however, it shall contribute upon the actual net proceeds of sale, with the addition of any amount made good as general average.

Passengers' luggage and personal effects not shipped under Bill of Lading shall not contribute in general average.

Rule XVIII—*Damage to Ship*

The amount to be allowed as general average for damage or loss to the ship, her machinery and/or gear caused by a general average act shall be as follows:

(a) When repaired or replaced, the actual reasonable cost of repairing or replacing such damage or loss, subject to deduction in accordance with Rule XIII.

(b) When not repaired or replaced, the reasonable depreciation arising from such damage or loss, but not exceeding the estimated cost of repairs But where the ship is an actual total loss or when the cost of repairs of the damage would exceed the value of the ship when repaired, the amount to be allowed as general average shall be the difference between the estimated sound value of the ship after deducting therefrom the estimated cost of repairing damage which is not general average and the value of the ship in her damaged state which may be measured by the net proceeds of sale, if any.

Rule XIX—*Undeclared or Wrongly declared Cargo*

Damage or loss caused to goods loaded without the knowledge of the shipowner or his agent or to goods wilfully misdescribed at time of shipment shall not be allowed as general average, but such goods shall remain liable to contribute, if saved.

Damage or loss caused to goods which have been wrongfully declared on shipment at a value which is lower than their real value shall be contributed for at the declared value, but such goods shall contribute upon their actual value.

Rule XX—*Provision of Funds*

A commission of 2 per cent on general average disbursements, other than the wages and maintenance of master, officers and crew and fuel and stores not replaced during the voyage, shall be allowed in general average, but when the funds are not provided by any of the contributing interests, the necessary cost of obtaining the funds required by means of a bottomry bond or otherwise, or the loss sustained by owners of goods sold for the purpose, shall be allowed in general average.

The cost of insuring money advanced to pay for general average disbursements shall also be allowed in general average.

Rule XXI—*Interest on Losses made good in general average*

Interest shall be allowed on expenditure, sacrifices and allowances charged to general average at the rate of 7 per cent per annum, until the date of the general average statement, due allowance being made for any interim reimbursement from the contributory interests or from the general average deposit fund.

Rule XXII—*Treatment of Cash Deposits*

Where cash deposits have been collected in respect of cargo's liability for general average, salvage or special charges, such deposits shall be paid without any delay into a special account in the joint names of a representative nominated on behalf of the shipowner and a representative nominated on behalf of the depositors in a bank to be approved by both. The sum so deposited, together with accrued interest, if any, shall be held as security for payment to the parties entitled thereto of the general average, salvage or special charges payable by cargo in respect to which the deposits have been collected. Payments on account of refund of deposits may be made if certified to in writing by the average adjuster. Such deposits and payments or refunds shall be without prejudice to the ultimate liability of the parties.

INDEX

235